PIERRE TOUSSAINT

PIERRE TOUSSAINT

ARTHUR JONES

DOUBLEDAY

New York   London   Toronto

Sydney   Auckland

PUBLISHED BY DOUBLEDAY
a division of Random House, Inc.

DOUBLEDAY and the portrayal of an anchor with a dolphin
are registered trademarks of Random House, Inc.

Book design by Caroline Cunningham

Library of Congress Cataloging-in-Publication Data
Jones, Arthur, 1936–
Pierre Toussaint / Arthur Jones.—1st ed.
p. cm.
Includes bibliographical references (p.) and index.
1. Toussaint, Pierre, 1766–1853? 2. African Americans—Biography.
3. African American Catholics—Biography. 4. Slaves—Haiti—Biography.
5. Slaves—New York (State)—New York—Biography. 6. Haiti—Biography.
7. New York (N.Y.)—Biography. I. Title.
E185.97.T7 J66 2003
972.94'04'092—dc21
[B]
2002041273

ISBN 0-385-49994-9

PRINTED IN THE UNITED STATES OF AMERICA

October 2003

First Edition

1   3   5   7   9   10   8   6   4   2

To three editors who brought out the
best in my storytelling:

❖

—Tom Fox, my dear friend and co-conspirator
at the *National Catholic Reporter* for almost
a quarter century (1980 to date).

❖

—Jim Michaels, editor of *Forbes*, the pal who
sharpened my writing, and the questions
I asked, just in time (1969 to 1985).

❖

—Desmond Fisher, my chum, the "Walker Cronkite"
of Irish television who, as editor of the *Catholic Herald*
in London, pointed my nose and prose
in the right direction (1964 to 1966).

ONTENTS

OUT OF SLAVERY

In 1789 the French West Indian colony of Saint Domingue sup-plied two-thirds of the overseas trade of France and was the great-est individual market for the European slave trade. It was an integral part of the economic life of the age, the greatest colony in the world, the pride of France, and the envy of every other imperi-alist nation. The whole structure rested on the labour of a half-mil-lion slaves.

In August, 1791, after two years of the French Revolution and its repercussions in Saint Domingue, the slaves revolted. The strug-gle lasted for 12 years. The slaves defeated in turn the local whites and the soldiers of the French monarch, a Spanish invasion, a British expedition of some 60,000 men, and a French expedition of similar size under Bonaparte's brother-in-law.

The defeat of Bonaparte's expedition in 1803 resulted in the establishment of the Negro state of Haiti which has lasted to this day.

C. L. R. JAMES,
THE BLACK JACOBINS, 1938

IN 1789, PIERRE TOUSSAINT, the subject of this biography, was eight. In 1803, he was a twenty-two-year-old slave and hairdresser in New York City, the sole financial support of his mistress, her two sisters, and three other slaves. Fifty years later, he died. At his death he was hailed as the most respected black person in New York City. He gained his freedom in 1807, almost literally on his mistress's deathbed. Wed in 1811, he and his wife, Juliette, adopted in 1815 Toussaint's infant niece, Euphémie, daughter of his deceased sister, Rosalie. As New York's leading coiffeur, he prospered as a businessman. He outlived all his relatives and most of his closest friends.

These facts, and C. L. R. James's historical facts regarding the French colony of Saint Domingue, constitute the basic details of the life of Pierre Toussaint, whose story follows.

A century after his death, his headstone was located in the Catholic burial ground in Lower Manhattan by a dogged researcher, seminarian, later Father, Charles McTague. That discovery sparked renewed interest in Pierre Toussaint, eventually leading to the formation of a Pierre Toussaint Guild to promote interest in him.

An excellent fictionalized account of Toussaint's life was written in 1955 by Arthur Sheehan and Elizabeth Odell. A second account, by Ellen Tarry, also fictionalized, appeared in 1981. Both relied, as does much of what follows, on Hannah Farnham Sawyer Lee's personal memoir of Toussaint published in 1854. Three New York cardinals have pressed Rome for Toussaint's canonization. It will come in time. Currently, Pierre Toussaint is waiting for a miracle, or two. The first miracle means beatification; the second, sainthood. Except for a passing mention, the events following his death and the quest for his canonization are not part of this book.

ONE

Saint Domingue, French Antilles, 1781

THE DOZEN OR SO HUTS, each with its small plot of land for cultivation, were placed within sight of the plantation house without much regard for organization or appearance. Typically, these huts would be close to the chateau, close enough so that someone with a loud voice could call from the rear of the huge tree-shaded mansion and attract the attention of servant-slaves who lived in them.

Yet the distance between the two forms of accommodation—the French chateau built in a tropical near-wilderness, and the huts on its northwest perimeter—was the widest humanity can measure. It was the distance between master and slave. It was the distance between the plantation-owning French aristocrats in Saint Domingue—today's Haiti—and the West Africans who toiled for them.

These Africans were a captive people torn from family, fields, and traditions; a people kidnapped, landed, branded, and worked to death in the fields before they reached midlife.

The slaves in these nearby huts were not field hands. They were the second-tier household servants. First-tier household servants had rooms in the chateau's internal slave quarters. Inside quarters were reserved for the "body servants," the intimate personal servants of the family: the ladies' maids and the valets.

These plantation chateaus, abutted by little hamlets of huts, were commonplace enough around the French colony of Saint Domingue, the crab claw–shaped western third of the island of Santo Domingo. At almost eleven thousand square miles, Saint Domingue was slightly smaller than the state of Maryland.

The mansions' styles were those of the French city and countryside, and few changes had taken place in their architecture to make them suitable for the Caribbean. The exception, in some, was that the corridors and windows tended to be wider to allow any cooling breeze to waft through.

That breeze was perennially laden with tropical scents: the heavy perfume of lush flowers and blooms, the after-rain aromas laden with dewy, moisture-soaked soils, blossoms, and leaves. Without thinking about it the inhabitants could tell what the weather was like, or recently had been, simply by sniffing the air. One variety of scents lingered after squalls and storms, another came with the tang from strong offshore winds. Cloying, perhaps, but always comforting and familiar for those born to it.

Smells linger long in the memory; one's nose rarely forgets the scents of childhood. Particularly the delightful smells from the kitchen, or those carried in on a breeze.

What breezes blew this day in 1781?

In the French part of the island of Santo Domingo—the eastern two-thirds were Spanish—there were rarely sufficient breezes to combat the unrelenting, stifling April-to-September heat and humidity. Rainfall ranged from twenty to one hundred inches a year, depending on the location. Temperatures rarely dropped below eighty-seven degrees Fahrenheit in winter and usually remained at or above ninety-five degrees throughout the summer. Not until October did the weather break, and in November the rainy season set in for most of the island.

Saint Domingue's (Haiti's) three provinces were the cultured, more closely settled North Province; the isolated, underpopulated South Province; and, located between them, the West Province where this chateau, L'Artibonite, was located. L'Artibonite commanded thousands of acres of the West Province's Artibonite Valley, irrigated by the 174-mile-long river of that name. L'Artibonite plantation owned hundreds of slaves to make it profitable. And made its owners as comfortable as French people could be when their real goal was to make enough money to live out their lives in Paris.

The West Province was bordered at its western edge by the sea, yet hemmed in by mountain chains that kept the rainy season at bay. The eighteenth-century plantations depended on irrigation from the Artibonite River for their abundant harvests. What precipitation came was borne in with the unpredictable but violent thunderstorms that could batter and howl with property-wrecking violence. Floods were common, and with that trick of fate that cruelly afflicts flood regions, droughts were not unknown.

Either temporarily in the L'Artibonite mansion's slave quarters, or more likely in one of the huts, was Ursule Julien Toussaint. She was in labor. The young woman, she'd be about seventeen or eighteen, was a chambermaid to the lady of the house, Madame Bérard du Pithon. This was her third child. In time and with seniority, Ursule would graduate to a room inside the house, just like her impressive and redoubtable mother, Zénobie Julien. Normally, Zénobie, who ran the chateau as a combination housekeeper and manager, would have been on hand to assist at the childbirth.

But this year, the slave Zénobie was in France. She went periodically, charged with transporting the Bérard children to Paris for their education.

Instead, Ursule's grandmother, the slave Tonette, was likely with her. Tonette had probably sent someone to the chateau for additional help with the imminent delivery. Perhaps Ursule's sister, Marie Bouquement, came. Bouquement often visited L'Artibonite with her mistress, Marie Elisabeth Bossard, from the Bossard plantation up north at Dondon in Marmalade. Ursule's two other young children would have been temporarily farmed out to play elsewhere. Her husband would have been at work.

Ursule's baby was a boy, christened Pierre Toussaint. ("Pierre" was for Pierre Bérard du Pithon, L'Artibonite plantation's owner.) Legend has it Pierre was born on All Saints' Day, November 2; hence his last name, Toussaint, French for All Saints. While possible, it is not likely. It would be too curious a coincidence. "Toussaint" was the paternal family name. Pierre's father is known to history as "Old Toussaint," and Pierre's sister, Marie-Louise, refers to their older brother (whose first name may have been Antoine) as "Toussaint."

In many Catholic cultures, people customarily celebrated their "saint's name day" rather than their birthday. That seems to be the case with Pierre Toussaint. (Forty years hence, Toussaint's adopted daughter, his niece Euphémie, in letters to her uncle Pierre, honors his birthday on November 2.)

Pierre's father, "Old Toussaint," was not one of the brutalized field hands, nor was he particularly old. Among the slave population, "old" was a relative term frequently used as an honorific once a man's hair turned gray. Few male slaves lived that long—at least half of Saint Domingue's male slave population was dead before the age of forty.

Five-year-old De Pointe (Aurore) Bérard, the white household's youngest child, was godmother to this newborn Toussaint. Child godparents were not unusual among French plantation families. In Pierre's case, the newborn would start out as a real-live baby doll for his five-year-old godmother, and grow into a playmate—simultaneously her constant companion and servant. There were other playmates, his siblings, Aurore's siblings, cousins (children of his aunt Marie), and the scores of other plantation families.

For slave children of household servants it was possible to form outside friendships on other plantations visited by the owners, or after church on Sundays, or in the streets around the town houses most plantation owners had in a nearby city. In the Bérards' case, the town house was either in St. Marc, the port city where they attended church, or more likely in Port-au-Prince, the colonial capital. L'Artibonite, the Bérard plantation, was in St. Marc parish, about fifty miles inland from Port-au-Prince and thirteen miles from St. Marc port.

Aurore Bérard, his little godmother, was one of the three people who most influenced Toussaint's early life. Of those three, she was the only one in the colony the day Pierre was born. Grandmother Zénobie was in Paris delivering the two older Bérard girls to their convent boarding school. Jean-Jacques Bérard, L'Artibonite plantation's oldest son and heir, who would later be master and mentor to Toussaint, was already at school in Paris.

To return home, Zénobie would soon undertake yet again the seemingly endless seven- to ten-week voyage from Le Havre to "Le Cap"—Cap François, Saint Domingue's cultural and commercial capital on the North Province's coast. There she would board a small barque to travel west around the top point of the crab claw, then east-southeast into the small port of St. Marc.

Zénobie's transatlantic traveling would not go on forever, and as the returned grandmother held her newborn grandson for the first time, she was aware that within five years, once Jean-Jacques was done with school, the end of her ocean journeying would be near.

Once Jean-Jacques completed his education and returned, the young Bérard would take over L'Artibonite from his father and run the fortune-creating family enterprise. Then his parents and the remaining brothers and sisters would move permanently to Paris, the ideal of every planter family in Saint Domingue.

Saint Domingue was a troubled land. The whites were there to exploit it; the blacks were there to be exploited and to create unimaginable wealth for the plantation owners. The mulattoes, those with mixed blood, were hated by the whites with an intensity greater than their disdain for the slaves. By far the majority of mulattoes were *gens de couleur,* free people of color. Ostensibly, *gens de couleur* had the same rights as whites. In fact, the white planters (known, along with the white colonial officials who ran the government and the military establishment, as *grands blancs)* worked extremely hard to deprive the mulattoes of any vestige of rights or independence.

The social pecking order was this: The colony was dominated by opportunists—in the top rank, the wealthy planters, who were in Saint Domingue solely to make money. Next in financial importance, but dominant in administration and tax gathering, were the royal governor—the absolute ruler, usually a retired military officer and an aristocrat close to the French court—and his chief bureaucrat, the intendant. They were there to pick the public purse—corruption was a normal perquisite of the job. Next in the pecking order came the *petits blancs,* the lower-class white workers, a category that included all the "lower orders," from plantation foremen and skilled artisans right down to the white riffraff. Fourth came the *gens de couleur,* a few of them freed slaves but generally mulattoes. There wasn't a fifth category—the enslaved were discounted. A grave mistake.

As an admixture, these groups constituted a volatile social chemistry. Like the king of France and his advisers, the *grands blancs* in Saint Domingue had no concerns about the colony as a dormant volcano. Yet Pierre Toussaint was born into a highly unstable racial-political-social tension that appeared quiescent solely because it had not received the final ingredient needed to cause combustion: the slaves tasting freedom.

The colony was deceptive. From the sea, a traveler on a vessel creeping slowly west on either the island's leeward or windward side approached Port-au-Prince or Cap François viewing misted high mountains, tropical forest, and plains. Throughout the colony, these mountains, productive with coffee shrubs, provided half of Europe with its favorite beverage. From Saint Domingue's lowland, plantations of sugarcane offered a manufactured vista where eighteenth-century Europe garnered a significant portion of its sugar to sweeten its coffee and cakes. Where there was no man-made crop, the island vista was of palms, tropical green foliage, flowers, and creepers.

The traveler saw a flowering, fertile abundance, a scene of wonderment for the first-time visitor. The view at night from the sea, if the vessel steadily turned into the port of Le Cap, was of the plantation houses illuminated across miles and miles of foothill and plain. The sugarcane factories sent flames roaring skyward from their boiling rooms into the darkness—sugar was more a manufacturing process than agriculture. For slaves, whether in fields or factories, it was a brutal harvest. Pierre Toussaint's birth coincided with that of the Industrial Revolution. And the Saint Domingue's sugar factories were as harsh a working environment as newly industrializing Britain's "dark satanic mills."

The seagoing traveler, gazing landward by day or night, would find in the nearing colony much to fascinate him. (Most visitors were males. This, though a place of some curiosity, was not a vacation spot.) On land the traveler would discover much to detest. One likable quality, however, was the colonial planters' open hospitality to their own kind. In an era when there were no hotels or comfortable lodging in the modern sense, the *grands blancs'* openhandedness to any visitor was legendary. Visitors were entertainment.

In Le Cap, as the cultural capital and financial center was known, squalor and culture lived side by side. If St. Marc, with about eight hundred full-time residents, and Port-au-Prince, population about eight thousand, could boast a few amenities—both towns, for example, had theaters—Le Cap, "the Paris of the Antilles," had almost everything Paris had except location. Of Le Cap's fifty thousand people, forty thousand were slaves. There were some eight thousand fashionable and stone-built houses. The finest of which, for those owners who chose to adequately furnish them, offered exquisite settings in which to wear the finest French fashions and imports, available in the city's commercial outlets.

For their entertainments, the wealthy colonial family and the professional governmental and commercial class could buy in Le Cap the same wines and many of the foods available in France itself. And there was more. From Paris to Le Cap's fifteen-hundred-seat segregated theater (mulattos sat in the third tier) came the latest theatrical and musical productions from Paris. Forty years before New York had its first serious opera, indeed its first decent theater, France's premier artists were appearing in Le Cap's excellent theater.

But this was a seaport. Le Cap's commerce-filled streets were also home to wandering swine, open sewage, foraging dogs, and never less than three thousand sailors from the cargo-carrying French mercantile sailing ships. Those vessels lined up for three-quarters of a mile along Le Cap's harbor front, their pointed prows sticking into the city like so many hatpins.

Seaport Le Cap was a city of booze, brothels, and brawls. There were moneylenders and gamblers, lawyers and forwarding agents, opportunists and the scum of all seaports: the drunks, losers, petty thieves, brigands, and ne'er-do-wells who'd washed up there and found no reason, or no way, to leave. They were men of all colors, though mainly white Europeans. Much later, they'd also be trouble.

The West Province (where Toussaint would grow to his early teenage years) was dominated by the political capital, Port-au-Prince, an unremarkable city prone to earthquakes. The huge West Province's estates were the largest in the colony; they had to be huge to justify the enormous investment needed to make them profitable and productive. This was not easy agriculture but irrigation-dependent and with unpredictable weather.

On the plantations of the Artibonite Valley, anywhere from three hundred to a thousand slaves was not unusual. Those field-hand slaves were housed nowhere near the main chateaus. Their slave camps would be on the outlying fringes farthest from the family mansion, so far away on these great acreages that their sundown singing, drumming, and dancing might only barely carry through the insect-noisy night to the chateau.

The third Province, the thinly populated South Province below the West Province, had little direct effect on Pierre's life, though it had a short yet important political role to play toward the colony's end.

As for newborn Pierre, who marked All Saints' as his feast day, which saints hovered over him—one more slave child in a colony that already had half a million? There was nothing saintly about being born a slave—freed from the womb straight into captivity.

His identity was that of the plantation. Slaves frequently were known by their owner's last name, or the plantation's name. There are letters to the mature Toussaint that address him as "Toussaint Bérard," after his owner, even though he was by then a free man. Haiti's more famous Toussaint, Toussaint-Louverture, the liberator of Saint Domingue who led the way to independent Haiti, began life as Pierre-François-Dominique Toussaint Bréda. Bréda was the name of the plantation on which he was born. (He was thirty-seven years older than L'Artibonite's Pierre Toussaint. The two Toussaints never met.)

❖   ❖   ❖

There is no actual record of when Pierre Toussaint was baptized, but it is certain he was. Bérard's daughter Aurore, in her letters to Pierre, always referred to herself as *ta marraine* ("your godmother").

Pierre Toussaint's life is the story of a child, a boy, and a man at first buffeted then scarred by the enormous sociopolitical shifts and revolutions of his day. He walked untainted through the plagues of yellow fever, typhus, and malaria, through seventy-three years of history as a telling reminder of civilization's greatest disgrace: slavery.

He was capable of rising above his slavery even when his Catholic Church and the society around him endorsed it. Despite the things he had to do to conform to society, he developed into a person constitutionally incapable of accepting many of the strictures of such a society or church—once he had decided on a course of action.

He was not a loner, but he was certainly independent. He would lecture a white woman, a valued client, on her materialistic values. On his deathbed he would tell a visitor who offered to bring a priest to hear his confession that he confessed to God, not to man. He could quote from Unitarian ministers as ably as he could the French Catholic clerics, or Scriptures whose writings he had early committed to memory. While nowhere is he on record as opposing slavery or working for its abolition, he helped countless people buy their way out of it. As an adult he supported numerous charities and endeavors when approached, but unless they were church-related, he joined no organizations.

Everyone who met him for whom records remain was uni-

formly impressed by Toussaint. As will be seen in the correspondence from his friends, something emanates from Toussaint's innate sense of personal dignity that is invariably
remarked on. He was an appealing personality, a cheerful and
trusted one. People of all ranks sought his counsel, and apparently took it. Yet this wasn't a stern, studious man or dour do-
gooder; he wasn't officious, nor did he take himself seriously.
He was funny, imaginative, and optimistic. And just as he never
missed daily mass, so, apparently, he never lost a friend.

In the very center of his Christian soul were his two core beliefs. The essence was his Catholicism. (In the surviving historical record, it is often his devout Protestant friends in those
anti-Catholic times who remark most favorably on his religious
practice. Fellow Catholics probably took it for granted.) His life's
work, too, was marked by his public witness to his faith based on
the beatitudes. He would quote, and did, from the Sermon on
the Mount, for he lived by its precepts. What comes out of the
early record suggests there is something Francis of Assisi–like in
Toussaint's sense of service. For he served all, not just some.

❖   ❖   ❖

Toussaint was not, however, anyone's fool. One of his white
friends later describes in detail just how shrewd a judge of char
acter Pierre became.

Further, if he was black and a slave, and suffered every con-
ceivable slight and offense meted out to Africans and those in
bondage, he shook it off. He never forgot he was black and,
later, had to constantly be alert to the possibility of kidnapping.
He was clever and, in time, wise. He was not without constant
burdens and losses, but he never let them deter him. He loved
as he lived—and those he loved, he loved to the fullest: his wife,
Juliette, who was as merry as he; his serious little Euphémie,
their adopted daughter; his closest white women friends, Mary

Anna Sawyer Schuyler and Catherine Church Cruger; his closest white male friends, Jean Sorbieu and Jerome Villagrand,
"best men" at his wedding; and his many black friends, Con-
stantin Boyer, Jean-Baptiste, Auguste Collon, and many more.
As their letters show, whether written by blacks or whites, his
friends loved him unreservedly in return.

These letters, as well as an early biography, are key to today's insights into Toussaint. In 1854, the year after Toussaint's
death, Hannah Farnham Sawyer Lee, sister to Mary Anna
Sawyer Schuyler, penned a 24,000-word *Memoir of Pierre Toussaint, Born a Slave in St. Domingo* (published in Boston by Crosby,
Nichols, and Company in 1854). It is bedrock material for
everything written since. (Later, in Chapter 13, there is a brief
but essential look at Hannah Lee's overriding influence on
modern perceptions of Toussaint. Some facts in Lee's book are
inadvertently erroneous and are dealt with at that time.)

Lee primarily used Mary Anna's notes to produce her Toussaint biography, and in this book, any unattributed quotations
are from Hannah Lee's biography. Beyond the biography there
are a few, quite slight, independent references to Toussaint from
those who glimpsed him late in his life, or whose forebears had
known him. His niece, Euphémie, as a child between seven and
fourteen, wrote him more than two hundred letters, short and
often charming. Though limited in their historic value, they are
descriptive as insights into the Toussaints' family life.

Extremely valuable to the record are several hundred more
letters from his friends, generally those resettled in France and
the Caribbean. Of those penned by Toussaint himself, only five
have survived.

There is a worrisome aspect to the Hannah Lee biography
concerning some presumptions she makes about Toussaint's attitude toward his own slavery. Again, there were circumstances
that affected her memoir, for Harriet Beecher Stowe's *Uncle*

Tom's Cabin, or, Life Among the Lowly appeared only two years before Toussaint's death. That book too often became the only frame of reference for those looking at Toussaint himself. It began the week Toussaint died in 1853. A *New York Evening Post* correspondent, reaching for some way to describe this unique African American from Saint Domingue, wrote: "Uncle Tom not an Apocryphal Character . . . Pierre Toussaint . . . if Mrs. Stowe could have been supposed to have known him, could have sat as the original of the portraiture to which she gave the name Uncle Tom." The writer knew even less about Toussaint than he did about Harriet Beecher Stowe.

To a newborn slave in Saint Domingue, this later involvement with white New Yorkers decades hence was irrelevant. He was a slave at birth on a steamy tropical island four thousand miles from the land of his forebears, the Congo. He was the forcibly enslaved child of forcibly displaced and enslaved parents and grandparents. What manner of people were his parents and grandparents? What was this baby's heritage that was greater than slavery?

If Grandmother Zénobie was any measure, his African ancestry numbered its share of impressive characters and capable people. Zénobie was more than Toussaint's grandmother. She was the archetype of the strong, cheerful, and gifted free women of color from Saint Domingue whose counterparts in Baltimore a half-century later founded the first congregation of black women religious in the world, and founded the second black congregation in New Orleans fifteen years after that.

This same inner strength is evident in Toussaint. His deep trust in God, his self-assured temperament, and the inner spirit of his character continually alerted and astonished not only his friends but especially those who met him unprepared. What was it? Why did these friends and acquaintances—black and white and mulatto from across a mix of social classes, geographical residences, and origins and beliefs—trust him so much, confide in him so intimately, turn to him so frequently, seek his help so openly, request his counsel and his prayers so desperately?

Toussaint was a momentary flowering. He appears to have represented something solid and good in his family and in himself. It was women like Zénobie, full partners with their husbands in an era when white women played second fiddle to their spouses, who, despite slavery, abuse, and disadvantage, kept their bearings and shaped their culture. It is the Zénobies who created slave and post-slave family stability out of their inexhaustible strength of character. They accomplished this in the American South as well as in the French colonies.

Toussaint was a beneficiary, and he apparently did not waste one drop of his inheritance. He stepped into life out of a tapestry that includes Ursule and Zénobie and great-grandmother Tonette; his father and grandfather (and perhaps his great-grandfather) were alive, too. It was a tapestry filled with colorful landscapes. He was raised in slavery on mother's milk, then fresh fruits, vegetables, fish, and sunshine.

He never lost his childish and childhood recollection of the sights and smells of L'Artibonite, nor did he ever lose his taste for the gumbo served by the cooks in the mansion's kitchen. A Chinese philosopher once averred that "patriotism is but the food of one's childhood." Toussaint was not alone in his taste for gumbo. In later life, his exiled Saint Domingue friends, white and black—onetime residents of New York later settled in France—were always pleading with Pierre: Could his wife Juliette please make some of her gumbo.

And crocks and jars of gumbo, or little sacks of seasoning, would be put on a *paquebot* from New York to Le Havre and make their way up to Paris and into French kitchens and from there as special treats onto the tables of their closest friends.

The baby Toussaint grew up cheerful and obliging, dignified, and with a great sense of his own worth. Those attributes have carried many people far in life. They are attributes which, along with his deep faith, have carried a slave baby's life and reputation two and a quarter centuries on into the twenty-first century.

Toussaint's major trait is not the fact that he was a slave, though that shaped his life. Nor that he was black, though that in many ways accounted for his strength of character. His prime attribute was something deeper. There was something in this boy that as a man would mark him as special to his friends. So special, in fact, that his dearest friend, the perceptive and competent Mary Anna Sawyer, the devout Protestant, toward the end of her life and Toussaint's, began in her letters to address him as "my St. Pierre."

Why did she see him as a saint? The search for the answer is the story ahead.

TWO

CATHOLIC SLAVEHOLDERS, CATHOLIC SLAVES

THE PREVAILING religious and social condition in the great plantation houses of late-eighteenth-century Saint Domingue was sloth. The inertia of these self-exiled, fortune-seeking French planters, many of whom quickly achieved the wealth they sought, resulted from the combination of an enervating climate, unprecedented affluence, a pining for "home" (France), plus nothing much to do except fend off sickness. "With possibly the worst climate in the West Indies," writes historian T. L. Stoddard, quoting a Saint Domingue government official, the planters' letters home "always mention . . . the writer's failing health."

As if remoteness, disease, and the weather weren't enough to smother initiative and compress the human psyche, over a span of generations the tropical climate even affected the physical appearance of planters bred in Saint Domingue. These *grands blancs* and their offshoots are depicted as pale, attenuated figures, as in a Goya painting—the same languid, graceful, even fragile white figures are stereotypical, too, of planter families in the antebellum American South. The Saint Domingue planter descendants were taller and stretched thinner than their peers in France. It was a mixture of fresher air than European cities breathed, more sunshine than northern Europe sees, and an abundance of fruits. The colonists' frailty was that of hothouse plants, blooms forced beyond their natural growth.

Sloth was such a curse it affected even the colonials' speech and gave rise to a drawling manner of talking that made it seem, visitors said, as if they were almost too tired to get their words out.

The native-born white planters were known in France as *créoles*, or colonials. "Creole" is used now for the pidgin French-African language heard in Haiti and New Orleans, or to describe mulattoes (*gens de couleur*) and a certain style of cooking. In the eighteenth and early nineteenth centuries, though, "Creole" meant only that the person was a white planter born in one of the French colonies.

In those colonies haste was not prized as a virtue. A Saint Domingue plantation house was a world of measured inactivity. Servants fetched and carried, and padded at somnolent pace barefoot down long airy corridors. Master and mistress, and the other ladies and gentlemen of the household, relatives or guests, bestirred themselves little. Nor had they cause to. There was no daily routine to speak of. Life was measured by the seasons, not by the clock. And the seasons were as predictable as they were unpleasant and unhealthy.

Visitors and chroniclers attempting to capture the lassitude and inertia frequently reach for the word *languor*. It suggests both a distressed mental condition, a longing for something or somewhere else, plus "a fatigue, a faintness, a drooping stillness."

"It was the burning climate of Saint Domingue that gave [the Creole] his mercurial temperament—his intense crises of reckless passion or feverish energy, followed by reactions in languorous apathy," wrote Stoddard. Life in Saint Domingue could be a living hell. It was death-ridden. Tuberculosis, then called consumption, was the great curse of the eighteenth and nineteenth centuries. If it was common in Europe, it was pandemic in the colonies. To that fear, Saint Domingans added the annual dreads of malaria and, particularly, yellow fever. These onslaughts snatched away children and family members at whim. They obliterated the armies that sought to pry Saint Domingue loose from this group or that. Yellow fever helped defeat Napoleon Bonaparte's plans for Saint Domingue quite as effectively as it slaughtered the British troops determined to add the colony to King George III's collection.

Europeans who sought colonial fortunes risked their lives in other ways, not least in travel between Saint Domingue and the homeland. Travel was treacherous not only from the weather and the poor quality of vessel and crew, but from "ship fever," louse-borne typhus. There were threats from other ships—pirates or the ships of those nations France was currently at war with, usually the British. Accidents on land were brought on by hurricanes in late summer, and dramatic thunderstorms at any time. Every few years, or decades, there could be an earthquake, often centered on Port-au-Prince, where the houses were accordingly built low and of wood.

But week-in and week-out, month-in and month-out, Saint Domingue life was mainly a response to the weather. Once the rainy season ended in April, the inhabitants of the pillared chateaus knew that the stewing humidity and scorching heat would torment them until the rainy season began.

The inside of these plantation chateaus could be bleak places—though not necessarily the one in which Toussaint was raised. Mansions might be totally devoid of quality furnishings, wall hangings, or personal effects. Eighteenth-century French visitors to Saint Domingue often noted the barrenness of the decor and the resultant pervasive air of impermanence. And there was a reason. It was as if the residents did not intend to stay once they'd made enough money, and couldn't be bothered to disguise the fact by making themselves truly comfortable.

Quite simply, most plantation families cared little about organized displays of wealth in their colonial homes; they preferred to reserve all outward manifestations for Paris. So their plantation opulence was a juxtaposed, almost comical mixture. The Toussaint-era visitor and commentator, Baron de Wimpffen, frequently quoted by historians, notes that in a country so rich there are "two kinds of plantations, one a picture of indolence in the last stages of wretchedness; the other [where] the pretensions of opulence [are] directed by the most execrable taste. Thus, you would sometimes meet an elegant carriage drawn by horses and mules of different colors or sizes, with ropes for traces, covered with filth, and driven by a postilion bedaubed with gold—and barefoot."

If the climate and lack of activity enervated the men of the family, it destroyed the inner composure and individuality of the women, the plantation ladies. One of the rare female travelers to Saint Domingue, the American visitor Miss Hassal, said the Creole ladies "have an air of voluptuous languor, which renders them extremely interesting. Their eyes, their teeth, and their hair are remarkably beautiful, and they have acquired from the habit of commanding their slaves an air of dignity which adds to their charms. Almost too indolent to pronounce their words, they speak with a drawling accent which is very agreeable."

When these planters' wives traveled to France with their families, however, they were ridiculed.

On their plantations in Saint Domingue the men had something immediate to talk about, money or trade prospects or reversals or expected shipments and exports. Or, as the revolu tionary unrest developed in France, there was politics. Or there could be sly references to the new mulatto mistress. Wives were for display and begetting the next generation in the family line; mistresses were for everything else. Five thousand of the seven thousand free mulatto single women in Saint Domingue were white men's mistresses.

The owners and male visitors reposing at plantations like L'Artibonite had the freedom to travel. They could remark on the need to go into town, and finally bestir themselves enough eventually to ride the thirteen miles to St. Marc. If adventure or business called, Port-au-Prince was fifty miles away, and could be reached by hard-riding on horses of dubious quality, or by the coastal boat from St. Marc. Hard-riding on horseback for ladies was frowned upon. For the men, grander financial dealings required a two-day boat trip—to Cap François.

Close to home, the Artibonite Valley plantation ladies indeed could go into St. Marc, and some would, for Sunday mass. Trips to Port-au-Prince or, blessed relief, to Le Cap were, for women, major undertakings. Trunks to be packed and a retinue of servants for company. Yet on their plantations, the world of these well-bred women was boredom.

Visitors and residents in Toussaint's day sketch an isolation that was physical in several ways. "The loneliness of the plantations" is a recurrent phrase. There was a great emotional distance along with the actual physical distance from France. In the colony itself, certainly in the sprawling West Province with its huge plantations, there could be considerable physical distance even from one's nearest neighbor, distance aggravated by poor traveling conditions on mere tracks, frequently washed out or uncared for.

On the plantation itself, there were the concentric circles of separation. The chateau with the intimate family and the slave house servants was the center. It was cordoned off from harsh reality by the outdoor slaves attached to the house. Then came the *petit blanc* class, the white overseers, mechanics, and skilled craftsmen who formed another barrier to further insulate the plantation lords and ladies from the source of all their wealth— the brutalized slaves. Around the *petits blancs* was a circle of the more skilled or trusted black slaves.

Then came the field hands.

Family members could, of course, breach these cordons any time they wished, to wander freely and safely among as many as a thousand slaves attached to a single plantation.

But of stimulation of mind, body, or spirit, the chroniclers of the day say there was little. Writes Stoddard: "The chief drawbacks to plantation life were monotony and loneliness. The strict regimen imposed by the climate and the unvarying cycle of tropical agriculture made the planter's existence one of deadening routine. He lived as on an island."

For the adults, the social highlight of the day was the hours-long evening meal. In a plantation like L'Artibonite, where the Bérards dined off "silver plate lined with gold," there would be at least one house servant to wait on each guest at the table, possibly more. The number of personal retainers was a colonial means of keeping social score. Biographer Hannah Lee wrote that in growing up to serve Jean-Jacques Bérard, Toussaint "lived in the midst of luxury and splendor; for the apartments of Monsieur Bérard, as he describes them, were furnished in a style of expense that exceeded even modern prodigality. All the utensils in his mistress's chamber were silver and gold."

In the early 1780s, the topics of dinner conversation would be insubstantial, familial, and gossipy, with variations on the theme of one day returning "home."

❖   ❖   ❖

How different was life for the slaves. For them, home was never again a possibility. And very few even had family. Toussaint was more fortunate—he was a fourth-generation baby and Zénobie occupied a privileged position in the Bérard household. Pierre's generation was already almost a century removed from the Africa of his forebears. Zénobie was personal maid and companion to the senior Madame Bérard, common enough on the great plantations, but she was also extremely competent and totally trusted (two of her gifts to her grandson Pierre).

Prior to her final round-trip to Paris to see the senior Bérards and their children permanently in France, Bérard *père* gave Zénobie her freedom. She had earned it. It meant she made her final trip to Paris voluntarily, returning to L'Artibonite as a free woman, satisfied to be majordomo, servant, and sage to young, single Jean-Jacques—mother to him and to the plantation.

❖   ❖   ❖

Whether in the French capital supervising and mothering her ward, Jean-Jacques, or in the chateau in Saint Domingue, Zénobie is seen as a solid pillar of common sense. She was literate, if barely. Handwritten notes in her not-too-well-formed lettering received by Toussaint in New York in the early 1800s survive. Zénobie was practical in the extreme. Though by the time she wrote those notes to Pierre the colony of Saint Domingue had been racked and ruined by rebellion and revolution, and had witnessed great insurrections that visited unimaginable cruelties on white, black, and mulatto alike, what Zénobie wrote to Toussaint about on one occasion was to request "a good pair of scissors."

Young Pierre seems to have been part of an extended family that crossed many plantation boundaries. The long-settled Bérards were slightly different from those who led "a remote and isolated plantation life"—the Toussaints, too, apparently had relatives and friends on some of these other plantations.

(This same family network among plantations was also the case for Toussaint's future wife, Juliette. When her family fled Saint Domingue with their owners it was as members of the extensive Noël and Gaston families, later influential in the black Catholic communities of Baltimore, Maryland, and, to a lesser extent, Wilmington, Delaware.)

The L'Artibonite Bérards had cousins in Port au Prince, possibly men in central government positions. In the plantation world, in addition to the Bossards of Dondon, the Bérards were close to white families, possibly the Sorbieus, Willagrands, and others whose youngest white children, contemporaries of Pierre, would in New York be among his lifelong friends. Toussaint had an older brother (here known as "Antoine") and a sister, Marie-Louise. He was followed five years later by Rosalie, Ursule's last child to survive beyond infancy. Ursule carried at least one child after Rosalie, but it did not survive.

During her childbearing months Ursule's chambermaid duties would be intermittent, for there were always more servants around than were needed to take up the slack. Pierre's godmother Aurore, for example, in addition to having toddler Pierre in regular attendance, had adult and girl servants like Madeleine, her wet-nurse, and Hortense, her personal lady's maid. There'd be plenty of specialized servants in the chateau, too, people like Old Cabresse, the seamstress.

Depending on the attitude of the plantation owners, Catholicism might or might not play a major role in the lives of some of the slaves. The personal and house slaves more so than the field slaves, for the personal slaves had greater mobility.

French planters were required by law to baptize their slaves, and they were encouraged to have their slaves' unions witnessed by the church. Slaves were to have Sundays and Holy Days free to attend mass. However, as France and its laws were two months away from Saint Domingue in good sailing weather (and a harrowing three months away in truly foul weather) most *grand blanc* planters, who detested restrictions of any kind on their treatment of the slaves, imposed their own laws and ignored the ones from France they didn't like. The exception was the tax laws, which were enforced on the spot by the governor, who helped himself to some of the money. Official corruption was rife.

To suggest the Bérards were more noble than their neighbors in how their slave field hands were treated is a temptation to be resisted. There is no proof. One can only hope the Bérards were among the minority of planters who lived up to the spirit of the slave-protection regulations issued by an earlier king of France.

Field-hand life was brutal. The Swiss traveler Monsieur Giroud-Chantrans, quoted by C.L.R. James, who visited a Saint Domingue plantation in 1785, when Pierre was about four, saw "men and women of different ages, digging ditches in a canefield, the majority naked or in rags. The sun shone down with full force on their heads. Sweat rolled from all parts of their bodies. Their limbs, weighed down by the heat. Exhaustion stamped on every face, but the hour of rest had not come. The pitiless eye of the Manager patrolled the gang, and several foremen with long whips moved periodically between them giving stinging blows to all who, worn out by fatigue, were compelled to take a rest—men or women, young or old."

It wasn't supposed to be this way. In the early seventeenth century, when colonies were first proposed and settlement got under way, King Louis XIII of France hadn't wanted slavery at all. It was Cardinal Richelieu who persuaded the king otherwise. (The mention of Richelieu is the first indicator of how often Toussaint's story conjures up some of the strongest characters in history.)

The cardinal softened the king's opposition by using religion as a tool. In 1626, when Richelieu issued the Royal Commission establishing the first French colony in the Antilles (in what is now generally referred to as the Caribbean), Catholicism was "established as the official religion and all inhabitants were to be instructed in the faith." King Louis was finally persuaded to accept slavery by those with a closer eye on their investments than their souls, through the stipulation that all slaves must be converted to Christianity. Consequently, French colonial charters were rigorous where religion was concerned.

In 1635, the Compagnie des Isles de l'Amérique was expressly instructed by Richelieu that Catholicism was mandatory. But Catholicism needed priests; therefore the pope had to be involved. And so he was. Pope Urban VIII, on July 12, 1639, approved the departure for the French Antilles colonies of four Dominicans to save the souls of the slaves. Any thought regarding the slaves' freedom escaped Church notice.

In Saint Domingue, these human beings were treated as chattel. They were branded, usually on each breast, and given a brief time—called "seasoning"—to acclimatize to the island's humidity and temperature before being put to work. Contemporary records say that at least a third of the slaves died during the "seasoning" period. The trip alone, along with the deprivation of their freedom, killed them. But by the seventeenth century they were dying under royal protection, for France's Louis XIV formalized slaves' rights in the 1685 Code Noir.

In 1720, when there were only 100,000 slaves, the augmented corps of priests had probably baptized about 50 percent of them. Slave numbers doubled in decades, the missionaries could not keep up. By the 1780s, 30,000 to 40,000 new slaves a year were pouring in. By then, as agricultural production itself doubled every three or four years (and investors' and planters' fortunes swelled beyond imagination), the demand for slaves exceeded the supply. With these soaring numbers, it was scarcely surprising that the percentage of baptisms dropped precipitously.

Africa could not keep up with Saint Domingue's demand for

slaves and some were smuggled in from other island plantations. Planters preferred to buy slaves rather than breed them.
It was cheaper. Breeding meant an unproductive seven or eight
years before the child could be usefully employed. And there
was the absence of the pregnant and postbirth mother to factor
in, if only temporarily. How different for the house slave. The
Bérards obviously welcomed the continuity where their house
servants were concerned. Field slave or house slaves, these
Africans frequently were people of quality. Modern research
suggests it was the slaves who brought the rice farming skills to
the Caribbean. They may have brought other knowledge the
whites used to advantage.

For what was the young Toussaint to be trained? For a role
as a personal servant, a valet, a gentleman's gentleman, certainly. Yet there could have been a second factor at work. There
was only one reason the French were in Saint Domingue, and
that was to make money. In Saint Domingue, millionaires, even
billionaires by modern measure, were present in their plenty.
The sole reason the French suffered through the monotony, the
dreadful climate, and the disease that claimed their children
and delicate colonial wives, was to quickly amass a fortune, then
return to Paris while still young enough to live a long, comfortable life enjoying their wealth. Someone had to manage the
plantation.

Pierre Bérard, the plantation master, was waiting for his
son, Jean-Jacques, to return from Paris in early manhood, as
equipped as he was ever going to be, to take over the huge estate. With the oldest son in charge of L'Artibonite, off the senior
Bérards would go. Jean-Jacques in turn, in the decades ahead,
could expect to marry and beget his own son, who would then
take over from him. Then it would be Jean-Jacques's turn to retire in wealth to France.

That was the Saint Domingue family tradition for generations of French planters. But there was also another system de-

veloping. The Jesuits, before they were suppressed and their plantations confiscated, had tried the alternative with some success. The idea was to educate and train bright, intelligent, industrious slaves to run the plantations. And the farsighted Jean-Jacques may have foreseen just such a future for Pierre Toussaint. (On the Bréda plantation, the other Toussaint—the Liberator, Toussaint-Louverture—was plantation steward, its administrator.)

Otherwise, in most ways, the pattern of plantation life into which Toussaint was born in 1781 was static. Life at L'Artibonite in the early 1780s for the family or the household slaves was likely little different from what it had been for their forebears a half century earlier.

❖   ❖   ❖

On the day he was born, unknown and unnoticed, Pierre Toussaint was about the two millionth black slave to arrive, one way or another, in the so-called New World. The first slave had been dragged out of Africa and shipped west not twenty years after Columbus first set foot on a lump of what became known as Saint Domingue. The explorer landed on Ile St. Nicolas, on the island he named Española (Hispaniola)—Little Spain. Ile St. Nicolas the French fancifully later dubbed "the Gibraltar of the Antilles."

When Columbus arrived, the million or so Arawaks who knew and claimed the land as home called it Hayti, meaning "mountainous country." It didn't matter what they called it. With Columbus's landing they had about fifty years left. It took only decades, not centuries, for Old World disease, brutality, enslavement, and outright slaughter to completely exterminate them. And in their plight, the Arawaks unwittingly became the trigger that brought Pierre Toussaint's forebears and those like them to Saint Domingue.

The plight of the Arawaks and other "New World" Indians

directly introduced black African slavery to this thoroughly exploitable hemisphere. It happened because the animist Arawaks, forced quickly into slavery on their island homeland, had an ally: the missionaries. Though to the Catholic Church these indigenous peoples were heathens and savages, that same Church—too late—tried to come to their rescue through the valiant efforts of Bartolomé de Las Casas and members of several religious orders.

To save the Arawaks, the idealist priest opened one of history's most egregious examples of the law of unintended consequences. Las Casas, born in Seville, Spain, migrated to Española and became the first priest ordained in the New World (1512). He was horrified by the Spanish treatment of the Arawaks and was a sufficiently good investigator and documentor of those atrocities that, in 1537, Pope Paul III issued *Sublimus Deus*, listing the Arawaks' rights and condemning the injustices against them. The Arawaks probably never heard about the Papal Bull—and were exterminated anyway because the Spanish in Española ignored it.

Las Casas, who proved his worth as an agitator for the oppressed Indians, wrote to the Spanish crown urging that the colonists be granted a license to import Africans. He later bemoaned his decision regarding the black slaves, writing that he was unaware the blacks "were as unjustly treated as the Indians." The importation of black slaves grew into the most sustained armada of human souls in maritime history until the voluntary mass migrations of Europeans to the United States in the nineteenth century.

The astute reader will immediately ask, if the pagan Arawaks could be (ineffectively, as it turned out) sheltered by the Church, by a pope no less, why were black Africans, under the guardianship of the same Church and pope, not also spared. The answer was an old one, and had its roots in the Muslim occupation of the Holy Lands that led to the Crusades.

In the eyes of Rome—and the Benedictine historian Cyprian Davis is a fine source on this—the Muslims were "infidels" (nonbelievers). Islam was the enemy, a force of unbelievers hostile to Christianity.

From the eighth century on, the growing Muslim hegemony over North Africa was not merely a threat to Christendom's territorial sway, it was a usurpation of "the one, true faith." Islam challenged Christian belief at its core. These "infidels" occupied the land of Jesus' birth and ministry, no less. (Plus, Muslims who captured Christians generally enslaved them.)

Muslims, however, didn't invent slavery for Europe. The word *slave* comes from *slavs*. Slavic people were a favored source of bound labor in early Roman times. What the Muslims did, many of them dark-skinned themselves, was embed the concept of African slaves in Spain and Portugal, both Christian countries. That's because the Muslims were not content to spread solely across the southern Mediterranean. They eyed and then firmly established themselves on the northern Mediterranean coast, taking up permanent residence in Portugal and Spain.

By 1492, when Ferdinand and Isabella drove the Moors from Spain (and those Jews they didn't boil in oil) and sent Columbus off on his voyage of discovery, infidel was synonymous with "Moors"—black North African Muslims. (The image of the Moor remains to the present day, in Shakespeare's *Othello*.) The black Moors brought African slaves to the Iberian peninsula, and enslaved other races when necessary.

Historian Cyprian Davis explains the convoluted thought process by which the Catholic Church came to accept black slavery. All black Africans from south of the Sahara were considered Muslims. And because Muslims captured Christians and made them into slaves, Christians were considered "to have a legitimate right" to in turn enslave the Muslims. The tragedy atop the villainy was, of course, that Africans south of the Sahara were rarely Muslim—Islam had not penetrated that far geographically by that time. Instead, the 1.5 to 2 million Africans the European slave traders wrenched from the Congo, Chad, Dahomey, and elsewhere—under the canard they were Muslims fit only for slavery—were in fact animists. In Saint Domingue as elsewhere, African native practices blended with the prevailing Catholicism to produced modern voodoo, what the colonial French knew as "voudou," from "vudu," the Dahomey people's term for animist beliefs and rituals.

Pierre Toussaint is a mere fragment within this vicious colonial enterprise, but Davis's account becomes more pertinent as Toussaint, first as a slave and always as a black man, remains a victim of periodic Catholic bigotry throughout his entire adult life. In that lifetime, American Catholic bishops, religious orders, and Catholic plantation owners, as people of their time, were slaveholders. Most with clear consciences, perhaps. Catholic Church teaching allowed their consciences to be clear. Catholic teaching did not prohibit slaveholding, only slave trading. The popes never declared slavery a sin until Pope John XXIII's firm and final condemnation in the mid-twentieth century.

Toussaint's faith was unshakable. His commitment to the Catholic Church total. He knew it was a bigoted institution. But even he was shaken when, though New York's most prominent black Catholic, he was subject to a racist rebuff as he one day entered (Old) St. Patrick's Cathedral with his wife. Despite subsequent lengthy apologies from the trustees, there is no evidence that Toussaint, who for more than a half century had attended the six A.M. mass daily at St. Peter's Church on Barclay Street, ever attempted to step foot in the cathedral again.

THREE

THE BÉRARDS

PIERRE TOUSSAINT'S SECOND FAMILY, the Bérard du Pithon clan that owned him, was a sizable household. There were eight Bérard children. The boys, in addition to Jean-Jacques, son and heir, were Lester, Des Glajeux, and Du Pithon. The four girls were Victoire, Félicité, Eulalie, and De Pointe (Aurore). Du Pithon, writing cordially to Toussaint in 1815, said he could not remember Pierre, "I was so young when I left St. Domingo that I should certainly not recognize your features, but I am sure my heart would acknowledge you at once."

It appears Pierre grew up with the younger two Bérards, and while he was never less than a slave in reality, in his earliest years was in actuality more or less just another playmate. One strong indicator of some early special quality about Pierre was that his older brother, Antoine, apparently was not similarly favored. All one can do is look at Pierre's later character and manner and conclude that, even as a little boy, Toussaint exhibited the bright, capable, cheerful, and willing ways that as an adult endeared him to his friends. When the mature Toussaint referred to his childhood days he saw them as idyllic.

Zénobie's presence was crucial. The grandmother, if one extrapolates from the few existing clues, was obviously his major role model. One can think of Zénobie as something akin to the butler in a nineteenth-century English manor (but one far less inhibited than, say, Anthony Hopkins in the movie *The Remains of the Day*).

The managerial and interpersonal skills Zénobie needed (and Toussaint later demonstrated) can today be seen in the authority, tact, and responsibilities required of, say, the in-flight purser on a New York–London–Hong Kong airline flight. His or her take-charge, crisis-solving qualifications must be coupled with a personable manner and a dignified strength of character to make the individual fully effective.

The grandmother's worth to the household provides insight into Toussaint's own later ability to wield a calm influence while bringing to bear imagination and authority delivered with a refined charm. Barely out of his teens, Toussaint's take-charge manner when disaster strikes the New York Bérard household is quite possibly a product of personality and temperament, but surely a personality wedded to a decisiveness and competence patterned on his early experiences watching his grandmother in action. (Her skills, lost to the historical record, must have been at their peak—and most severely tested—when revolution, upheaval, and constant bloodshed tore Saint Domingue apart. How good was she? All we have to go on is that during the slave uprising, working alongside Jean-Jacques and his other staff and managers, she ensured the survival of the entire family.)

At L'Artibonite, the bond between the domestic slave and plantation family could not have been more intimate. Grandmother Zénobie wet-nursed the two older Bérard children. Because it was not uncommon, in eighteenth- and nineteenth-century Europe, for an infant to actually live with a wet-nurse for the first two or three years, similar practices were followed in the colonies. (As late as the 1870s, for example, the young Winston Churchill was raised by his live-in "nana," Mrs. Everett. Churchill saw his mother perhaps three or four times a week, just before bedtime. His father he saw less than once a week.)

The nursing brought women like Zénobie closer to their young charges than were the children's natural mothers. And naturally the nurse-child affection was two-way. All the time Jean-Jacques was in Paris without Zénobie, "he constantly wrote to her, sending her presents and retaining his early affection."

In a mirror image of this, Pierre basked in the Bérards' affection. That the Bérards were kindly masters explains Toussaint's own deep and nostalgic feeling for his early childhood. Toussaint was one of the lucky ones. But his situation was not unique. Historian C. L. R. James (speaking of Toussaint-Louverture, though the comment could easily be applied to Pierre Toussaint) remarks that "circumstances conspired to give him exceptional parents and friends and a kind master." Being a "kind master" could well have been a Bérard family tradition, for James also says that the earlier planters, those who founded the colony in the late seventeenth and early eighteenth centuries, were people of simpler and more modest tastes. And the Bérard family habits and style may have persisted down to Jean-Jacques's generation.

Further—and this must not be overlooked, for the Bérards may have been among them—not all Frenchmen considered the African slaves to be crude brutes. Chroniclers as different as Baron de Wimpffen and author Hilliard d'Auberteuil, admired many African slaves as voluble and intelligent human beings. *Grand blanc* planter Auberteuil wrote a book on the topic. It was immediately banned in the colony, and probably didn't make him too popular among the majority of planters either. Had the Bérards similarly felt the African slaves were intelligent and ca-

pable human beings, L'Artibonite's governing family would
have been in a distinct minority, but not totally alone.

Without proof it is risky to assert too much about the
Bérards' personal qualities. Yet is one clue to the Bérards' character Toussaint's own rounded personality? Possibly. His formation came at the hands of both his own family and the Bérards.
It is reasonable to presume that Jean-Jacques had a strong hand
in Toussaint's teenage training and further education, even if
Jean-Jacques did this at Zénobie's quiet urging. On some subjects Jean-Jacques himself may have tutored Pierre. After all,
when young Bérard returned from Paris at barely twenty, he
had his books and time on his hands. Like many a student fresh
from academic pursuits, Jean-Jacques may have enjoyed having
the boy, a temporary surrogate son, as a protégé to mold intel-
lectually. While doing that—if, in fact, he did—Jean-Jacques
could still have put Pierre under the tutelage of a priest for
other topics of instruction. (Did history repeat itself forty years
later when Toussaint and his wife took orphaned and abandoned African boys into their home to see them trained, educated, and prepared for life? Didn't Toussaint regard the white
child, little William Schuyler, almost as his own son?)

In the Bérard family, regular religious practice appears to
have been a norm, and religious learning had some place in the
family's makeup. Aurore Bérard's later letters to Toussaint are
pious in the extreme. On a more religiously cultivated and educated level, Pierre was familiar with the New Testament, and
could quote from it at length as well as from the best French religious minds admired by aristocratic French Catholics. It would
not have been Zénobie, or his mother, Ursule, who supplied
Pierre with the sermons of Bossuet and Massillon, or the max-
ims of John of the Cross. They were either already in the L'Artibonite library, in Jean-Jacques's luggage when he returned
from Paris, or, somewhat less likely, on the bookshelf at the local
rectory.

Throughout his life, Toussaint quoted freely from memory these and other works. His level of Scriptural and theological familiarity was an attainment far greater than that of the average lay Catholic in Europe and North America, even into the late twentieth century.

Only the parish priest or Jean-Jacques, not long returned from the grand liturgies and religious certainties of high church France, could have inculcated such appreciations. It was not piety, but learning, and classical learning at that. It meant Toussaint had a solid background on which to draw—lessons of history and religion intertwined to produce a formed mind. Admittedly, this was Catholicism totally allied to royalty, what became known as the Ancien Régime. But there was no other brand available. Decades after Saint Domingue's disintegration, Toussaint's friends in France, particularly Jean Sorbieu, would write to him at length of French Catholicism's great displays, and mock the preaching and liturgies that satisfied New York's "Irish savages."

The Bérards' religious practice—if Bossuet and Massillon came from their library shelves—would expect and demand sermons that were impressive, intellectual, and oratorical tours de force. This high-minded appreciation also anticipated grand liturgical rituals. In New York, in the 1800s, Toussaint's Saint Domingue and French friends paid subscriptions of one gourd (about a dollar then, about $25 today) each calendar quarter to regularly bring a visiting French priest to St. Peter's Church on Barclay Street, just so they could have occasionally the style and content of ritual and preaching they enjoyed. Was there, during Toussaint's boyhood, a hint of this French intellectual tradition present in the parish church of St. Marc? Very likely, if the planters were fortunate with their assigned priest, or capable of influencing which priest served them.

Of the French Catholic preachers Toussaint committed to memory, Jacques-Bénigne Bossuet (1627–1704) was a French

bishop, noted preacher, and classical scholar. In the age of Louis
XIV, Bossuet's fame as an orator was such that he was known as
"the voice of France."

What would have made him popular with the people like
the royalist Bérards was that Bossuet believed equally in religious absolutism and the divine right of kings. That didn't mean
Bossuet fawned on royalty. Bishop Bossuet preached against,
and counseled Louis XIV against, his mistresses and his engag-
ing in adulterous behavior. Louis argued that kings were above
the law. Bossuet agreed, but not, he told the king, above the law
of God. Toussaint certainly understood such distinctions.

Thirty-six years younger than Bossuet, Jean-Baptiste Massillon (1663–1742) was also a bishop and preacher. Bossuet
himself admired Massillon's sermons. Both men preached set
pieces, lengthy, scholarly sermons on Lenten topics, royal funerals, and moral themes. Bossuet, however, was friendly with
Protestant scholars and seriously interested in Christian unifica-
tion—at least for a while. But then, toward the end of his life,
Bossuet turned somewhat savage, condemning everything from
people to theater. It is not clear as to whether Toussaint's comfort with people of other faiths stemmed from reading Bossuet
or from his own personality. Knowing Bossuet's works, Toussaint would have taken to heart only that which made sense. Yet
if there were Protestants in Saint Domingue, they kept very
quiet about it. Later, in New York, Toussaint committed to
memory writings of one of the Channings, who were American
Unitarian ministers. That Toussaint continued to memorize sermons and speeches later in his life strongly suggests a fertile and
inquisitive intellect.

Another author Toussaint read was St. John of the Cross
(John de Yepes, founder with St. Teresa of the Discalced
Carmelites), who lived from 1542 to 1591. He was a solitary by
temperament and opportunity, and his works, such as *The Dark*

Night (of the Soul), reflect this. Nonetheless, he was regarded during Toussaint's boyhood as he is today, as a spiritual master with much to contribute to life on the path of perfection.

These sixteenth- and seventeenth-century churchmen were not the only ones to influence Toussaint's life. Cardinal Armand Jean du Plessis, duc de Richelieu (1585–1642), it can be argued, was the reason slaves were baptized. Though a priest and bishop, Richelieu had only one passion—to centralize French power under the monarch. To do that, as prime minister, Richelieu played many a cunning game. Under his tutelage, the monarch stripped the aristocrats of their political power, which also meant that they lacked political patronage. And without patronage there were few fresh ways to keep the family coffers filled. This meant that their sons had to seek their own ways to make a fortune. As there were now very few opportunities for them inside France, the noble houses looked outside France, toward the new colonies.

It was the cardinal's fixation on an all-powerful monarchy that led to this active promotion of colonial expansion. He was not content with just centralizing power; he wanted to strengthen it. And in foreign affairs he wanted a French navy so strong it could cow, or at least deter, the British—and that cost money. The colonies in the French Antilles, in turn, held promise as a source of that money. A flourishing colonial agricultural machine could send back immensely profitable goods, with planters able to pay high taxes, and the colonies themselves could be a ready market for French goods. Further, a large merchant marine to import the colonial goods meant shipyards and trained sailors. Richelieu's political and colonial ends fit with the junior aristocracy's lack of means.

In Europe, the right of primogeniture ensured that everything went to the first son, leaving the second and third sons casting about for careers. They needed money to live as French lords, as did their eldest brother. Saint Domingue presented them with such an opportunity, which is one reason its history is filled with aristocratic names.

There were nonplantation jobs, too. *Grands blancs* served as high-ranking government officials, and the military establishment needed officers. Though there were no nobles among the professional-class functionaries (lawyers, accountants, shipping firms)—those jobs were deemed beneath their dignity and beyond their skills. Saint Domingue was big business, with plenty of middlemen busy in a two-way trade that saw raw sugar and coffee headed to Europe on ships that brought French goods back to the colony.

❖   ❖   ❖

The Bérards possessed a family name common to several areas of France, including Paris and Montpellier in Languedoc. Wherever the Bérard family originally hailed from, and from whatever social station, the Saint Domingue Bérards, once they'd begun to make money, considered Paris home. Just as many modern Americans, regardless of their state of origin, intend to live in and become New Yorkers or Washingtonians or Angelenos, so most *grand blanc* planters had their eye on a life of leisure in the French capital as the reward for their efforts.

Richelieu may have wanted colonies, but it was not the king or the cardinal who saw to it that Saint Domingue was initially settled by the French. French and English pirates preying on the Spanish New World gold fleets achieved that.

The French presence on what was a Spanish-claimed island came about because by the 1620s, a century and a quarter after Columbus landed, some French privateers, pirates, and ne'er-do-wells decided on Tortuga, six miles off the northern coast of Santo Domingo, as a good base of operations. Settled on Tortuga, the pirates raided Santo Domingo's northern plains for meat—readily available from the thousands of wild cattle that roamed loose, descendants of cattle brought by the first Spanish colonists. From their island fortress, the Tortuga French made famous a new word, "buccaneer," from *boucan,* the way they smoked their beef—by barbecuing it over an open pit.

Gradually, some Tortugans, along with others sailing the Caribbean, simply began to appropriate land in what became Saint Domingue's North Province. They did this without so much as a by-your-leave to the Spanish authorities far to the east—an administration that rarely had either the force or the will to take steps to oust the French squatters two hundred miles away. The French squatters became legal when, by the 1697 Treaty of Ryswick, the Spanish ceded the western third of Santo Domingo to the French. The French called their portion Saint Domingue—and the land rush was on.

Here's what the French had gained: the top pincer of crab claw–shaped Saint Domingue is the North Province—a peninsula, about 50 miles long and 40 miles wide that juts out toward Cuba, 70 miles to the west. The big block of land that is the West Province is the muscle, the stout hinge for both the top pincer and the lower pincer, the South Province. The South Province's peninsula is about 150 miles long, and varies from 20 to 40 miles wide. It points toward Jamaica, 170 miles distant.

The two pincers form a huge bay, the Gulf of Gonaïves. The West Province's western edge is on the Gonaïves coast. The French established their new political capital, Port-au-Prince on this shore, to the south. On the same shore but far to the north, the Artibonite River flows into the Gonaïves waters. At roughly midway between Port-au-Prince and the mouth of the Artibonite is St. Marc, the major city that served the Bérards. The West Province backs into the border with Spanish Santo Domingo.

What attracted would-be planters by the hundreds and then thousands to Saint Domingue was obvious. As one nineteenth-century scholar explained: "In richness and variety of vegetable products the land is not excelled by any other country in the world. All tropical plants and trees grow in perfection, and nearly all the fruits and vegetables of the temperate climates may be successfully cultivated in the highlands. Among the indigenous products are cotton, rice, maize, tobacco, cocoa, ginger, native indigo, arrowroot, manioc [cassava], pimento, banana, plantain, pineapple, artichoke, and yams." The important crops became sugar-cane, coffee and indigo—essential as a blue dye.

This was an unoccupied paradise. The Arawaks were all dead. The land was there. The newcomers took it.

The French turned their favorite port, the North Province's Cap François, from a "back door" of the Spanish colony into the "front door" of the new French colony.

If, as seems likely, the Bérards of Toussaint's era were fourth-generation Saint Domingans, then Founder Bérard was probably born in the 1660s or very early 1670s, and he would have been working his plantation by the late 1690s or early 1700s. But why, one wonders, were the Bérards in the West Province? It is quite possible that, by the time Founder Bérard decided to try his hand as a colonial planter, the North Province lands were all claimed—or too expensive to buy. Or, equally possible, the Bérard family may have had connections to those in government service in Port-au-Prince. We know there were Bérard cousins living in the political capital. Perhaps these relatives were quick to advise Founder Bérard to lay claim to lands in the West Province at a time when it was still being pioneered.

Certainly, Founder Bérard and his original backers obtained title to thousands of acres in the Artibonite Valley, the foundation of the family fortune. He was early enough to obtain land enough, yet where did he gain the knowledge essential to irrigation-dependent farming on a flood-prone river valley? Twenty-first-century scholarship suggests it was the slaves from

agricultural West Africa, and not their masters, who brought
the requisite tropical climate farming knowledge to Saint
Domingue.

Much of the plantation's early period may have been farming by trial and error. Tradition has it that Toussaint's forebears
were from the Congo—a land of fishermen and farmers. That
would mean they knew agricultural methods suitable to tropical
conditions. Even if Founder Bérard had some agricultural
knowledge, it would have appropriate for Europe's temperate climate; it would scarcely have prepared him for Saint
Domingue. (As pure conjecture, the parents of Toussaint's great-
grandmother Tonette, or those of other early slaves, could have
brought with them the sort of knowledge a fledgling planter
needed to tackle the Artibonite wilderness and subdue it for successful farming. Certainly someone other than Founder Bérard
had a hand in shaping the acreage into productive land.)

The economics of French colonial enterprise worked this
way: To seventeenth- and eighteenth-century Europe, a colony
was simply a business venture. It was nothing more than a fac-
tory, and the planters were its managers. This was true of any
colony, whether one is speaking of the thirteen original colonies
in North America, or the earlier Spanish ones. Someone was
putting up money and funding a settlement from which they
would—they hoped—reap a profit. They weren't certain quite
how the profit would be gained, but they knew the land and resources were there for the taking, forcibly or otherwise.

The other player in the colonial game, besides those who
provided investment money for ships, supplies, and tools, was
the monarch, the king. The monarch owned outright all land
claimed in his name. He, or she in the case of England's Elizabeth I, would issue a charter, just as corporations today are
chartered. The colonial investors, occasionally nobles but most
often wealthy domestic businessmen, frequently assisted young
nobles and the higher born to set up shop as planters—the pre-

sumption being the young nobles and their near kin were a better risk than the average Frenchman. Other potential émigrés included people fleeing religious or political persecution or the law.

As far as the European monarchs and their advisers were concerned, the colony and the colonial people had no rights. The entire establishment existed simply to create commercial activity for the native land, and to be taxed on its exports as well as its imports. The colony could trade only with the home country, and carry its goods only on the home country's ships. Later, founder Bérard could well have been among protesting planters who caused one Saint Domingue governor to complain, "these people have risen against the King's authority and the Company. They demand tax exemption, free trade with all nations, and a republican liberty." It was a widespread feeling in all of Europe's colonies.

When French San Domingue's planters began to vigorously protest ever higher levels of French taxation, when they petitioned to overturn French laws that forbade them from trading with other countries, when they derided the ban that prevented them from setting up industries to make products the home country instead sold to them, when they complained because they were deprived of representation in the French government—those French planters were only doing what the American colonists did vis-à-vis the detested government of King George III of England.

It was a common standoff. In the king's eyes, colonials had no rights. Yet all colonists wanted the same things: freedom to trade with all comers, less taxation, more rights, and more representations.

The founding Bérard had stepped into a colony that was corrupt from top to bottom. Financially corrupt at the top because the governor was corrupt; morally corrupt at the bottom because of slavery. The *grands blancs* planters' grievances may have been real enough, and they may, in their dealings with the monarch in France, have been royalists to the core. But they were arrogant royalists.

That arrogance was obvious when Louis XIV bowed to missionary pressure and issued the slave-protecting 1685 Code Noir. Many wealthy planters simply dismissed it as irrelevant. To them it was not a church-state conflict, it was a church-commerce conflict. The planters knew there was no power in Saint Domingue that would enforce the Code Noir. The succession of local governors understood whose money actually filled their wineglasses and bought their Brie, so they sided with the wealthy planters.

To its credit, the Church wouldn't back down. The missionary priests, the Jesuits, Dominicans, Capuchins, and Trinitarians, continually pressed the monarchy for protections for the slaves. They wanted, in historian George Breathett's phrase, "a policy of religious protectionism, a policy designed to make secure and maintain a purity of faith among converted slaves."

The planters hated the policy and, where they could, ignored it. Time and again the Church fought back. A Church council was held in Martinique. It laid down the rules: Slaves could not be worked on Sundays or feast days. It was the sort of ruling one hopes the Bérards wholeheartedly supported.

Most slaveholders returned the fight (the Bérards and like-minded others could, through inertia, simply refuse to get involved). The slaveholders charged that the Church was interfering with commerce, therefore with secular affairs. Both priests and planters turned to the king. The monarch sided with the priests. He issued an order saying colonials who opposed the clergy's aims were "anticlerical," and to be anticlerical was a grave charge. Criticizing the Church for protecting the slaves became a punishable offense, for which the royal administration in Paris developed a sliding scale of fines.

For opposing basic religious freedoms for the slaves the

plantation owner was fined sixty pounds of tobacco. (Tobacco was frequently used as currency in Caribbean and North American seacoast transactions. When Pierre Toussaint later wants to help his sister, who had fled Saint Domingue for Cuba, he sends tobacco, not money. Tobacco was readily convertible into any local currency.) The fine for a second offense was ninety pounds of tobacco, and a third offense meant a loss of the slaves, who would be seized and handed over to a more "Christian" slaveholder. That was the letter of the law.

But there is no evidence these regulations were ever enforced.

And yet, the law's significance to Toussaint's life cannot be discounted. If the royalist Bérard family comported itself as practicing Catholics in a place and time when few did, they could have lived up to the spirit as well as the letter of the Code Noir. If a Bérard felt this way about the rights of the slaves, it meant he was philosophically far ahead of the temper of the times. This same Bérard was also in a moral quagmire. Breathett explains. The Church's high degree of agitation on the slaves' behalf creates a paradox, said Breathett, for "a God who insists on equality presents something of a quandary if one is seeking to convert a slave. It would be difficult, if not impossible, to instill principles of a religion, which emphasizes the equality of all men under God, in persons denied basic human rights."

Yet Breathett makes a parallel point: that in the late seventeenth century, when this religious protectionism was first being tested, "there existed no abstract conception of the dignity of man." That concept was still almost a century away.

The chateau that Founder Bérard or his successors built in the Artibonite Valley was sizable enough. Its remains are still detectable, though barely. Locals to this day insist that some of the huts in the area date back to the original slave huts. The land is still healthy and fertile, which means the garden plots could have produced an abundance in slave days.

Certainly the slaves needed their gardens. Saint Domingue could not feed itself or its slaves. Nearly all food was imported. When, during the Seven Years War (1756–1763), food failed to reach the colony because the British halted French maritime commerce, thousands of slaves simply starved. Historians generally agree that when slaves were not working, and despite their general exhaustion, they did cultivate small plots.

Founder Bérard and his fellow planters were creating what would become the wealthiest colony the world had ever seen. Picture any period of unprecedented prosperity in the United States—the onset of the railroads, the automobile, movies, television, the heyday years of Silicon Valley. Saint Domingue matched or exceeded it. In moments of surging wealth creation in Europe or the United States, the stock market, banking, steel, beer, or advertising created millionaires by the score; so, in Saint Domingue, the coffee and sugar, the indigo, cocoa, cotton, and hides did for French venturers. But it didn't stop. In Saint Domingue it grew and grew, decade after decade. Generations of French venturers kept wallowing in wealth beyond their expectations. Saint Domingue's output was not static. As the century stormed ahead, the value of Saint Domingue's exports kept doubling. And the pace was quickening—from 1786 to 1789 (as Pierre moves from being a boy of five to one of eight), "the planters doubled their productivity." Rewards at this rate kept attracting additional investment wealth.

Everyone in France with money wanted to participate. In those same three years, 1786–1789, historian T. Lothrop Stoddard reports, a vast amount "of French capital poured into the island for investment—a hundred millions [a half-billion in twenty-first-century dollars] from Bordeaux alone. The returns were already splendid and still greater were expected."

This golden situation—much wealth already in hand plus the prospect of ever-mounting fortunes—was the bequest the father, Pierre Bérard, handed over to L'Artibonite's fourth owner, Jean-Jacques. The father, Pierre, had lived and prospered during Saint Domingue's golden years, when the colony was all profits and little trouble. The same would not hold true for Jean-Jacques.

The only major internal island traumas in Pierre Bérard's time had been those inflicted by the runaway slaves, known as maroons, who lived in the high forests. In the 1750s, when Pierre Bérard was a young man, there had been the famed and feared Mackandal maroon uprising. Normally, the maroons, living in groups of anywhere from a dozen to a hundred, would swoop down from the hills to raid isolated plantations. Hunting primarily for food supplies, they would kill, rape, and pillage before stocking up on provisions and disappearing back into the hills. Often enough they persuaded some of the plantation slaves to join them. The planters were not idle in retaliating, just ineffective. Saint Domingue had three forms of armed military: the French regiments stationed in the colony under the governor's command, a militia, and the "volunteer" police force, the *maréchaussée*. This latter, compulsory service for the mulattoes, was a local guard expressly established to seek out runaway slaves and keep local order. Invariably, though, by the time there had been a raid and the *maréchaussée* summoned, the maroons were back in the mountains where they were safe.

Mackandal's uprising was different—and devastating in its intent. A charismatic voodoo leader, Mackandal built a vast network of contacts throughout the plantation world's slaves. He gradually put into place a plan whereby, on a given day, all the white plantation owners would be poisoned. Poisoning was a common retribution used by slaves with bitter grievances against their owners (as if slavery wasn't grievance enough). The slaves best situated to poison their masters and mistresses were the women. And on plantations, the slave girls and women often had good reason for revenge: rape and sexual abuse.

On this score, if Toussaint is the example, the Bérard males maintained a certain moral probity around the chateau. Pierre Toussaint was not of mixed blood (though his wife, Juliette, was), and there is no evidence or suggestion that the male Bérards were involved in sexual impropriety with their household slaves. Outside the chateau, their religious convictions could have kept them away from adulterous couplings and *gens de couleur* mistresses.

With no Mackandal to worry about, and, for whites, in a setting of wealth, luxury, and indolence, little Pierre Toussaint grew up with his own siblings and cousins and young Bérard playmates. Like Mary with her Little Lamb, wherever his godmother Aurore went, Toussaint would probably go, too. The large house with its creepy attics and upstairs "box rooms," and plenty of space under the roof, was probably the indoor playground.

More significant, the little Toussaint may have been in attendance when the youngest Bérards received their initial nursery education before inevitably being shipped off to France. During the periods when Zénobie was at home and in charge, the possibility is quite high that Toussaint attended whatever schooling was being made available. Outside the chateau classroom, childhood life was to be enjoyed.

For Bérards and Toussaints, this colonial idyll began to shatter in July 1789 with the storming of the Bastille. The French Revolution had broken out across France. The horror-filled waves of "Terror" that dispensed death and dispersed families were four years ahead for France, but only two years ahead for Saint Domingue.

FOUR

GUILLOTINES AND BOILING SUGAR, 1788—PART I

BY LATE 1788, the Bérard family had happily settled in Paris, unaware of what lay ahead. Comfortable in their new life, Monsieur and Madame Pierre Bérard, well situated in a grand home and with a fine fortune to draw on, began the delicate social interplays necessary to get their daughters suitably married. One daughter, Eulalie, soon became Madame de Bercy. Zénobie, who had accompanied the family to France, possibly remained in the capital long enough to attend the wedding. The boys, their education done in a few years, would be expected to find brides in good families and, if they chose, careers.

In the French capital, the Bérards' high hopes for the future were real enough. They could not imagine that, within six years, both Monsieur and Madame Bérard would be dead, hounded to death during "the Terror" by agents of the Revolution. The Bérards' fortune and Paris home were confiscated, the children left to fend for themselves as best they could.

All this would have been beyond belief as, late in the summer, Zénobie headed home to Saint Domingue. Teeth gritted, for this was her tenth transatlantic crossing, Zénobie endured the nearly two months of what another transatlantic traveler of the time called "the customary hardships of a small vessel, ill-provisioned and inadequately manned."

Jean-Jacques Bérard would want to be at Cap François to greet and escort his old nurse, his other mother, back to L'Artibonite. There'd be no reason why Jean-Jacques, with a couple of other personal servant-slaves, would not have taken seven-year-old Pierre on the small coastal sailing ship from St. Marc to Le Cap to welcome his grandmother back home. It would be a glorious adventure. In Saint Domingue, as for the Bérards in Paris, these were golden days. The last of them.

Ship arrival dates in the eighteenth century were approximate—they were always "give or take a week or two." And as planters did not operate by the clock, Bérard would allow plenty of time in Le Cap to await Zénobie's arrival. He'd travel with his entourage probably a week or so in advance of the best date for expected arrival. Accommodation was not a problem. Either Jean-Jacques had his own town house in Le Cap, or he would stay with friends. As mentioned, hospitality among the planters was part of the social code. Monsieur Bérard and his slaves would be assured of a comfortable place to stay.

Once they had settled in at Le Cap to await the ship's arrival, Pierre would be exposed for the first time to the life of servant-slaves in a big-city setting—big city by the standards of the place and time. There'd be two emotions welling up in the seven-year-old. The first was the anticipatory joy after all this time, perhaps two years, of seeing his grandmother again. The second would be seeing Le Cap for the first time, the grandest city in all the Caribbean, "the Paris of the Antilles."

After the provinciality of St. Marc and Port-au-Prince, and the isolation of the plantation, Toussaint would have marveled. The three-quarters of a mile of cargo ships lined up at the harbor front, their prows jutting over the heads of pedestrians. The constant activity and noise of loading and unloading as dockers and sailors worked the cargo; the agglomeration of whites of all social standing milling around in the city streets, competing with the pigs and chickens and dogs that also claimed the malodorous thoroughfares. What a sight for any child from the countryside.

Pierre wouldn't see the worst of Le Cap, of course, but if there were slave boys his own age in the household, they'd have known and told him. His head could easily be filled by the naughty stories—plus tales of seagoing adventure. It was a context within which the local parish priest could easily find material to rail against. Young Toussaint would see only the best of Le Cap, including Holy Mass on Sundays in the only church in the whole of Saint Domingue with a lock on the door. The churches in the other towns and cities of Saint Domingue were generally left bare and unlocked—possibly because there was nothing in them worth stealing. As Pierre knelt in Le Cap's church with the openness of a child still in the age of innocence, did he ever ask God why he was a slave? Or if he would always be one? If he did ask, perhaps returning grandmother Zénobie was part of the answer. She was a free woman.

With her arrival, Pierre's head would quickly be filled with new stories—accounts of his godmother, Aurore, and the other Bérard children. Zénobie could relate what it was like to be a truly free black person. In Paris, for the first time in her life, this intelligent, capable woman of African heritage was able to walk the streets as an equal, in a city she regarded as the capital of the world. She would know in herself, and see in the eyes of those she met, what it meant to be fully accepted. She could recount to Pierre and the other members of the family what it felt like to be deferred to in restaurants and shops, to sit next to whites in a Paris theater.

In the Paris of the 1780s, Zénobie thrilled to the experience of such genuine freedoms, her rights acknowledged by French whites of every social standing. Paris was, in major measure, a city without an entrenched racism (though that did not mean there were no bigots).

Presumably, Zénobie's deeply moving tales of freedom would have stirred the souls of all her black listeners. They'd know that out in the wider world there was something other than slavery for Africans. Pierre probably locked Zénobie's visions of Paris away in his heart, for nearly twenty years later, Toussaint, living in New York, started to organize his affairs with the view to moving permanently to the French capital. Like many grandmothers, Pierre's had a direct way about her, and when asked for advice, her response would be clear and direct: "Earn your freedom. Work hard. Do what you're told. Please at every opportunity, and your master will grant your freedom as my master granted me mine. Only your master can grant it. Serve him and you serve yourself. Serve him in such a way he cannot fail to acknowledge except by freeing you from bondage."

Though Pierre admitted years later that he always had a quick temper, gradually he learned. He applied himself to his household duties and learned in order to serve in different ways. (There could be a dignity to it. The English author Anthony Burgess calls this "the dignity of service"—the satisfaction that comes from any work done well. The character-building strength comes from the tribute one pays to oneself in personal dignity for having achieved.) Toussaint cleaned his master's boots, polished the silver, and learned to brush dust and dirt and mud from outer clothing—women took care of men's linens, their shirts and underwear.

Even by age eight or nine, Pierre would have been schooled

in the simpler tasks of the valet, possibly by Zénobie or by an older manservant, perhaps his own father. He would learn to pour drinks, wait at table, carefully awaken a sleeping person, draw drapes, and carry hot water to his master's chamber. Yet there was every expectation that for him (and, one senses, within him) there would be more to life than this. That expectation was based on other Toussaint attributes. He was bright and entertaining, an accomplished musician and a mimic. Not simply someone good at parroting the mannerisms of others, but an intelligent and incisive mimic who got under the skin of the person he was portraying. This seems to have had negative results, since as an adult he would cease his mimicry, realizing its potential for harm as well as amusement. It was, he decided, "something better left to the young."

For Toussaint, the gift of mimicry had an unexpected life- and values-shaping quality to it. It gave him insight into people. The young boy who watched people—mainly adults, one presumes—so as to later imitate them in order to amuse saw into people. In studying them he learned about human foibles and strengths, and these insights gave him a deep compassion. And this discerning compassion—remarked upon in his adult years by those closest to him—was one of his special qualities.

> He had a wonderful insight into character, and a wonderful tact in classing his friends. To some, even where he was sincerely attached, he was never communicative, for he knew they were not judicious. To others, with whom he had daily communication, he was careful not to commit himself, for he knew they were not sincere. But there were others to whom he gave his whole heart as though he truly believed them little lower than the angels.

In terms of affection, Toussaint was color-blind. As an adult, his special love was reserved for his wife, Juliette, and his adopted daughter, Euphémie. Among those friends to whom he "gave his whole heart," however, were the white women Mary Anna Schuyler and Catherine Cruger. His ease of dealing with all colors and classes was probably the result of reciprocity as well as personality. He was open and appealing. Despite his status as a slave, whites and blacks, free and slave, returned his openness. One senses this from his earliest recorded reminiscences—those regarding Jean-Jacques's first wife.

On Zénobie's return to Saint Domingue, the chateau was no longer a household brimming with children. By the early 1790s there is the stately young couple, Jean-Jacques and his fragile new wife, taking their place in local society. The huge mansion is home now to only themselves and their visitors—relatives from Dondon, or his wife's family from Port-au-Prince.

The chateau hummed along under Zénobie's dictates. But something else had followed from France in her wake—news. A letter from Paris took about three months. It had to first make its way from Paris, an inland city, to a port, usually Le Havre. There, handled by a family friend or acquaintance, it would wait for the next "packet" (*paquebot*) headed to Le Cap. From Le Cap, the letter would be transshipped on a smaller vessel down to St. Marc, and then carried to the plantation. In the late eighteenth century no one said "bad news travels fast." All news traveled equally slowly. Though bad news certainly was making its way from Paris.

By November of 1788, as Pierre Toussaint turned seven, the profligate French monarchy was collapsing into bankruptcy. There were two reasons for the pending financial collapse, profligacy in Louis XVI's court, and generosity in constantly advancing millions in loans to Benjamin Franklin for the American cause. Yet it was the expenses associated with the monarchy's vanities that caught history's attention. Vanities such as gardeners having to change the colors of all the Versailles flowers between morning and afternoon by digging up thousands of potted white blooms and replacing them with potted blue blooms—an extravagance beyond belief when segments of France faced starvation.

As the monarchy weakened, the aristocrats began maneuvering to regain some of their lost might. The king had agreed to call into session the Estates-General—the French assembly—for a huge grievance meeting. There had not been one for more than a century. Louis realized he had to do something. At the lowest end of the feudal social scale, the peasants, hungrier than ever, had begun to revolt. These 1788 history-changing events—the physical bubblings that joined with intellectual rumblings, revolutionary enlightenment, and republican theories and feelings—would not be slow to translate themselves from Paris to Saint Domingue.

The French colonies in the West Indies were more or less France in microcosm. All the splits in France would in time be mirrored in Saint Domingue, Guadeloupe, and Martinique. Drop the lighted revolutionary torch into this incendiary mixture of mutual hatreds—slavery and suppression—and no one was safe. Conflagration was as inevitable in Saint Domingue as it now appeared to be in France. And yet Jean-Jacques, no doubt guided in some things by Zénobie, and watched in all things by Pierre, would be able to keep the plantation on a fairly even keel during much of the most chaotic colonial revolution in history.

Young Bérard would struggle on through years of Saint Domingue's upheavals, shifting allegiances, internecine fighting, and the welcomed—by Bérard—invasion by the British. What crushed Bérard was the successful emergence of Toussaint-Louverture.

Jean-Jacques's ability to maintain a functioning plantation business in the midst of insurrection and war shows his father had made an excellent choice in handing it over to him. Yet even as one marvels at Jean-Jacques's dexterity and courage, one cannot move beyond the key fact that his entire livelihood and thinking were ruled by the need to have slaves and keep them under control. With that reminder, it is fair to add that after 1790, Jean-Jacques heroically labored in a war zone. But it is was heroism tempered by the actuality of the wrongful and sinful slavery he was trying to prolong.

Was the growing Toussaint, knowing what he did, at times trapped in a duality that defied his own attempts at rationality: How can one be loyal to a master who nonetheless personified a system one despised? Did this ambivalence gnaw at Toussaint? Any historical allusions that might help answer the question are fragmentary: "He prized liberty for the slave, yet was never willing to talk on the subject," wrote biographer Hannah Lee a year after Toussaint's death. Another fragment is from a later book.

Frances Sergeant Childs was the niece of the American Jesuit Father John LaFarge. When LaFarge's mother was a young woman, Toussaint was her coiffeur. Obviously, Mrs. LaFarge had talked to her son about Toussaint. LaFarge, in turn, passed on what he knew to his niece, Frances, for her 1940 book *French Refugee Life in the United States*. Here is Childs's comment: "On her deathbed, Madame Bérard gave Toussaint his freedom, and when he married he paid for his wife's freedom, as he had already paid for his sister's, so that slavery went out of his personal life. He remained, however, always conscious of and loyal to his race, conceiving it not as a handicap to his advancement, but as the framework in which his life's work was cast."

❖   ❖   ❖

The constant contrasts in Toussaint's young life are astonishing. His education alone is a wonderment. Convention has it that Pierre, working in the house at servant's duties never explicitly spelled out in existing records, was a favorite. His handwriting develops to a quality clearly that of an educated person. The penmanship exhibited in letters to his aunt Marie Bouquement is elegant. His written and spoken French was always superb.

The Jesuit Father Margat, a priest of the colonial period, said the properly taught slave spoke better French than France's own artisans and peasants. And well they might if, like Pierre, they learned their French from the educated, aristocratic elite. Margat described well-educated slaves as "extremely well-educated" and said that they had "the highest understanding of Christian principles." (Pierre's namesake, Toussaint-Louverture, though educated and a great planner, was a man who could dictate excellent reports and memoranda yet was not fluent in French.) Eugen Weber, author of *Peasants into Frenchmen: The Modernization of Rural France,* notes that of France's 28 million population at this time, the number who spoke standard French was surprisingly small—perhaps only three or four million. The remainder spoke their local languages or patois.

A major component of the esteem in which Toussaint's eventual New York friends would hold him had to do with this social refinement. Key to this was the perfection of his spoken French and his French manners. Superbly spoken French was, in effect, entrée into a particular niche in upper-class society. (A modern comparison might be that of the well-educated Englishman in American society. He is noted less for his English accent than for the correctness of his grammar, his enunciation, and the range of his vocabulary.) It was as an entertaining and capable "Frenchman" in New York that Toussaint would gain acceptance in the parlors and boudoirs of the important families. Quite simply, his slave status was secondary among educated New York whites; it was his French refinement combined with his skills as a coiffeur that provided his entrée.

❖   ❖   ❖

A French upper-class household of that time, if it had books, would have a small selection that ranged from Abbé Raynal to Benjamin Franklin. The popularity of Franklin's best-selling *Poor Richard's Almanack*—in French, *Bonhomme Richard* (1777–1778)—stemmed in part from its homely advice and in part from Franklin's presence in France as the American ambassador. The French had plenty of books of adages, little moral essays of their own. These cautionary tales, moralistic in the extreme, were an essential part of upper-class education at the time. Raynal, by contrast, in his *Histoire philosophique et politique des établissements et du commerce des Européens dans les deux Indes,* created a philosophical view of the New World to match North American Franklin's practicality. Many of these books, either in French or English, would also be in the libraries of the East Coast American elite. This elite conducted much of its social life in the French language.

The average educated Frenchman's view of North America came from J. Hector St. John de Crèvecoeur's *Letters from an American Farmer,* widely read in upper-class French homes. Practicing Catholics, or those who aspired to be, would have a New Testament and other religious reading. The same volumes may have been on Bérard's shelves, too.

Toussaint would be able to understand the developing African-French patois, later known as Creole, but there was no opportunity for him to learn other languages. In New York, from sheer necessity, he learned a functional spoken English, but there is no suggestion of fluency. He struggled to read English. His friend Mary Anna Sawyer Schuyler could neither speak French easily nor write it. She apologizes in one instance for her inability and suggests to Toussaint that he show her letter, written in English, to her son to read—if Toussaint couldn't work his way through it.

Throughout his working life, the bulk of Toussaint's coiffeur clients either were French or spoke French. It was the refined language of the day in all European society. (And until America's own revolution, North America, too, was somewhat European in that regard.) Paradoxically, for the teenaged Toussaint, isolated and insulated at first at L'Artibonite until the bloody upheavals began, the opportunities for literary pursuits were probably superior to worries about survival.

However, the revolutionary rhetoric in France spread and turned to violence as its influences circulated in Saint Domingue. By the late 1780s, pamphlets from the Paris-based Amis des Noirs (Friends of the Blacks, an offshoot of British antislavery agitation), plus the revolutionary writings of Tom Paine (the 1789 "Declaration of the Rights of Man") were available in the colony and a major topic of white and mulatto conversation. These writings and reports would be accessible to literate slaves.

The traveler Baron de Wimpffen, knowing the education level of some slaves, particularly house slaves, spoke with alarm at the carelessness of plantation masters who talked freely in front of their slaves of the agitations in Paris. Those masters brushed aside de Wimpffen's concerns. They told him they'd keep their slaves subdued using the methods that had always worked—brutality-induced fear. They had a catalog of cruelties that ranged from splattering the slaves with boiling sugar to burying them up to the neck and smearing their heads with sugar so they'd be eaten alive by insects. Variations included stuffing the slaves with gunpowder and igniting the fuse, or whippings so severe the slaves died or were permanently disabled. Mutilation was another deterrent. Castration or the loss of ears or fingers or a hand was dealt out speedily as punishment. The very real threat of these complex tortures and death kept the majority of slaves fully subdued.

After the fall of the Bastille on July 14, 1789, Royalists began fleeing France for safe harbor in Germany, England, and the United States. By this time the senior Bérards, in Paris, must

have felt they'd headed to the wrong place and should have remained where they were. They could not know that equally revolutionary events would soon be loosed in Saint Domingue.
There was no safe harbor in the colony either.

Toussaint was almost nine when the doors of the Bastille
Prison were thrown open. He was ten when the initial great
slaughters began in the colony as social, political, and racial allegiances shifted more often than the seasonal hurricane's
winds. And the political gales caused greater damage.

The internal sociopolitical situation in Saint Domingue during this period was complex, and the various groups, always dis-
trustful of one another, kept changing sides. Then there were
the problems caused by slow communications—what happened
or was ordered in France didn't reach Saint Domingue until
three or four months later. (It is from this time in French history
that modern politics gained the terms *Right* and *Left* to describe
political ideologies. Today's usage of those terms stems from the
period in the revolutionary French assemblies when conserva
tives/reactionaries [Royalists] sat on the right, and the revolutionaries [Republicans] sat on the left.)

Because what happens to Toussaint was the result of the
convoluted politics of the times, a brief sociopolitical chronology
of the tumultuous years immediately ahead in France and Saint
Domingue may keep the tale from becoming too complex:

  ❖ 1791: The earliest slave insurrections come to Saint
      Domingue. In effect, and for dazzlingly intricate reasons,
      these grew until they produced modern Haiti.

  ❖ ALSO IN THE EARLY 1790s: The future Liberator,
      Toussaint-Louverture, emerges as a force. He switches al-
      legiances several times, siding variously with the *grands
      blancs,* the Spanish of Santo Domingo (the other two-
      thirds of the island), with the French Republican govern-
      ment forces, and finally against those same forces.

❖ AUGUST 1792: In Paris, French peasants storm the Tuileries, imprison the royal family, and dissolve the national legislative assembly. A new parliament, the National Convention, is summoned.

❖ 1793: "The Terror" begins. In January, Louis XVI and Marie Antoinette are guillotined. Mob vengeance against the Royalists, the aristocracy, the planters, and anyone who caught their disfavor was merciless. This was when Monsieur Pierre Bérard was seized and imprisoned. The Terror began the mass exodus from France to the United States and elsewhere. Historian Frances Childs notes the exodus included "truly all sorts, Royalists and Republicans, Catholics and Masons, courtiers and artisans, priests and philosophers, slaves and freemen." A decade ahead, from among these émigrés and refugees, along with those from Saint Domingue, coiffeur Toussaint would find customers—and some lifelong friends.

❖ 1793: "Firing of Le Cap." Saint Domingue's cultural capital is torched and sacked by former slaves. It spells the end of white planter hopes of ever seizing control of the colony. This is the point at which Toussaint's future wife's family, the Noëls, most likely fled Saint Domingue for Baltimore.

❖ ALSO IN 1793: The British invade Saint Domingue and rule much of the West Province, where Bérard and the other *grand blanc* Royalist planters welcome them—for it meant the continuation of slavery and commerce.

❖ 1797: It becomes obvious to Jean-Jacques Bérard that Toussaint-Louverture would soon oust the British. Bérard, his wife and her two sisters, plus five black servants including Toussaint, his sister Rosalie, and his aunt Marie, a freewoman, leave for New York. As Louverture conquers the West Province and drives out the British, many more of Toussaint's relatives and friends are up-

rooted. The Pacauds—his sister Marie-Louise and her
husband—leave for Cuba. Santiago de Cuba becomes a
major haven and Saint Domingue a refugee dispersal
point. The refugees flee to wherever they feel they can
achieve freedom or find work. Marie-Louise's husband,
Antoine, apparently goes to Portugal.

The French Revolution was essentially Republican versus Royalist politics, the Enlightenment versus the Ancien Régime of
royalty plus church.

In Paris in 1789 and 1790, the assembly called initially for
the abolition of slavery, but more concertedly favored full colonial citizenship rights for the mulattoes. Yet in 1790 abolition
was overwhelmingly rejected on the ground that Negroes were
property, and property rights were inviolable.

At a meeting in France attended by the Saint Domingue mulatto leader Ogé, the French priest Abbé Grégoire cleverly
sought a way around that impasse on behalf of mulattoes. He
proposed the vote be given in Saint Domingue and other
French colonies to all those over the age of twenty-five who met
the property qualifications. Such a step would have included
practically all of Saint Domingue's mulattoes.

Back in Saint Domingue, at a special assembly in St. Marc,
not thirteen miles from where Bérard and Toussaint lived, the
grand blanc Royalist planters howled with anger when they
heard Grégoire's proposal. Even so, Ogé, who had returned to
the colony from France, asked for the decree's promulgation.
When the Colonial Assembly refused, the mulattoes rose in
protest in many parts of Saint Domingue, particularly the
Bérards' West Province, where mulatto plantation owners were
most numerous.

This St. Marc assembly was dominated by Royalists, and
Jean-Jacques almost certainly attended. The Royalist *grands
blancs* ignored the Republican colonial officials, like the gover-

nor and the intendant, deciding instead that they would recognize only direct royal authority. In one sense the meeting was unauthorized because those colonial officials had not summoned or approved it, but this was Saint Domingue, not Paris, and the white planters were not about to be deterred.

Bérard still "earnestly wished to preserve a neutral position; but he found this impossible. His immense property became involved in various ways." If one thinks of how the American Civil War was at times a running skirmish ranging across several states, and if we apply that to Saint Domingue's insurrections and slave revolt, L'Artibonite plantation could not avoid being part of the conflict when the mulatto uprisings hit the West Province.

Any one plantation was capable of mounting a temporary force to repel invaders. Hundreds of slaves, possibly loyal if they'd been relatively well treated, could form a first line of defense as attackers swept through. There might be a cordon of armed whites—the overseers, mechanics, and others—plus the men of the household, including the male household slaves, to protect the family. The troops, militia, or *maréchaussée* might come to the rescue of a besieged plantation if its friends were inside.

These were the difficulties through which Bérard and his family and the growing Toussaint and his family lived for the next six years.

There was always the possibility, of course, that when times became oppressive, Bérard and a chosen few from the household could temporarily abandon the plantation for Port-au-Prince or other places that offered greater safety than a fairly remote plantation.

But as biographer Lee states, Bérard was attempting to remain politically neutral. If this is so, young Pierre Toussaint witnessed it. Perhaps the reasons behind the neutrality were described to him by Jean-Jacques, and may explain, in the mature Toussaint's New York days, Pierre's penchant for exempting himself from the fray. This detachment was certainly heightened by his sense he was a Frenchmen and guest in the land of the Americans. It may also offer a partial explanation for his reticence on making his opinion known on public issues—one presumes "reticence," the existing record is quite incomplete in covering many areas of his life.

In the United States, Pierre more or less identifies himself as French in political situations. It may be he had modeled himself on where the Bérards were politically, even as Royalists, though that cannot be said with certainty. It is unwarranted to suggest Toussaint held the same opinion as the Bérards as to slavery. Had Toussaint remained in the colony beyond 1797 and not been taken to New York, undoubtedly his attitude toward slavery and Saint Domingue independence would have surfaced quite clearly—for he would have been forced by circumstances to take sides. A seventeen-year-old slave boy when he left the colony for America, he appears to have left behind its issues as too painful to explore in public.

Bérard was not able to maintain his neutrality for long. The St. Marc assembly effectively took over the government in the capital. The unpopular governor was overthrown by the Royalists, and a new governmental council was formed. The entire West Province, where Bérard lived, immediately accepted the new council. The mulattoes, in full revolt for being denied the rights of citizens, had taken to arms. One historian summarizes that this mulatto uprising was "defeated by foul weather and few forces." Ogé was caught and, as a reminder of the depth of the racism, put to death on the opposite side of the public square from where whites were put to death.

Throughout the colony, Royalist planters now faced a more ominous problem than political differences—restless slaves.

Meanwhile, back in France, the news of Ogé's fate finally reached Paris, and when the Paris revolutionaries learned of his

treatment—for he was popular in Paris—they turned more vigorously than ever toward mulatto rights. The mulatto lobby in
the French capital would soon contend, presciently but abor-
tively, that the whites needed free mulattoes to side with them
to keep the slaves down. Saint Domingue Royalists wanted none
of that: Mulattoes were not to be given their freedom.

This is still at a time when the Republicans are holding the
king a virtual prisoner. Now, with the king under duress, there
was another split in Saint Domingue. The French Revolution
had forced the colonial whites to take sides. The *petits blancs*
were revolutionaries, Republicans (with red cockades in their
hats), and the *grands blancs,* the planters, were Royalists (sport-
ing white cockades). It had reached the stage where white men
were killing each other now—and the slaves saw their opportunity.

The whites, as historian Stoddard comments, failed to see
that their only chance to keep the colony functioning was by
uniting. They couldn't; the political and social differences were
too sharply drawn. Consequently, the French colony was slip-
ping over the edge with increasing momentum.

The situation teeters in both Paris and Saint Domingue. In
the colony, the slaves were holding forest meetings by night and
participating in regular insurrections by day. The militia and
maréchaussée were kept busy quelling the revolts through vicious
reprisals, tortures, and executions. Similarly, each attempt at
mulatto gains was brutally beaten down by Saint Domingue's
Republican *petits blancs* and poor whites, or by armed force from
the Royalist planters, or by the governor and his troops.

Toussaint's boyhood was now one in which "the Negro
stockades were garnished with the skulls of prisoners killed after unspeakable tortures, while the tree-lined roads leading to
the white 'camps' were festooned with the bodies of hanged
rebels." When the mulattoes erupt they "fashion White Cockades out of the ears of their dead enemies, rip open pregnant

women and throw infants to the hogs." This was only one of the many atrocities against women and children, on all sides—and, as some of the more fastidious commentators correctly state, some are simply too horrifying to relate.

Toussaint had every reason to be horrified—and terrified. And the worst was still to come.

FIVE

RELIGION—AND REVOLUTION, 1788—PART II

IT HAD BEEN A TIME for final good-byes at L'Artibonite in early 1788. Aurore and her young siblings had left Saint Domingue for good. There would be no need for the girls to return. Unless one of them married a planter, there would be no need to leave Paris ever again. The boys, as young adults, might return to the island to seek their fortunes, and potentially they could use L'Artibonite as a base from which to go into business for themselves. But the parents' years in the colony were done. That part of their life was over. Zénobie had gone with them, but only to see them settled, and then she returned to Saint Domingue for good.

Toussaint must have been bereft. The seven-year-old's playmates—particularly his adored, bossy godmother, Aurore, now twelve—were gone, leaving a sense of loss that would remain with him for the rest of his life. It would be the first of a wave of losses over the next sixty-plus years. The Bérard family's departure was simply a precursor of much worse to come. In retrospect, the best the observer from two centuries later can remark is that, as a slave, Toussaint was indeed fortunate to have some pleasant memories. Nightmare would supersede idyll. Saint Domingue was heading into a bloodletting terror.

Bérard *père* handed L'Artibonite over to Jean-Jacques during a surge of productivity, prosperity, and profit. Indeed, there were fresh avenues for profit beyond just shipping to France. The home government had yielded and certain ports, like Port-au-Prince, were entrepôts—free ports from which plantation products could be exported to other nations, such as the United States with its huge market. Because of this new avenue of commerce, Jean-Jacques developed New York connections.

Greater productivity demanded more and more slaves. Africa itself was unable to meet the demand, so brigands were stealing slaves from places like nearby Jamaica and selling them in Saint Domingue. Meanwhile, the growing disparity of numbers in the colony staggers the imagination. By the 1780s there were 32,000 whites, 27,000 mulattoes, and an acknowledged 450,000 slaves—meaning there was a deliberate undercount of slaves. Since slaveholders paid a poll tax based on a per-head slave count, there was reason to fudge the numbers. Later researchers have suggested there could have been as many as 700,000 slaves when the insurrections started. And right up to the very end of the colony, even as it was going up in flames, slaves were still arriving at the rate of 30,000 to 40,000 a year.

What defies modern credulity is that neither the revolutionary government in France, which would soon rule the colony, nor the *grand blanc* planters or the *petits blancs* and white riffraff, nor the mulattoes running their own plantations or the French investors, nor the governor or the intendant could see what was likely to happen: that a breakdown in the vile existing order, which depended on white unity, would bring about the colony's total disintegration. There was no deep-seated realization that the hands that would eventually wreak the vengeance and rip the land from colonial France were black, were slave—hands that had nothing to lose. That the colony would be taken over by people whose lives were already forfeit.

Equally blind to the situation was Pierre Bérard. He left Jean-Jacques in charge, apparently content at his son being solely responsible for the family's fortune from that moment on. To both father and son the future held nothing but the promise of ever greater returns.

How quickly the world turned.

Revolution accelerates change, but not without first inflicting great misery. In brief, over a ten-year period, four political ingredients stirred up the tumult that changed Toussaint's life.

First, the French Revolution promised equality to all French citizens, including those in the colony, regardless of color (though initially the revolution reneged where slaves were concerned).

Next, in Saint Domingue, the *gens de couleur* (mulattoes plus a small number of blacks), free under French law, were denied that equality by the *grand blanc* planters. In response, the *gens de couleur* protested. Their protests triggered a violent reaction from the Royalist whites, the planters.

Third, the slaves were drawn into the ensuing white-mulatto struggle. The slaves realized slavery was not immutable, that the whites were not united, and they rose against all the whites.

Finally, liberator Toussaint-Louverture, at the head of a slave army, seized the initiative, declared a republic (but not yet an independent one), and led the slaves toward eventual freedom from France. Napoleon Bonaparte sent twenty thousand troops to subdue Louverture, but during peace negotiations Louverture was seized through trickery. The Liberator died in a French dungeon less than a year before independence was declared.

Basically, all the violence in the early years originated in whether the *gens de couleur* were to be given equal rights in the colony. Historian Frances Childs wrote, "the free mulattoes, often educated and wealthy, shared the white man's scorn of the Negro, yet [the mulattoes] were deprived of all civil and political rights." These mulattoes were Bérard's neighbors. When the troubles worsened they were happy to unite with the whites to deny equality for the slaves.

Mulattoes were significant within the Saint Domingue non-slave structure. In the West Province, the *gens de couleur* were a large part of the plantation-owning elite. In the 1780s, Bérard father and son would have witnessed, even if they did not support, the continued erosion of rights for once-free mulattoes. Neither father nor son apparently was aware of what the mulatto response to that erosion might be. (Toussaint's later easy relationship with *gens de couleur* in New York may provide a clue that the Bérard family's dealings with their neighboring mulatto plantation owners were not strained or hostile. However, as Toussaint was comfortable with people of every race, perhaps this was not a Bérard trait.)

The increasing proscriptions against the free mulattoes' rights were already under way at the time of Jean-Jacques's birth in 1766. But the erosion of their rights accelerated. Originally, mixed-race offspring in Saint Domingue were free if the white father claimed them as his. This stems from the fact that in the late seventeenth and early eighteenth centuries, the shortage of white French women in the colony made the white-black liaisons likely, if not inevitable. The mixed-blood children were factored into the practicalities. Long before the French had a legal claim on the land, the leading buccaneer, in an effort to provide white women for men he wanted to turn into planters, emptied the Paris prisons, hospitals, and streets of prostitutes and had them shipped over to Saint Domingue.

The commentators of the day drolly remarked that most of

these women were ill-suited to and probably incapable of child-bearing in the tropics. And one can imagine that even some pirates probably preferred the single state to the female options provided. Once slavery began, the slave women were mistresses and only very rarely wives. And the mulatto women were even more rarely wed by whites.

Male mulattoes, whether they wanted to or not, were required to serve for three years in the *maréchaussée,* the local guard—never as officers, only as rank and file. The mulattoes had to provide their own uniforms, arms, and horses—and got nothing out of the experience beyond the capacity to organize as a fighting unit—something the whites hadn't actually considered. Once out of the *maréchaussée,* however, the mulattoes were forever after forbidden to carry firearms unless, as sometimes happened, they graduated into the militia.

Gradually, in civilian life, professions previously open to mulattoes were closed to them. If they were not already landowners, they were now deprived of a living, and took to moneylending and vice in a big way. The screws were tightened—*gens de couleur* were told they could no longer marry whites, they could not wear European clothing, they could not attend functions where whites were present. Many of these mulattoes were, as plantation owners or moneylenders, extremely wealthy.

Like the *grands blancs,* the mulattoes sent their children to France to be educated, and traveled there themselves. And that was the most painful rub, for in France they could do everything they were forbidden to do in France's colony. In Paris, the *gens de couleur* could educate their children alongside the "best" white children, go where they chose, wear what they chose, do what they chose. The galling contrast between the conditions the mulattoes enjoyed in France and the restrictions they faced in Saint Domingue was simmering and festering, a boil waiting to be lanced.

Prosperity was the mulattoes' best revenge. Through their

legal and illegal enterprises, the mulattoes made fortunes to rival those of the wealthiest whites. And because the planters were engaged in cyclical agriculture, they frequently had to go into debt until the receipts for the next harvest were received. It was, therefore, to the mulatto moneylenders, the bankers, the planters turned. The *grands blancs'* existing animosity toward these mixed-bloods was thus compounded. And if the *grands blancs* were gamblers, their gambling debts were held by the mulattoes, too.

So vicious was the white racism, so fearful were the white planters of the taint of slave blood, that Saint Domingue's residents were required to report the degree of black blood in them, even down to one part black to 127 parts white.

The colony literally seethed with multifaceted colonial hatreds. The *grand blanc* planters despised the *petits blancs* who, with the revolution in France, instinctively became Republicans while the planters remained Royalists. Most whites loathed the tax-happy governor and the intendant, and were disgusted with the mulattoes. Mulattoes were a constant reminder to the *grands blancs* that the white community was the thickness of a bedsheet away from being part-colored. Furthering the fomenting brew, the governor and intendant generally distrusted one another and competed for power. The high officials were derisive toward the *grands blancs* and supercilious toward the *petits blancs*. The *petits blancs* hated equally the planters, the mulattoes, the governor, and the intendant. The mulattoes feared and hated the *petits blancs* and detested the *grands blancs* with whom they wanted equality. As social groupings, this entire body was united on only one point: They all hated and despised the slaves.

This was the tinderbox on which Jean-Jacques Bérard was to fashion the family's future. The tinderbox Toussaint was helpless against. Pierre and the entire plantation were totally dependent for their safety on the skills of Jean-Jacques Bérard, his leading employees, and Zénobie.

❖   ❖   ❖

In France, the country whose fortunes constantly affected Toussaint's life, the scene was different but also constantly shifting.

The French Revolution was antimonarchist, antiaristocratic, anti-Catholic, and anti–colonial planter. The Bérard family was permanently settled in Paris before Pierre Bérard truly grasped the extent of the peril leveled against his family. One optimistic precaution he took as the Republicans rose to power was to change the children's names so they didn't appear so aristocratic. At this time Pierre's godmother, De Pointe, became Aurore. (Two decades after the Revolution, when Pierre and his godmother Aurore renewed communication, she signed her first letter to the mature Pierre "De Pointe [Aurore]," and thereafter, "Aurore.") The record does not provide the new "Republican" names of the other Bérard children.

❖   ❖   ❖

What may have buttressed, in Saint Domingue, the idea of blacks and mulattoes having equal dignity with whites was the influence of the more progressive elements of the Catholic clergy. Though the Jesuits were suppressed in 1763, almost two decades before Pierre was born, the effects of enlightened missionary Catholicism may have lingered in some quarters. (The Jesuits' plantations were confiscated and given to the Capuchins and Trinitarians who succeeded them. Historian George Breathett remarks, "the suppression of the Jesuits warned other orders not to be too dedicated to the slaves and thus undermine the colonial society's foundations.") The Jesuits were dedicated; tradition has it that once suppressed, some of the priests took to the hills and remained with the maroons and agitators. As the revolution succeeded, if there were still Jesuits in the hills, theirs may have been an early form of liberation theology carried to a successful conclusion.

Others had a more negative view of the Saint Domingue clergy. The visitor Baron de Wimpffen saw the clergy living in comfort, taking concubines, raising large numbers of their own children, celebrating mass in empty churches, and accumulating fortunes. He said that while there were priests of merit, "truth obliges me to avow they are not numerous."

Historian Breathett disputes this general view. He contends that the fact that Catholicism thrived for three generations following the successful 1801 revolution (even though the Vatican refused to recognize the new republic for sixty years) speaks highly of "the intensity of Catholic indoctrination." He holds to this view even when other "historians denigrate the quality of the clergy" in the colony. Judging from the religious devotion and fervor of exiles like the Toussaints, the Noëls, and the Montpensiers, Breathett may be more correct. He adds, "the maintenance of Catholicism in any fashion during the period 1801–1860 is a clear indication that this form of religious worship made a significant impact on black Haitians."

Catholicism survived the slave revolution as a religion that apparently functioned with a strange mix of accepted priests, fugitive priests, and "slave priests." Sometimes these latter were slave catechists acting as missionaries or, it is hinted, as regular priests. Even before the revolution slaves of both sexes held positions as parish officers (beadles), men and women responsible for the everyday operations and organization of the parish. Catholic slaves did much catechetical work at the traditional after-sundown slave gatherings when, after slave labor and tending one's plot were finished for the day, there may have been a little time before sleep. If slaves were catechists, was Toussaint's mother, Ursule, a catechist? Or Zénobie? Could Pierre's knowledge of the New Testament have come that way? It is simply not known.

The possibilities provoked, however, are tantalizing.

❖   ❖   ❖

There was a two-tier racist society in matters like the theater; was there also a two-tier society in the church with priests who ministered specifically to blacks? If so, was there an elementary "black church"? Further, if there was a two-tier church, or priests ministering to blacks as Catholics within the one parish, did those blacks have their own music? Toussaint was particularly musical. Did he and Juliette, when they gathered with black friends and relatives on festive occasions, play and sing not merely festive songs but songs born in Saint Domingue that were religious or sacred?

Was there an enlightened attitude toward mulatto-white relationship sometimes in part based on grounds of common religious acceptance—all Catholics together? The races did pray together in church. In 1792, when whites and mulattoes together successfully defended Port-au-Prince against a slave army—and the whites (temporarily) accepted mulattoes as equals—they celebrated first with a huge banquet (paid for by the mulattoes) and then walked "arm in arm" to mass where they all sang the Te Deum.

There was no enlightened attitude toward the field slaves. Indeed, the reverse was true. By Pierre's teenage years, worried colonial officials finally moved to ban sundown meetings. Not without reason the authorities were finally becoming fearful of mass gatherings of slaves. The laws also were being sharpened in other ways. A free mulatto could no longer marry a slave without permission. Churches were now closed to slaves after sunset. Next, growing ever more alarmed, the government began to send mixed signals. At one time slaves were forbidden to act as beadles or work as catechists. Then a royal edict followed that stated the bans were not aimed at those well-prepared in the faith.

At L'Artibonite, as the 1780s became the 1790s, Jean-Jacques had his hands full. Despite the gathering storm, the young Bérard was doing well as he "successfully cultivated the plantation, treading in his father's footsteps, and with appropriate patriarchal care, exacted a due proportion of labor, which he rewarded with kindness and protection. Wealth flowed in upon him." Yet as master of L'Artibonite, Jean-Jacques Bérard also needed a wife.

Either as a love match, or one arranged out of pure suitability and availability, young Bérard began courting his teenage cousin who lived in Port-au-Prince. Her name is lost to history. "He was tenderly attached" to this cousin, who "had resided much on the plantation, and partook of his attachment to the slaves, particularly to Zénobie and her descendants."

Possibly early in 1793, when the young lady was eighteen and Jean-Jacques was twenty-seven (Pierre was about twelve), the couple wed. But unlike Jean-Jacques's mother, the new Madame Bérard was not robust.

"I remember her when the bridal took place," said Pierre Toussaint later, in his earliest directly quoted recollection. "She was very pale, her health was always delicate, but she looked so lovely and we were all so happy. Rosalie [Pierre's sister] and I were never tired of gathering flowers for her, and we used to dance and sing for her amusement." A year after the marriage, however, the young chatelaine of L'Artibonite "began to droop." It was tuberculosis.

"I can see her as she lay upon the couch, panting for air—all so beautiful, outside and in," said Toussaint. "Then Rosalie and I would stand at opposite sides of the room and pull the strings of a magnificent fan of peacock feathers, swaying it to and fro, and we would laugh and be so gay that she would smile too. But she never grew strong, she grew weaker."

Young Madame Bérard expressed a wish to return to her family home in Port-au-Prince. Jean-Jacques immediately agreed, hoping the sea air might bring some benefits. She took

Pierre and Rosalie with her. But her decline was rapid; a month later she was dead. She was barely twenty. Toussaint for the first time had attended someone through ill health and into death— it would not be the last. He developed a skilled and comforting manner with the dying (what the Scottish islanders in their Celtic prayer-life refer to as a "soul-friend"). And whether the person was a poor woman dying from the plague, or a priest in Toussaint's own home expiring from "ship fever" (typhus), he ministered with grace, and bestowed, according to existing letters, a spiritual ease.

All this lay in the future. The young mistress's gradual decline into death had prepared Toussaint for life.

For the young widower, Jean-Jacques, there were further woes. His wife's decline was a symbol for the colony itself. As she slipped away, Saint Domingue reached the edge of its precipice. In the next five years, as Toussaint entered his early teenage years, and Jean-Jacques his thirties, the French Revolution and the colony's own eruptions and insurrections would send an entire way of life down into the sea.

The French colony would disappear with such completeness it might never have existed. In time, with the exception of a few elderly widows, not a single white would survive.

SIX

THE BLOODY BOYHOOD

HANNAH LEE TELLS OF A MOMENT, the only such time on record, when Toussaint, long a Manhattan resident, commented on what he had witnessed in Saint Domingue. Pierre's revelation came during a conversation on the fight for abolition in the United States. The information is thirdhand. The woman he addressed (not Lee) later seems to reflect that Toussaint's reaction was conflicted:

> He seemed to fully comprehend the difficulty of emancipation, and once, when a lady asked if he was an Abolitionist, he shuddered and replied, "Madame, they have never seen blood flow as I have" (*Ils n'ont jamais vu couler le sang comme moi*).

Given that abolition was a major issue during his latter New York decades—his biographer, Bostonian Hannah Lee, was a confirmed abolitionist—Toussaint was probably frequently asked this

question. He had, it seems, developed a stock answer to cut discussion short. He did not say he was not an abolitionist. Rather,
he feared the same nonstop bloodletting that he had lived
through in Saint Domingue would erupt in the United States. He
replied with an observation, true at its essence, that abolitionists
in the United States did not know what they were getting themselves into. He shuddered at the price that would be paid in
blood. Toussaint was correct, of course. Eight years after his
death, the bloodletting began. It was the American Civil War.

Nonetheless, there is an element to Lee's quotation that
must be explored. It takes a great deal to make a self-controlled
grown man "shudder." To shudder is an involuntary action. Accepting, as I think one can, that abolition as a topic must have
surfaced many times when whites talked to Toussaint, even if he
was prepared for the question, he could not control that involuntary shudder. The teenaged Toussaint had witnessed atrocities that were now suppressed so deeply in his psyche he could
do no more than issue a stock phrase—and physically recoil at
the recollection.

Saint Domingue's bloodletting scarred him. What specific
incidents and events actually traumatized Toussaint during pu-
berty and into adolescence, from age eight to sixteen, is unknown. Part of this chapter's task, then, is to see what he may
have witnessed. (In the accounts that follow, unless otherwise
noted, the quoted and paraphrased sources are from historians
T. Lothrop Stoddard or Thomas Ott.)

In Paris on May 15, 1791, the Constituent Assembly made
the move that triggered events which, within six years, forced
Jean-Jacques Bérard from Saint Domingue and landed Pierre
Toussaint in New York City. On that date France's revolutionary
ruling body specifically granted citizenship rights to mulattoes.

The news had to travel first to Le Havre by overland coach.
Then it languished for upward of twelve weeks on a slow-
moving vessel battling headwinds to Port-au-Prince or Le Cap.

From either city, the news of the expressed rights of the mulattoes circulated throughout the colony. From the decision to the bloodshed took three months—unbeknownst to San Domingans, June, July, and August of 1791 ticked away as a silent and dreadful augury.

There'd already been two mulatto uprisings in Saint Domingue by the time news of mulatto freedom came. However, "before the whites could protest, a tremendous Negro revolt broke out on the North Plain, surpassing in horror any previous uprising on the island." On August 22, on the North Plain beyond Le Cap, the slave leader Boucman suddenly appeared with six thousand black troops, risen slaves. Boucman first struck the "the scattered white population" of the northern plantations who "offered no resistance. The men were at once killed, often with every species of atrocity, while the unfortunate white women were violated—frequently upon the very bodies of their husbands, fathers and brothers."

All remained quiet in the city of Le Cap itself. Then, just before dawn on August 23, 1791, "a stream of disheveled fugitives waked Le Cap to terror and affright," while behind them in the still darkened sky, the great North Plains "in a lurid glow bore ominous witness" to the fugitives' tidings. The slaves were burning canefields and plantations, and this disheveled band "were but the survivors of a frightful massacre." Le Cap was a port with few fortifications on the landward side.

"In the half-light of dawn" a National Guard reconnoitering party from Le Cap "was suddenly overwhelmed by a horde of Negroes whose ghastly standard was the impaled body of a white child; only two or three of the soldiers escaped to carry the dreadful tidings." Another account states that "the slaves had joined the rebellion." It spread like wildfire. "Young children transfixed upon the points of bayonets were the bleeding flags" as 100,000 risen slaves destroyed more than 300 plantations on the North Plain.

There were in Le Cap ten thousand whites and their forty thousand slaves. In effect, however, "*grands* and *petits blancs* were cornered in Le Cap" both by their own slaves and the tens of thousands more outside the city.

Though grossly outnumbered inside the city, the enraged whites and their allies in Le Cap began containing the city slaves, while their troops went on sorties into the plain to capture Boucman's insurgents. Warring slaves were practically "nude, or in tatters, or grotesquely decked in [seized] rich apparel." They were armed with guns, knives," and kitchen utensils. Trapped, Le Cap's *grands blancs* suddenly found themselves with unexpected allies: many mulattoes "took firearms from the king's store" and fought alongside the whites to kill the attackers. The mulattoes hoped that this display of solidarity with the whites would convince the *grands* and *petits blancs* that the *gens de couleur* were worthy of citizenship and equality. (Those hopes were futile.)

As the North Plain bloodshed continued, Saint Domingue foreshadowed what was to come in France. If the guillotine soon would never stop in Paris, in Le Cap six gallows were operating night and day. Le Cap's whites were nonstop hanging the risen slaves the troops captured, plus any other unfortunate city black they happened to seize. The brutality was intended to send a message also to the forty thousand blacks inside Le Cap. It did. Outside the city, Boucman's forces were gradually repulsed.

The horror spread. As whites now turned to eliminate the newly enfranchised mulattoes, the West Province "plantations suffered particularly severe damage, and the excesses against humanity were as terrible as those in the North Province." This was when Pierre may first have actually seen "blood flow."

There would be more reasons to shudder.

In this decade, by the time Bérard and Toussaint quit the colony, more than one-third of all the people in Saint Domingue were dead. As many as 2 million people were slaughtered, nearly all of them black or mulatto. The whites lost several thousand; the black lost almost 2 million. The overall toll translates into roughly 200,000 people being killed annually. It means 500 deaths a day, day in and day out for ten years, in a place the size of Maryland.

Black and a slave, Pierre Toussaint had reason to shudder.

Unfortunately for this account, so many questions cannot be answered. In these years, just where was the Toussaint family of slaves? How did they come through unscathed when the Artibonite Valley, the West Province, and their major cities—St. Marc, Port-au-Prince, and Le Cap—were all in various stages of violent upheaval? Was Bérard away on occasion fighting with the White Cockades, which seems likely? If so, in his absence, were the L'Artibonite household slaves, the Toussaint family, forced to witness atrocities by the victors in local skirmishes—atrocities meant to quell any idea household slaves might have about rebellion, freedom, or equality?

All this is possible, though the fact that all the Toussaints escaped with their lives becomes exceptional.

Atrocity stories had always traveled around the colony like lightning. They were as ancient and as prevalent as Saint Domingue slavery itself. Toussaint would have heard, as would all slaves, of the individual brutalities affecting those they knew. Matching cruelty against cruelty forgives neither side, and while there's little sense in comparing this atrocity against that barbarity, the blood lust was rooted in a reaction to prevalent experience. The infant impaled on a spike as a "regimental flag" by slaves in revolt was quid pro quo for the violations forced upon generations of slaves, and their children, and their infants.

The barbarities had plenty of precedence. If a white woman was mindlessly slaughtered, she may or may not have been the type of plantation mistress who, dissatisfied with the meal her slave cook prepared, had the cook immediately thrown into the oven and burned to death. Historian C. L. R. James mentions the white chatelaine whose husband ogled a young black slave. The chatelaine had the young woman summarily beheaded by another slave.

The blacks unleashed on whites in a single decade a century's store of collected tortures suffered since the colony's inception. The whites retaliated in kind. The mulattoes? They fared as badly as the slaves but for a different reason. The slaves were despised, but the mulattoes were hated for the white blood in their veins—and envied for their financial success. At this point, as in the immediate past, it was the mulattoes who suffered most.

When Paris got the disjointed news of the North Province massacre, probably from a ship's captain who'd sailed as the attack got under way, the assembly presumed the revolt had been caused by their decision to grant freedom to the mulattoes. So the assembly nullified those freedoms granted only four months earlier. That decision, when news of it reached Saint Domingue, provoked more mulatto uprisings, focused primarily in Bérard's West Province.

Now Bérard and Toussaint were caught up somewhere in the middle of a "three-way civil war among whites, mulattoes and blacks, especially in the West Province, where the *gens de couleur* revolted."

As always in looking at Bérard's and Toussaint's plight in these years, the mulattoes remain key.

The tenuousness of allegiances has already been seen in the fragile unity in Port-au-Prince between whites and mulattoes as they repulsed thousands of risen slaves. The slaves waited, well removed from the city. This was the occasion when whites and mulattoes "went arm in arm to Mass and sang the Te Deum." This was as much victory for the white and mulatto slaveholders as it was for the mulattoes alone.

In the North Province, the Colonial Assembly in Le Cap

was the opposite of jubilant that the mulattoes had freedom with leadership over thousands of black slaves. Angry northern whites feared the mulattoes outnumbered them and would take over everything. The South Province, going through its own upheavals, eventually sided with the North and was a key to the final outcome years later.

Bérard still wanted to continue the Saint Domingue dynasty. It was his role and duty in life. Pierre, black and a slave, was fastened to the Bérard coattails; wherever his master went, the slave must follow. Whatever Bérard said or believed, Toussaint, at this point, must echo. Whatever Bérard endured, so must Pierre. Many white Artibonite plantation owners held strong and fast throughout. They were always, backs against the wall, even in extremis, on the wrong side of the moral issue. They grouped together in mutual protection societies when danger first loomed. Bérard likely joined with other strong men of his region under the leadership of the powerful planter Humas de Jumecourt and West Province planter Coutard. These whites allied themselves as junior partners with mulattoes to form a Royalist-slaveholding "confederacy for the West." Now all that was done; the mulattoes were the masters. The West's *grand blanc* Royalist planters had one remaining solution: invite the British to conquer the colony and continue the slavery—but that was still a year away.

The confederacy's fortunes had swung from successes to disasters. The courage of these men and their families, however they survived, was never in doubt. Their cause—prosperity based on slavery—was never in doubt either. And no amount of courage made that cause defensible.

A double betrayal was soon under way. Learning that the mulattoes had their freedom, the slaves who pressed Port-au-Prince now demanded their freedom, too, or, failing that, the slaves demanded that the whites surrender the mulattoes to them.

The perfidy now becomes astonishing. The mulatto army holding Port-au-Prince with the whites chose the bravest slaves and offered them their freedom if they would lead the other slaves back into slavery and keep them in order. The offer was accepted and 100,000 slaves returned to work. (Having the slaves back on the plantations was the planters' final major success.)

As soon as the slave threat receded, the second betrayal occurred: The whites reneged on their promise of equality to the mulatto. The mulattoes had betrayed the slaves; whites now betrayed the mulattoes. And in November, the Port-au-Prince Colonial Assembly quickly reversed itself and withdrew mulatto equality.

The predictable happened: Insurrections, battles, and bloodshed began all over again as mulattoes of the West Province once more revolted. The mulattoes again emerged supreme at the head of a slave army. A bloody whirlwind swirled around the heads of the Toussaints and the Bérards. Pierre's family—great-grandmother Tonette, grandmother Zénobie, mother Ursule, his siblings Marie-Louise, Antoine, and Rosalie—were in constant danger of the worst sort of atrocity and death. How could Pierre not be affected?

For twenty-first-century observers, the military and political intricacies now become meaningless. The decisive battles and the made and broken alliances matter to the colonial historian, but they add nothing to the Toussaint story, which must deal in the broad outlines. The simple fact is that by the end of the 1791, "white power was effectively broken in the West and South Provinces. Whites [and this would include Bérard] were disarmed and at the mercy of their *gens de couleur* conquerors."

Then, from Paris, came the decisive legal blow against the Royalist white planters. In April 1792, Paris gave Saint Domingue mulattoes and free Negroes the same political rights as whites. "The white Santo Domingans submitted for the moment, unable to do anything else, but they realized their agony had begun." Yet the sentiment in Saint Domingue was adamant when it came to the French government's anticipated next step: freedom for the slaves. In October 1792, the president of the Le Cap Assembly publicly warned, "we have not brought half a million slaves from the coasts of Africa to make them into French citizens."

In that same month, October, Saint Domingue learned that in August, peasants had stormed the Tuileries, imprisoned the royal family, and dissolved the legislature. In France, the Republican French government was strengthening its grip both on the nation and its colonies. It lived up to its earlier pledge and confiscated the lands of those who'd fled France. That left a lot of Frenchmen and their families (Toussaint's future clients and friends) stranded in New York City. In the United States in 1792, reports historian Ott, the concerns centered almost solely on the effects the Saint Domingue civil war might have on its own southern plantations, where "slave revolts were feared."

Paris responded to the colony's continued bloody insurrections and divisions by sending out six thousand soldiers and three new commissioners. One commissioner, Sonthonax, was notoriously anti-Royalist and viciously opposed to the *grand blanc* planters. He was determined to rid the colony of them. Completely in favor of full rights for mulattoes and blacks, he took over the North Province and ran it as a virtual dictatorship. It was Sonthonax who, in 1793, would finalize the whites' downfall. The event—"the Firing of Le Cap"—was one of the greatest incendiary-based slaughters in history prior to the unleashing of modern airborne weaponry. Even after the "Firing," Bérard, for four more years, hung on. That was possible because the British had arrived at Port-au-Prince.

But the most important event in the Toussaint story at this moment was that, in Saint Domingue, Toussaint-Louverture stepped firmly onto history's page.

❖   ❖   ❖

Louverture began by organizing slaves and former slaves into an army. There was also a more formal armed struggle under way for Saint Domingue. The Spanish in Santo Domingo (the other two-thirds of the island), Royalists and Catholics themselves, were determined to help the *grand blanc* Royalists and mulatto monarchists defeat the forces of godless revolution. The Spanish offered the Saint Domingue blacks guns to fight the French government. (Which, commentators note, was something of a psychological breakthrough for the slaves. For the first time they understood that whites were willing to use blacks to kill other whites. There was not, after all, an indissoluble monolithic white supremacy.)

Liberator Toussaint-Louverture allied his army with whomever he felt would aid his cause. He served the Spanish as an officer in their forces, fighting the French Republican government troops. Then he switched sides and eased himself into a position of leadership in the French forces, thus fighting French Royalist forces and mulattoes. With that accomplished he sent a delegation to the French government in 1792 informing them of his actions on behalf of France. His ability to change his allegiances—like his lightning ability to change tactics when commanding troops—gave him his nickname. He was a man who always saw "the opening" *(l'ouverture)* best suited to his aims.

In January 1793, King Louis XVI and his queen, Marie Antoinette, were guillotined. The Reign of Terror had begun. In the United States, the first republic in the hemisphere, everyone sided with the French Republicans and cheered the downfall of this European king. In Boston, a theater ran six shows a day based solely on the seizing and beheading of Louis XVI. The audiences loved it. Paradoxically, the United States continued to welcome the aristocratic refugees from the Revolution's death-dealing Terror. But Britain and France were now once more at war. Readers of Jane Austen's novels will recall the tension, the English expecting a French invasion any moment. In English villages, the nobility and gentry crowded into their pews in the chapels on their estates or the churches in their villages. Having seen what was happening to the aristocracy in France during the Terror, the English nobility were praying the peasantry would not revolt and do the same to them.

In all likelihood it was late this year, 1793, that Jean-Jacques (and twelve-year-old Toussaint) learned that Pierre Bérard, long under surveillance by the forces of the Terror, had been imprisoned by the revolutionaries and the family fortune confiscated. Bérard may not have heard this news for many, many months. But once he did, how helpless he must have felt on his parents' behalf, and how anxiety-ridden the Toussaint family, too, must have been. There was simply nothing Bérard could do. There was no one with any authority he could turn to. His siblings in Paris were left to survive as best they might. Their relatives, too, would be under duress or suspicion.

After six winter weeks of captivity in a Paris dungeon, Bérard senior was released, no reason given. The surveillance continued. But the experiences, the likely deprivation through loss of food, privacy, and hope, sapped the resolve and physical stamina of both Monsieur and Madame Bérard. The Bérard parents died shortly afterward.

Toussaint's godmother, Aurore, later told Pierre that in order to survive they'd been forced to use what little share of money the siblings had salvaged—by selling their parents' few unconfiscated possessions—to take the lease on a tobacco kiosk on a busy street. For the next twenty years, in all weathers, Aurore worked fourteen to sixteen hours a day. Historian Frances Childs notes, "The Revolution had grown increasingly radical and ruthless"—the Christian religion was suppressed, a new calendar with ten days to the week imposed. Non-Republicans were fit only for the guillotine. On what charge, if any, Pierre Bérard was arrested is immaterial. Just being a wealthy planter would create suspicion enough of Royalist sympathies.

Twenty years beyond these events, forty-nine-year-old Aurore, still operating her small tobacco kiosk, wrote to Pierre, in her letter that reunited them, that "the Revolution deprived us of all our property. My father was one of the victims of that frightful period. He and my mother died of grief."

Young Toussaint's reasons for grief were multiplying. The continuing gruesome atrocities must have had him wondering and praying over what would become of them all. He had no reason to presume he and his family would survive when so many had already been killed. The white plantation period was drawing slowly but inexorably to its close. Two events sealed its fate, one in 1793, the other in 1804. The first was the "Firing of Le Cap" and Sonthonax's actions that immediately preceded it. The second was the decree issued by Jean-Jacques Dessalines, Haiti's new leader, to slaughter all the remaining whites. (The action was followed to the letter with the exception of a few elderly widows. The former white colony became all black.)

Sonthonax had earlier begun a forcible expulsion of the whites. He began rounding up whites from all over the North Province—the only one he controlled. He stripped them of their valuables, pushed them onto ships in Le Cap's harbor, and ordered them gone. Stoddard tells of Le Cap businessman Monsieur Aubert who urgently tried to get his family and some possessions out of the colony. His firm did a great deal of business with Stephen Girard in Philadelphia, whom he kept apprised of what was happening at Le Cap. He told in 1793 of "the destruction of our commerce," of his papers "thrown into the street," of not knowing where his partners were. His wife, children, and some money and possessions he managed to get aboard a Girard ship, the *Polly*. Shortly after it sailed, but before it escaped the bay, Sonthonax's forces seized it, and the Auberts "lost everything." Aubert took Girard's other vessel, the *Sally*. It, too, was seized and searched. Aubert, who arrived in the United States penniless, told Girard he'd spent forty-five years in Saint Domingue and lost a fortune (in today's money more than $150 million).

The French government, growing frantic over the deteriorating situation in Saint Domingue, sent over a new colonial governor, Galbaud. The governor's treatment at the hands of Commissioner Sonthonax triggered the final, truly devastating event.

Commissioner Sonthonax had the mulattoes' support, and the new governor, Galbaud, sought to gain the whites' support. The battle lines were drawn, the stage was set for the climax. Then Sonthonax caught out Galbaud in a legal impropriety.

The situation, in brief, was this: Sonthonax learned that Governor Galbaud, contrary to French law, owned property in the colony he governed. Challenged, Galbaud admitted the fact and accepted that because of this breach he must leave his post. He quit the capital, Port-au-Prince, and sailed to Le Cap prepared to leave. But Sonthonax's treatment of the whites in Le Cap—and, by extension, his treatment of Galbaud—ushered in events that triggered the end of the white colony.

Despite the fact that Galbaud had agreed to leave, Sonthonax's mulatto troops in Le Cap began bullying any whites they came across. Sonthonax's soldiers insulted and injured sailors from the French fleet under Galbaud's control, as well as mariners from the fleet of merchant ships—some of them under the U.S. flag.

There were many French troops and merchant sailors aboard vessels lying at anchor out in the bay who also knew of this treatment. On June 19, Galbaud's arriving vessel was cheered by naval officers and sailors, and merchant mariners.

This was their answer to the bullying by Sonthonax's mulatto soldiers. Galbaud landed in Le Cap with two thousand sailors of the fleet at dawn on June 20, 1793.

Once Galbaud landed, many of the French navy and merchant sailors from the fleet in the bay came ashore with him. It was time to pay Sonthonax's men back for the bullying. Fighting broke out. Soon whites, those who sided with Sonthonax, were fighting other whites, Galbaud's troops.

Sonthonax had the French National Guard, the mulattoes, and free blacks. Governor Galbaud had his troops, his marines, many of the merchant sailors, all the *grands blancs,* and perhaps a few *petits blancs* who were anti-Sonthonax. The conflict rapidly deteriorated into furious house-to-house fighting throughout Le Cap. Throughout the night, through the next day, and again into the night, Galbaud's disciplined troops successfully pushed Sonthonax and his allies out of the city to beyond the city's limited fortifications. All that lay behind Sonthonax was the darkened North Plain and the slaves. This was the point at which Commissioner Sonthonax tipped the scale and created "the Firing of Le Cap."

Sonthonax sent emissaries out into the North Plains. Ott describes how these emissaries reached the blacks' leaders and said Sonthonax had promised them all the plunder they could take, plus their freedom, if they invaded Le Cap. The blacks had no reason to resist the commissioner's offer—Sonthonax threw open the barricades.

Thousands upon thousands of "frenzied" slaves then roared into the city killing and looting with abandon. Galbaud and his troops were forced back to the harbor. Though it was night, "harbor and shipping lay as bright as day in the awful glare of the burning city. Those of the white population not huddled along the quays were dying amid their burning homes. Next day a full fifteen thousand more rebels poured into the city and Galbaud, recognizing the case was hopeless, set sail for the

United States. Every ship that could keep the sea followed his flag, and soon the great fleet, with ten thousand despairing refugees aboard, dropped the empty harbor and blazing city below the horizon. Fortunately the voyage was fair, and when this tragic armada cast anchor in Chesapeake Bay, the sufferings of the wretched refugees was over."

Childs's account of the end of the colony as a white bastion concluded that Governor Galbaud "was not strong enough to control the situation." She conjectured that conditions in the colony by that time were so acute the same disorder and denouement "might well have occurred with or without Galbaud." She chronicles how "Galbaud's forces retreated gradually to the fleet which already held the Commissioner's deportees, while the destitute white refugees piled into both warships and merchant craft. The fleet, loaded to the gunwales, set sail on June 23 and early July dropped anchor in the Chesapeake."

In one of those ships, described as a "guineaman," were the black Catholics who would lay the foundation stone for the Black Catholic church in the United States. And in all likelihood, Toussaint's future wife's parents were aboard.

As the last ships sailed out of Le Cap, the cargo of newly impoverished multimillionaires left behind the source of their fortune and headed toward destitution. Those who couldn't leave in time were victim to the now familiar reprisals of torture, rape, and death.

In the West Province, Bérard, still at L'Artibonite, was fighting to preserve what planters like Denis Cottineau de Kerloguen and the Marquis de Rouvray were leaving behind: huge plantations that represented the bulk of their fortunes. In modern terms, Cottineau de Kerloguen lost $50 to $75 million; de Rouvray $40 to $50 million.

The personal tales may be moving, but what the escaping whites suffered was minor discomfort by comparison to the barbarity off which, either directly or indirectly, they'd all lived.

Perversely, once these planter-refugees arrived in America, the U.S. government, which favored a slave economy, contributed generously to alleviate the refugees' misery. By 1794, the U.S. federal government was supporting from public funds some two thousand ousted Saint Domingue slaveholders and other exiled whites.

Back in Le Cap: "for four days and nights," wrote Monsieur Carteau, watching from the heights overlooking the North Plain, "fire consumed this rich and famous city. We were stupefied. In this uncertainty we waited impatiently the outcome of this tragic event; although we whites, so long the butt of the Commissioners' injustices and cruelty, had the keenest dread of that which lay in store." Wrote another, "all the whites are leaving for New England who can possibly get away." (New England was how the colonists often referred to the United States; Canada was known as New France.)

Barely a week later Sonthonax granted equality to the blacks of the North Plain. Back in Le Cap, fires burned and embers smoked continuously for a further three weeks. The looting continued until there was nothing left to take. Then the city was empty. Burned out and empty. The former slaves who had pillaged were gone. They were now free in name. A century of white presence in the north colony was little more than a pile of ashes and smoked-stained cooling masonry.

Meanwhile, the British, always France's implacable foe, had waited offshore for an opportune moment, or an invitation, to invade. It came when the West Province planters urged the English to step in and take over the French colony. Bérard had chosen his side. His decision sealed the fate of L'Artibonite plantation. The British landed in Saint Domingue in September 1793.

In the West Province, under British protection, planters like Bérard tended the harvests and tried their best to continue business through the two ports to which they still had access, St.

Marc and Port-au-Prince. But the Royalist and mulatto planters did not underestimate the skills of the Saint Domingue revolt's true rising star, Louverture. He was advancing on the West Province after he "took Dondon without a fight." When he marched on Marmalade, the mulatto commander deserted to Louverture with twelve hundred troops.

To Jean-Jacques Bérard and his fellow *grands blancs,* Toussaint-Louverture was the enemy. There was more or less a territorial deadlock. The British, who had come in through Port-au-Prince, held much of the West Province's southwestern portion; Louverture held the rest. By exporting the plantation's produce through Port-au-Prince, Jean-Jacques was able to keep the family enterprise functioning. But even under these conditions, a plantation chateau was no place for a single man determined to continue the family tradition. His mind turned once more to matrimony.

His choice was Marie Elisabeth Bossard Roudanes of the Dondon plantation. The Bossards and the Bérards were familiars, possibly she was his cousin. Marie Elisabeth was twenty-one; her husband, Philippe Pierre Roudanes, was dead— perhaps killed in the fighting. Her father, Louis, was dead, too, cause not known. Possibly both were killed when Dondon fell into Louverture's military hands. At that point the remnant of the Bossard family likely fled to the West Province to be under British protection. This possibility is strengthened by the fact that Marie Elisabeth's sister, Marie Anne, was married to Colonel Dessources of the St. Marc regiment, who had placed his troops under British command. The Toussaint records also mention a "Michelle" Bossard. This may have been an alternate name for Marie Anne (there was already one Marie in the family), or Michelle could have been a cousin.

The mother of Bérard's future bride, Lady Marie Anne Fleury, after the marriage, went to live in Cayes and survived for almost a quarter century. The three girls may initially have taken refuge with their mother, or gone to L'Artibonite plantation, where there would be room also for Colonel Dessources plus their retainers. L'Artibonite seems the more likely destination, given that Zénobie's daughter, Marie Bouquement, was Marie Elisabeth's maid and previously her wet nurse.

Late in 1796 (in all probability), Jean-Jacques and Marie Elisabeth were wed.

In the decade ahead, Toussaint's new mistress was to become a focal point of his existence. She is central to the first ten years of the Toussaint story in America. He, at the time of the wedding, is approaching fifteen. Though in age still a boy, he would by now have taken on most of the duties of a more mature gentleman's gentleman.

As for the colony itself, its several fates from this point become less important to the Pierre Toussaint account. For Jean-Jacques, the situation during the years 1794–1796, though far from static, likely affected him less than had the constant insurrections of the previous six years. He operated under British protection, as did a huge portion of the West Province.

By 1797, however, yellow fever was decimating the British troops. Port-au-Prince was ravaged by it. Jean-Jacques Bérard was sharp enough to realize that Toussaint-Louverture was growing strong enough to defeat the fever-weakened British and could unify the colony. Bérard, as a man identified with those who had supported the British occupation, anticipated there would be troubles enough in the year or so immediately ahead once Louverture arrived—not least for those white planters who had called England to their aid. It would be wise, Bérard decided, to leave Saint Domingue for a while.

For years Bérard had been trading with New York using Yankee merchantmen sailing out of that city. Using his contacts there, he rented a furnished house in lower Manhattan. Then he transferred sufficient monies to America to enable him and his family to live well for a year or two. He would take his wife, Marie Elisabeth, and her two sisters, Madame Dessources and Mademoiselle Adélaïde Bossard.

The fleeing whites, even Bérard in his least calm moments, wondered if all was lost forever. And if so, would there be compensation for the seizures of the plantations and the flourishing businesses? The question of reparations was to drag on for forty years. (As for the slaves and *gens de couleur* retainers, it was due only to "the Almighty's heavenly goodness," Toussaint's black friend Auguste Collon wrote him years later that he and his family "survived the atrocities, and a further several years of tribulations and penury, a consequence of the nomadic life to which I, perhaps too imprudently, subjected my family.")

To serve them in New York, the Bérard entourage would have five black servants, four of them slaves: Pierre, fifteen; his sister, Rosalie, ten; Hortense, possibly in her late twenties, who was formerly Aurore Bérard's personal maid; and Old Cabresse, a seamstress in her fifties. Marie Bouquement, forty, Pierre's aunt, was given her freedom by the Bossard sisters in 1796, probably just before the Bossard-Bérard marriage. Bouquement's freedom papers do not list Marie Elisabeth as a Bérard. The fact that both Pierre and young Rosalie went to New York was probably Zénobie's doing—looking out for the youngest members of the family in an otherwise threatened country.

Pierre and Rosalie, without knowing it, were saying good-bye to their parents and siblings forever. Marie Bouquement would leave her children behind. Zénobie, Ursule, and the other family members would remain. Of the nine people departing L'Artibonite, three of the four whites would return, only to quickly die there. Of the slaves, only Marie Bouquement would again see Saint Domingue—in a desperate and unsuccessful bid to find her daughter, Adèle. Then she, too, sadly, would return permanently to New York.

The siblings Pierre and Rosalie were leaving their family forever. To their horror-filled late childhood would be added the anguish of homesickness, separation, and loneliness. It was the lot of thousands of French-speaking exiles from France who had already flooded into the seaboard cities of the United States. Now the French colonies added their final émigré populations to those same French-speaking communities.

Pierre was about to face enormous burdens in a land whose language he couldn't speak, where the climate was usually cold and damp and gray-skied. It was a place where, within four years, only his abilities, energies, and faith stood between survival and total desperation.

SEVEN

NEW YORK, NEW YORK

AT THE END OF THE SUMMER OF 1797, Pierre Toussaint, walking behind his master, Jean-Jacques Bérard, and the Bossard ladies, along with the four other servants, disembarked at a New York wharf close to Wall Street. The fifteen-hundred-mile voyage from Le Cap to New York had taken three weeks.

The entirety of the city into which Toussaint stepped is what today is called Lower Manhattan—for ease, say everything below today's Chinatown. Apart from that there were a few outlying settlements to the far north, such as Greenwich Village.

President George Washington had just finished his two-year term and the second president of the United States, John Adams, who had lived in Greenwich Village during Washington's presidency, when New York City was the nation's capital (1789–1790), succeeded him.

Toussaint didn't know it, and had been promised otherwise, but Lower Manhattan would be his home for the rest of his life.

The moment his feet hit New York's cobblestones Toussaint became part of U.S. history, as well as French and Haitian history. That is the immigrant reality.

There was no vainglory in Toussaint. Not at any time in his life would he have speculated that the world that opened up for him in America might serve later generations as a window on his times. He was not conscious that he was the type of person or his the type of life through which subsequent Americans and Haitians might examine their own story. Yet his story is a means of illuminating the shameful history of American slavery as it existed in the United States, the Catholic Church, and general society.

His arrival in the United States is crucial. Toussaint's story, at this point, becomes an American tale.

Had Pierre stayed in Saint Domingue, lived a life of equal industry, cheerfulness, goodness, and caring for others, he would still have been a good example of a decent, Christian man. He would have been free and kept pace with his times, but he would have been just one more freed man. He may even have pined for some of the lost benefits his particular servitude had provided. Or he may have found, with his education, his winning ways, and organizational ability, a distinctive role for himself in the development of the new nation called Haiti.

In any event, he *was* in New York, and the city had different tests for his determination than the trying world he had left behind. In the United States his servitude continued—everything continued. In Saint Domingue, the rebels were exorcising white hatred by gradually eliminating the whites. So in America, the white slaveholders, frightened by the French colony's example, tightened their grip. For a black, slave or free, the United States represented the same social denigration and brutal ostracism with which Toussaint had lived in Saint Domingue—conditions Haiti's ex-slaves would soon consign to the bonfire of history.

He arrived in New York when it was still a small town rebuilding itself from the charred city the British had left behind at the end of the Revolutionary War. When he died more than half a century later, it was *the* metropolis, the country's preeminent city. Despite periodic setbacks and panics, the city was booming. In Toussaint's first twenty-five years as a New Yorker the population doubled and doubled again.

With what astonishment and, as a typical sixteen-year-old, with what sense of adventure did Toussaint step into this new world? Surely the first thing he noticed was that it was a white world. The racial mix was topsy-turvy compared to the world he'd come from—an overwhelmingly black world where only one-tenth of the population was white. In New York only 15 percent was black.

The next difference was also immediately obvious. From the chatter around him as he left the gangplank, he noticed the language was different. Simultaneously, there was a different texture to the place—the smell, the feel, the noises, the sights, the tastes. The dress was far more somber than the colorful colony they'd left, and if the city was overcast, as it often is, it seemed a dismal place with its dark and damp air heavy with wood smoke from a thousand chimneys.

Not all of these things would assail him, some would entertain him. He was, after all, a young man who looked at the world with curious eyes. Nothing in the record suggests Toussaint was a fearful person. Cautious, yes, but with the good-natured unflappability that comes from temperament (or, in some, from a deep, cheerful faith).

Another big difference from the land he'd left was the absence of trees. Toussaint had left a land of trees for a land of houses. And worse, New York was damp, smoky, smelly, and dank. The wind didn't carry many fragrances, and at its worst it was malodorous rather than sweet, with a strong tang of sewage and soot. (There were defenders of New York even then who spoke lyrically of the place, stressing the pleasant breezes that blew across the Hudson River from the fields and farms and flowers of New Jersey.)

The sailing ship that brought the Bérards and Toussaints, as it docked, pointed its prow straight up Wall Street, the city's major and most prestigious thoroughfare. While city records do not show where the Bérards—and therefore Pierre Toussaint—actually lived when they first arrived, Wall Street was the way to their new home, and it would lead them into a lot of surprises. The worst would be the weather. No matter what the season, these temporary exiles—as they thought of themselves—had been accustomed to blue skies. Gray skies, rain and snow, and a chilling damp would be the new regime. In summer there was heat, certainly, but it was the heat of a congested and foul city.

Met by friends or business contacts, the Bérard party, traveling by coach—baggage following behind in a cart, probably with Toussaint riding on it to safeguard the family possessions—made its way five blocks up Wall Street, past Trinity Church, to Broadway (then still often referred to as Broad Way). Wall Street was "the most fashionable place of residence and, with Federal Hall (built with lottery money) there, the center of political life of the United States." Jean-Jacques Bérard and his little entourage would pass the home of Alexander Hamilton, who lived at No. 57 Wall Street. The slave boy riding on the luggage cart could not have imagined that he would meet Hamilton, and come to know Hamilton's wife and grandchildren well—as their coiffeur. Along Wall Street, Hamilton's neighbors were the business and political elite, intermingled with some ordinary professionals, artisans, and craftsmen.

Expansion was everywhere in this part of town. Barely a decade earlier, in 1785, returning New Yorker Samuel Beck, back from France, had "found it a neglected place, built chiefly of wood, and in a state of prostration and decay. A dozen vessels in port; Broadway from Trinity Church inclusive down to the battery in ruins, owing to a fire when occupied by the enemy. The ruined walls of the houses standing on both sides of the way, testifying to the poverty of the place, five years after the conflagration. Although the war had ceased, and the enemy departed, no attempt had been made to rebuild. In short, there was silence and inactivity everywhere." To illustrate how bustling and industrious the city quickly became, before the 1780s were out one resident wrote, "House building in abundance, and house rents remain high." To such a new or recently built house were the new arrivals headed.

If the Bérard coach turned right to head north up Broadway, it would immediately pass Little Queen Street, where once had resided Aaron Burr, the man who, seven years later, would kill Hamilton in a duel. Burr wasn't in Little Queen Street for long. After Vice President Adams vacated Richmond Hill Mansion for Philadelphia, Burr moved into the mansion.

The new arrivals would see homes large and small on Broadway itself, a higgledy-piggledy mix of workshops where the owner lives above the premises practically abutting mansions in spacious grounds. Those spacious grounds would offer the only touch of greenery the Bérards and Toussaints, accustomed to lush flowered and forested surroundings, would see. Tree planting was generally banned in the city except in front of churches and public buildings. Perhaps, once he was settled in, Toussaint, longing for greenery and flowers, sought relief from barren New York by looking through the railings at Richmond Hill Mansion. Mrs. Adams described the grounds as abundant with "venerable oaks and broken ground covered with wild shrubs. I have prohibited the grounds from invasion and sometimes wish there were game laws. The partridge, the woodcock, the pigeon are too great temptations. Cultivated shrubs included shaddock, citron, lemon, olive, lime and green bay trees; [there] is large myrtle, box leaf, small myrtle, tea plant, pomegranate, creeping ceres, Arabian jasmine, balm of Gilead, rosemary and lavendar."

As the Bérard party progressed, they passed the business of John Miller the hairdresser, located for a while at No. 3 Broadway. The innocent Toussaint did not know an apprenticeship and a life of hairdressing awaited him. There were breeches-makers and peruke (wig) makers. Widow Colley's boarding-house once occupied No. 56 and Mrs. Sebring's was at No. 63.

The grim, gray city was one of cobbled streets with wood or redbrick-faced houses. If the little band headed farther up Broadway, to Barclay Street on the left, they'd glimpse St. Peter's Catholic Church just a block in. Given the prevalence of low houses of the day, the church roof could have been visible from a carriage on Broadway. On the streets jutting off Broadway, the new arrivals would see many white women going about their day, some attended by slaves. Adult white women out-numbered adult men in the city two to one—there had been a war on, with all its attendant dislocations and casualties.

The Bérard coach and Toussaint cart passed taverns and a brass foundry, the sheds of harness makers and coach-builders, attorneys' offices, fruit shops. Another hairdresser, Peter Mc-Kinnion, long shared No. 100 Broadway with John Charlton, M.D. No. 133, the final house on Broadway at that time, had be-longed to John Jay, the antislavery advocate and anti-Catholic governor of New York.

Beyond the relatively broad thoroughfares like Wall Street and Broadway, the streets tended to be narrow and cramped. Some were even too narrow for two handcarts to pass each other. Like St. Marc or Le Cap, in some areas of the city dogs ran loose, chasing the pigs that foraged amid the muck. There was plenty of noise. Residents complained not only of the pigs but of the constant tolling of church bells for funerals. The bells began the moment the cortege left the house and didn't cease until the bur-ial grounds swallowed up the deceased—possibly an hour later.

Somewhere in a gentrified area, Bérard found himself face

to face with his new home, a typical upper-gentry four-story brick-faced frame row house of decent but not excessive proportions. At most it was probably twenty-five to thirty feet wide, though quite deep, possibly forty or fifty feet. In the style of the day, three or four steps, brownstone or cast iron, led up to the front door. Still outside, at street level, to one side of the main steps were steps descending to a windowed cellar. This is where the kitchen, storage, fuel, and some slave or servant quarters were located.

The Bérards would enter the main door onto a small vestibule with a tiled or planked floor and a stand for hats and wet cloaks, then go on through another door leading into the hallway. The internal dimensions would not impress anyone accustomed to a mansion. There'd be a stairway to the right, narrow in the style of New York houses, with a front parlor door to the left and, along the corridor, a second room to the left, for use as a sitting, sewing, or reading room. The person entering the house faced another door directly ahead along the main hallway. Open that door and the new arrival is in the main downstairs room. This is a room the width of the house, with a prospect looking out to the rear onto a medium-sized garden with a tiled patio or slabbed walkways and plantings. Pause at that door and, to the right, descend the inside staircase to the basement and the kitchen.

In most houses this main rear room would be the dining room and, often, an extra "day room." When not in use, the table would be sided—folded and placed against the wall to allow more space. Upstairs, at the next level, the layout of the first floor repeated itself. The third floor would be divided into bedchambers (in the parlance of the times, hence chambermaid), and the top floor (not the eaves) would contain additional bedrooms. Under the roof there'd be servants and slaves—those not sharing the cramped rooms off the basement kitchen.

If the main room on the first floor was kept permanently as a dining room, the main day room would be on the floor above it.

In the walls of the halls and rooms were niches for vases and ornaments to allow decoration without encumbering the narrow space. Furniture would be set sparingly. Houses at this time were underfurnished by today's standards. There were no bathrooms. The contents of chamber pots and commodes were emptied into big pails by the servants. The city sewerage system, according to contemporary accounts, "consisted of slaves, a long line of whom might be seen late at night wending their way to the river, each with a tub on his head." It is not likely such a task awaited Toussaint, menial help on a contract basis would be brought in for that unpleasant work. Apart from Old Cabresse the seamstress, the slaves Bérard brought from Saint Domingue were personal and immediate to the household.

Like the outgoing household sewage, the population's incoming drinking water was carried on people's heads or shoulders, or delivered in carts. Fresh (or reasonably so) drinking water in those times was colloquially and accurately referred to as "tea water." Water for making tea was potable water distinguished from that used for washing and scouring. In Lower Manhattan, it had its own source, the "tea water spring," marked as such on city maps. Afternoon "teas" or "chocolates" were primary social functions of some importance in the former British colonies.

No bathrooms meant no baths. Not only were New Yorkers more drab than the colorfully dressed folk of French Saint Domingue, they were probably smellier, too. Off Broadway, on Crown Street, Henry Ludlum kept a bathhouse "with warm and cold water of sufficient depth for both ladies and gentlemen"— separated bathing, of course. Heating Henry Ludlum's bathhouse, or the house in which the Bérards and Toussaints now lived, meant wood for the fireplaces. These commodities, too, needed to be hauled to the fireplaces on each level of the house each day, and the ashes carried down each morning.

Householders were supposed to take care of the street in front of their dwelling and the city crews were expected once a week to collect the dirt and trash. Unlike the long line of slaves who carried the middens to the river at night, the street cleaners were not noticeably reliable. They came under the control of the "watch," the rudimentary city-run "police force." More threatening to a boy like Toussaint than the failure to police the street cleaners was the fact that the watch had a racist reputation. Its 1780s high constable James Culbertson had done nothing when his night watch beat the black freedman Raphael until his kidneys issued blood. Culbertson was removed for total neglect of his duties.

The watch was likely corrupt and certainly inept. It had all the capabilities of a Gilbert and Sullivan police force. A farmer who made his way into the city reported he had been set upon by "a gang of villains." The next day those he identified turned out to be members of the night watch. In the manner of other police chiefs in history, the high constable claimed the watch was "on important secret service for the city." The high constable was also responsible for keeping the streets free of pigs, "but he seems to have escaped that duty." The newspapers were occasionally filled with letters and impolite rhymes ridiculing the high constable and his men. Meanwhile, the city by night and day was victim to "footpads" (muggers or highway robbers), who in the New York City newspapers were always referred to as "wheelbarrowmen from Philadelphia."

In their new dwelling the Bérard women would have the furniture rearranged as the trunks containing their clothing were unpacked. The meager possessions of Toussaint and the slaves would be stuck in a corner of their rooms, as the everyday tasks were immediately allocated. Toussaint, who would quickly have to acquire sufficient English to assist with major marketing, would also be required to check the "intelligence" offices. These were the news centers of the day, and they carried the latest information from around town as well as details of the ships arriving from around the world. Those coming into New York from Saint Domingue were of particular import. Such vessels meant, for the Toussaints, letters from home. Pierre's mother, Ursule, and his aunt Marie were both literate. A letter from Ursule shows a slightly better grasp of written French than even Zénobie's.

❖   ❖   ❖

Had Pierre Toussaint been born in New York City rather than Saint Domingue, he'd still have been a slave but probably wouldn't have been a Catholic. Saint Domingue was a Catholic country. If there were any French Protestants in the colony, they had the good sense to keep quiet about it and function as if they were lapsed Catholics, which is probably what a not insignificant portion of the colonial Catholic population was. In New York, however, not only were there very few Catholics, there was a high degree of anti-Catholicism, a hostility that grew markedly worse throughout Toussaint's lifetime.

Until the mid-eighteenth century, Catholicism had been banned in New York. This was in marked contrast to Maryland, for example, where so many black refugees from Saint Domingue landed. Maryland was already at least 30 percent Catholic (and 20 percent of those were slaves).

Toussaint's life was dramatically played out under two very different proscenium arches. On the Saint Domingue stage, the backdrop was brutal slavery and glittering fortune-making. On New York's stage, the backdrop was a bigotry quick to provoke violence and kidnapping—though New York City added for most the chance of possible economic advancement through skill or opportunism.

American Catholicsm, as it developed in the decades immediately ahead, accepted the racism and slaveholding. Quite simply, and to its shame, American Catholicism reflected the social
mores of the day. In future years, Catholic bishops, and communities of men and women religious, were slaveholders along
with the rest of society. Indeed, the year Toussaint arrived in
America, so did the first Carmelite nuns from Europe. And as
their first novices entered the "carmel" to become nuns, they
brought slaves with them as part of their dowry.

What all this means is that whatever excitement Toussaint
found in New York City was offset somewhat by the four strikes
against him: he was black, a slave, a foreigner who didn't speak
the language, and a Catholic.

❖   ❖   ❖

Because religion is a constant theme in Toussaint's life, anti-
Catholicism is a major factor in his story. Anti-Catholicism was
not present everywhere and at all times in colonial America.
In Maryland, for example, Catholics were at one point more
numerous than Protestants (more Catholics than Protestants
signed up to participate in the Catholic Lord Cecil Calvert's
1634 proprietary colony). And Maryland's Catholics brought in
a law of religious tolerance (which, when the Protestants gained
the upper hand, was ignored, and legions of Catholics, by the
time Toussaint arrived, fled Maryland for the new frontier—
Kentucky).

New York was Dutch and Protestant. So Protestant, in fact,
that, in 1643, when the Jesuit priest Father Isaac Jogues visited
the city (then called New Amsterdam), he found only two
Catholics among the approximately eighteen hundred inhabitants.

Forty years later that would be two Catholics too many for
German-born Calvinist Jacob Leisler, who, in 1689, successfully

led an armed rebellion against New York's British Catholic governor. Having unseated the governor, Leisler instituted a strict policy of religious intolerance. Colonial New York duplicated the repressions under which Catholics in England suffered during what are known as "the penal times" (during which, those caught at or suspected of Catholic practices were heavily penalized, frequently tortured, and sometimes put to death). In America, under Leisler, Jesuits ministering to New York State Indians had to flee. After Leisler's "rebellion," London sent out a new governor who had Leisler executed. The British government didn't object to Leisler's anti-Catholicism—to the contrary, that was state policy—but it did object to colonials taking upon themselves insurrections against duly constituted governors, Catholic or otherwise.

With a new governor, anti-Catholicism was intensified and a vicious bigotry ensued. One example speaks to many: During the mid-eighteenth-century English-French war over who would own Canada, Catholic "French Neutrals" in Acadia (Nova Scotia) were expelled. Some arrived in New York. Incredibly, to modern sensibilities, simply because these Acadians were Catholic, the adults were immediately forcibly indentured as servants and their children shipped off to other states as wards of Protestant families. (This alacrity in taking displaced, orphaned, or poor Catholic children and sending them to Protestant homes in other states persisted in New York well beyond the first half of the nineteenth century. It ceased only when the Catholics gained political power in the city.) Other "Acadian neutrals" went to Louisiana, held on to their Catholicism, and today are known as Cajuns, a corruption of Acadians.

Though details of Catholic life in eighteenth-century New York are scant, what was known did not augur well for black Catholics like Toussaint. In 1741, there was a slave insurrection in New York City known as the "Negro Plot." There were immediate reprisals and executions. What actually happened is not clear. One line of argument is that there was a slave insurrection, another says there was no true insurrection and the whole thing was cooked up to deliberately discredit blacks and Catholics. The result was the same either way: Spanish Catholic Negro slaves (from St. Augustine, Florida, then a Spanish colony) were executed along with a Protestant clergyman who was suspected of being a Catholic priest.

The Negro Plot intensified the suspicions of anti-Catholic New Yorkers and heightened the fears of New York's slave owners. An 1813 map of New York even contains historical sites, such as sites nos. 56 and 55, respectively, "Plot Negroes gibbeted" and "Plot Negroes buried here." The gibbet, close to the natural swampy drainage area called "The Collect," is shown on the map replete with a tiny drawing of a man hung.

Into the second half of the eighteenth century, Catholic priests were outlawed, and Catholics who sheltered them were liable to a £200 fine (in excess of $5,000 in today's dollars). However, the fact that the law was on the books suggests that somewhere, furtively, Catholics were meeting in the city. Elsewhere in the state there were Scottish Catholics who had fled following Bonnie Prince Charlie's defeat at Culloden Moor. They were in New York's Mohawk Valley with their pastor, Father John McKenna. (McKenna became the first president priest in the state in a century.) The Scots wisely maintained a safe distance from the bigoted city. However, a courageous Jesuit, Father Ferdinand Farmer, began to slip into Manhattan periodically to secretly say mass in a loft on Water Street for a brave handful of clandestine Catholics.

❖   ❖   ❖

The Revolutionary War brought the first publicly visible Catholicism to New York City. French Catholic officers and men who came to fight the British on America's behalf had Catholic

chaplains in their regiments. These chaplains publicly celebrated mass for the Catholic soldiers. But the colonists' victory
over the British brought no great reason for local Catholics to
celebrate—the first American flag run up a staff in the city to
mark the victory had American colors on one side and "No Pop-
ery" on the other.

In 1777, New York State made religious freedom a staple of
its constitution. Now, at least, the Jesuit priest Farmer could
openly visit the city where José Ruiz Silva, a wealthy Portuguese
wine merchant, opened his home for mass. Gradually a little
community formed—at most two hundred Catholics. Whatever
freedoms John Jay, New York's first post-Revolution governor,
approved of with one hand for his fellow Americans, he tried to
take away from the Catholics among them with the other. He
even proposed an amendment to the naturalization clause of
the New York State constitution that would exclude foreign-
born Roman Catholics from citizenship. It was not adopted.

Seven years later, in 1784, the French consul, Hector St.
John de Crèvecoeur (whose work, *The American Farmer,* Toussaint
likely read in the French original), organized some trustees
to establish a church. The Spanish consul general, Thomas
Stoughton, advanced one thousand pounds, and his business
partner bought the leases of five lots on Trinity Church Farm.
Contributions came from several quarters, including Charles III
of Spain. Other funds came from wine merchant Silva, doing
business at No. 1 Beekman Street; chandler Andrew Morris on
Great Dock Street; grocer Gibbon Burke on Water Street; up-
holsterer William Mooney on Nassau Street; merchant Charles
Naylor on Williams Street; merchant George Harwell on Water
Street; and grocer John Sullivan on Moore Street.

In 1785, the Spanish ambassador, Don Gardoqui, laid the
cornerstone. Because of Charles III's generosity, Gardoqui was
granted a reserved pew. St. Peter's Church, the mother church
of New York City, was consecrated that same year. Gardoqui was

a popular figure in the city. He entertained lavishly at his residence, Kennedy House, and was regarded, according to the otherwise anti-Catholic John Jay, who had known him in Madrid, as "chatty and sociable."

By the time Toussaint arrived in the city, the migration from France had doubled and redoubled the city's Catholic population. Irish Catholics who fled their abortive 1790s rebellion were in turn augmented by tens of thousands more seeking jobs. To them, in the 1820s, were added thousands more who came to dig the Erie Canal. French Catholics, however, always regarded the Irish-dominated American Catholic church as a second-rate affair with poor preaching and mediocre liturgies. Toussaint's friend Jean Sorbieu refers to these Catholics as *Irlandais sauvages,* Irish savages. Not until the 1840s did New York's French families build their own church, where they could have their preferred glittering high masses and sermons that were feats of oratory preached in their own tongue. Pierre Toussaint was the first person to make a donation to the proposed "French church," as the new St. Vincent de Paul parish was known. He, however, stayed ever faithful to St. Peter's.

Though united in name the United States was not, in the late eighteenth century, a geographically united continental mass. Louisiana and Mississippi belonged to France (and briefly to Spain) until the 1803 Louisiana Purchase. Mississippi was claimed by Catholic France as early as February 13, 1699, when French nobleman Pierre Lemoyne, Sieur d'Iberville, touched land in Biloxi Bay, and his chaplain, Recollect Father Anastasius Douay, said the region's first mass on the beach. Where Lemoyne's expedition lifted their heads to Heaven in praise of their Triune God and saw sky, today they'd see towering bayfront gambling casinos crammed with worshipers whose trinity is three bars, three bells, or three dollar signs.

Both Louisiana and Mississippi were bastions of slave Catholicism with some freed black and mulatto Catholics. Many

Saint Domingue mulattoes and free blacks uprooted themselves as the colony collapsed, sensibly headed for French New Orleans. Among them was Toussaint's sister, Marie-Louise Pacaud, who fled first to Cuba and then moved to New Orleans. Three decades hence, in the 1830s, driven out by bigotry and joblessness from American cities in the north, many more free blacks decided to call New Orleans home.

❖   ❖   ❖

The first black Catholic in what would become the United States was an explorer. Historian Cyprian Davis tells of the black Catholic Esteban (a native of Azamor, Morocco) who accompanied the Franciscan Fray Marcos de Niza, sent north from Mexico (New Spain) in 1539 to evangelize the Indians. "In 1539," writes Davis, "four men, members of Governor Alvar Núñez Cabeza de Vaca's expedition, arrived in Mexico after a harrowing trek through lands that are now Florida, Texas, and Arkansas. They were all Spaniards—three were white, and the fourth was black." Three years later, Esteban the Moroccan was with Fray Marcos in the role of scout. Accompanied by friendly Indians, Esteban would forge ahead deeper into the present-day American Southwest and report back to Fray Marcos whether the places he visited were of lesser or greater importance. This he signified by varying the size of the woven twig crosses he sent with the Indian messengers.

At the city of Cibola, however, Esteban was detained overnight by the Zuni and the following morning put to death. The Indian messengers reported to Fray Marcos that the Zuni would not believe that a black man was the emissary of white men.

Thirty years later, in 1565, and three thousand miles away, there was the start of a sizable black Catholic colony on the east coast. Again it was Spanish in founding—today's St. Augustine,

Florida—starting as a Spanish military outpost in the New World. Blacks were part of the population, both slave and free. Those numbers were augmented a century and a half later, "especially after 1700," writes Davis, when the Spanish colony invited slaves from the nearby colonies of Georgia and the Carolinas to escape to St. Augustine. There, "provided they converted to the Catholic faith," they were freed. In 1763, when Spain gave up its Florida colony to the British, the entire Spanish colony more or less decamped to Cuba, leaving St. Augustine practically deserted. Though not before some of them had been implicated in New York City's Negro Plot.

❖   ❖   ❖

Toussaint was not just Catholic, he was a slave and black. In his world, racial bigotry was joined to the anti-Catholicism. When Toussaint arrived, New York City was second only to Charleston, South Carolina, for the number of slaves within the city limits. During the Revolutionary War, when the British occupied New York City, blacks arriving there were considered freed men and women. It was a temporary sanctuary at best. When Cornwallis surrendered to Washington's forces, not only did the New York Tories, who had supported King George III's forces, have to flee the city for their lives, so did the runaway blacks who had sought sanctuary under the British. With the British troops gone, slave masters from Virginia, the Carolinas, New Jersey, and elsewhere flooded into the city looking for their property.

Like the Tories, many runaway blacks went to Canada where St. John, New Brunswick, and Shelburne, Nova Scotia, initially welcomed them. Within a handful of years, events—and whites—turned against the blacks, culminating with race riots. More than a thousand of the former slaves, which suggests how numerous they must have been in New York City, fled Canada back to Africa, to settle in Sierra Leone.

Not everyone in New York hated the slaves and endorsed slavery. Long before Toussaint arrived, the Quakers in Manhattan had freed their slaves, but the general slaveholding populace was neither impressed nor inspired to do likewise. Slaves were about fourteen percent of the city population. In 1799, after a decade of much debate and many false starts, the New York State legislature passed the gradual Manumission Act that compelled slaveholders to "free any children born to slaves after July 4, 1799." In a further act, passed in 1817, slaves born before 1799 were to be freed a decade later, on July 4, 1827. The Quakers were the predominant group in the New York Manumission Society, which opened a school for slave children provided they were over nine and could spell words of one syllable.

❖   ❖   ❖

The city that awaited Toussaint bustled. Despite periodic panics and recessions, trade, finance, and domestic manufacturing and services were multiplying almost exponentially. Slaves were cheap workers (white women were not much more expensive), and newly freed slaves moved in droves to New York City from their place of original enslavement—undoubtedly as word got around that the city's climate toward blacks appeared at least marginally better than elsewhere.

And while free blacks lived in pockets scattered throughout the whole city, they were crowded on the east side, where there were plenty of casual and menial jobs. Yet while the picture seems a little optimistic, behind the scenes whites were brutalizing even freed blacks. And the jobs blacks held were soon threatened—Irish immigrants pouring into New York who didn't want to dig the canal wanted the jobs blacks had.

Toussaint quickly understood what all New York African Americans already knew: New York was a dangerous city. For

Toussaint there was the added factor that he was a Catholic as well as a slave. New York and neighboring New Jersey could be as cruel as Saint Domingue. Historian Shane White remarks, "ever willing to differentiate themselves from the South, New Yorkers displayed a remarkable myopia about the continued existence of slavery in and round their city." White describes slaveholders in New York and New Jersey as no less willing to beat and mutilate their slaves than slaveholders elsewhere. In New Jersey in 1792, an inquest into a slave woman's death revealed that she had died after "a most barbarous and inhuman whipping, a more painful death than she must have suffered can scarcely be possible."

Moreau St. Mercy, who chronicled slavery in Saint Domingue and later lived in the United States, wrote of a New York apothecary he saw "repeatedly whip a little mulatto" who was chained in an attic on a bread-and-water diet for stealing some drugs. The seven-year-old slave was first flogged and then given salt to eat before being locked away and deprived of water.

The treatment of slaves was regulated by a New York State act passed February 22, 1788, which provided that "every Negro, mulatto or mestee [mixed race] who was a slave at that time should remain so for life, unless manumitted, and that the children of slave women should be slaves. Only slaves under fifty could be manumitted, and even then there had to be a certificate signed by the Mayor, the Recorder and two aldermen that the ex-slave was capable of supporting himself and would not become a charge on the city. Those freed by their owners' wills were free, but the estate had to be responsible for the former slave's welfare."

The list of proscriptions affecting master and slave appeared endless. As White mentions, selling any slave brought into the state after June 1, 1785, was punishable by a fine of one hundred pounds, plus the slave would be freed. Anyone who bought a slave to remove him or her from the State of New York faced a similar punishment. Employing runaway slaves and working them without the master's consent meant a daily fine of $12.50, a sum at least double the weekly wage of most New Yorkers. Selling liquor to a slave brought a fine of forty shillings. A slave who struck a white person was to be tried for petit larceny; a jury trial for slaves was reserved for capital cases only. The master was punished if the slave was begging.

Local papers ran scores of advertisements offering rewards for valuable slaves. George DeWan quotes the chilling May 13, 1805, advertisement in the *Suffolk* (Long Island) *Gazette:* "For Sale: A Negro woman, in every respect suitable for a farmer— she is 25 years old and will be sold with or without a girl four years old." There were bounty hunters, known as "blackbirders," avidly seeking runaways. And when they couldn't find runaways, they had little compunction about kidnapping any blacks they could find—slave or free—and selling them into slavery. For decades, because of the risk of kidnapping, Toussaint had to watch out for himself and his fellow slaves and family.

Into this world, with his French master, had come the teenaged Toussaint. He was a unique example of a slave, for he was a refined young man. He could serve as a servant, and would serve as a hairdresser, yet no matter the slights, he never felt permanently demeaned. As a Christian he had a sense of his own worth.

He exuded a strong, unpretentious aura of personal dignity. He had a charm to his manner, mischief in his makeup, and, one suspects, a highly developed, slightly distanced, and amused tolerance of New York society. He was a born mimic, and some of these New Yorkers might have unconsciously provided him with some characters whom Toussaint probably parodied to entertain his black friends.

All this in a New York of which John Quincy Adams could say, for "all the opulence and splendor, there is very little good breeding to be found. They talk loud, very fast, and all together. If they ask you a question, before you can utter three words of your answer, they will break out upon you again—and talk away."

Young Toussaint might be a slave, but that didn't mean there wasn't a lot going on to keep him amused—as well as keep him busy.

EIGHT

THE BÉRARD HOUSEHOLD,

1797–1814

NEW YORK CITY IN MID-FALL might be smelly and damp, chilly and dismal, but for the three fine ladies of the Bérard household it was socially exciting indeed. And a lot safer than Saint Domingue.

At the close of the eighteenth century, the social set in Manhattan was all too delighted to continue to make room for elegant, witty, and refined French beauties—whether in flight from the Terror in Paris or the Terror in Le Cap. Prime among those extending a welcome was the large, landed, and wealthy Schuyler family.

This family, headed by Washington's famous Major General Philip Schuyler and his wife, Catharine Van Rensselaer, within a few years would take Pierre Toussaint to its collective heart. Four years before the Bérards arrived, the Schuylers and their seven children had quickly wrapped their protective arms around the young Madame de La Tour du Pin. Patriarch Schuyler, by now a senator from New York, called the young woman "my sixth daughter." (If the general sounds a little overwhelming, it may be so. Four of his five daughters eloped—presumably rather than face a discussion over their choice of husband.)

Certainly twenty three year old Madame de La Tour du Pin was in a class of her own—a character out of a gothic novel. Her father was one of King Louis XVI's closest allies. She was rebellious, and she was brave—and almost forty years younger than her husband, whom she'd wed to escape her domineering mother. Arrested even as her father was trying to save the king from execution, Madame de La Tour du Pin wriggled out of captivity, secured passports for herself, her husband, and her children, and made it to America. There, her breeding, gaiety, and energy paved the way in New York society for French-speaking latecomers like Madame Bérard and her sisters.

The three Bossard sisters were of an age with some of General Schuyler's family, and the Bossard-Schuyler social relationship is the most probable route of Toussaint's entrée into the Schuyler circle, as well as the homes of New York's finest, as coiffeur.

It is not possible to overestimate the significance of the Schuyler family in Toussaint's life. He did not remain merely a coiffeur to the Schuyler women. His two closest white friends were members of the family—Catherine Church Cruger was the general's granddaughter, and Mary Anna Sawyer Schuyler was the second wife of the general's oldest son, Philip Jeremiah.

First Catherine: The general's strong-headed daughter Angelica eloped in 1777 with the British businessman John Barker Church. The couple left for England where Angelica became a fashionable and celebrated "grand country house" hostess—much portrayed by leading artists in England of the day. Angelica and John Church and their daughter, Catherine ("Kitty"), returned to the United States the same year Toussaint arrived, 1797. The Churches built a fine mansion in New York and led a sociable life. Catherine became a particular favorite of Toussaint and his circle of friends, who, because most of them were French-speakers, spelled her name "Quitty."

Catherine, General Schuyler's granddaughter, married Peter Cruger, a grandson of Nicholas Cruger, who, by 1777, had become the biggest merchant in New York City and was the owner of Cruger's Island on the Hudson. Catherine and Peter Cruger spent much of their married life in France, returning to New York for occasional visits. Catherine Cruger could have been one of Toussaint's clients even before she was married.

The second beautiful and lifelong relationship was with Mary Anna Schuyler. Eavesdropping on her conversations with Toussaint through her letters, we realize the depth of their mutual knowledge of each other. Further, knowing how well she understood and admired Toussaint gives special credence to Mary Anna's observations regarding goodness—indeed, saintliness. They met because one of the young Toussaint's Schuyler clients was Mrs. Sarah Rutsen Schuyler, wife of Philip Jeremiah, the elder Schuyler son.

Around 1805, Sarah died, possibly while giving birth to the couple's fourth child—and third son—Stephen. Toussaint would have felt the loss keenly for he quickly made friends with the entire family in the households he visited.

Philip, thirty-three, father of four children between the ages of two and eleven, remarried. The new bride was twenty-one-year-old Mary Anna Sawyer, daughter of Dr. and Mrs. Micajah Sawyer of Newburyport, Massachusetts. In the casual style of letter writers of the day, she was known variously as Mary Anna by her parents, Maryann by her brother William, and Mary Ann (or Anne) in much subsequent writing. She signed all her letters "M.A.S." Mary Anna and her sister, Hannah, were married in a

joint ceremony—Hannah to a successful businessman and en-
trepreneur named George Lee.

Both Mary Anna and Hannah were educated, articulate,
and lively. Hannah, who late in life became Toussaint's biographer, was a well-known author of best-selling fiction, plus books
on religion and art. Self-confident and witty, the Sawyer sisters
were at home in America's highest society.

Mary Anna, on entering her husband's family, was not out
of her social depth, only out of her Boston milieu. The couple's
time was divided between their Rhinebeck, New York, estate
and their New York town house. It does not stretch the imagination to suggest that Toussaint, though only five years her senior, added to Mary Anna's confidence not only as her confidant
but because he knew the people in New York society and could
help her succeed in her new role of wife, stepmother, and society hostess.

In some ways Mary Anna was barely more than a girl suddenly responsible for four children and, periodically, a busy social whirl. She was soon doing the New York City and New York
State social rounds as her husband proudly showed off his new
wife in the homes of the wealthy and fashionable. She was a
cheery and unselfconscious writer. On March 3, 1807, shortly
after her marriage, she wrote her parents from her new family
home in Rhinebeck, "we are well and I think very happy in each
other. Our children are good and their parents wise enough to
appreciate rational enjoyments without grasping at more than
falls to the lot of mortals. Tomorrow we dine and spend the
night at Chancellor Livingstons—this is showing ourselves to
you in our much dissipated point of view—these visitings will
soon be over and we shall again be as domestic and retired as
you are.

"But now," she told her parents, "they are all giving us dinners as we are new married people, and as our neighborhood is

not the most compact the consequence is half the time they give us their beds. We should hardly think of riding twelve or fourteen miles to make a call yet one or two have visited from that distance."

In the succeeding four years, Philip and Mary Anna had three children of their own: William, who died at age twenty-two; Sybilia, who died in infancy; and George Lee, who survived into ripe old age. Toussaint and Mary Anna became dear and devoted friends, a relationship that lasted almost forty years. As will be seen, she saw something so special in him she began taking notes of what he said.

Throughout her life, with total confidence, assured of his guidance, prayers, and understanding heart, Mary Anna poured out her deepest woes and griefs to Toussaint. An early example comes from around 1814. Mary Anna has been to the home of her stepdaughter, Catherine, Mrs. Samuel Jones, who has not long been wed. Mr. Jones is dying, apparently from yellow fever. Mary Anna has returned home and needs to unburden herself.

Her letters are written in French, but not by her. Mary Anna is in the habit of asking others better versed to pen the French for her. She sometimes wrote to Toussaint in English but knew he struggled with reading that language. "You will not find," Mary Anna notes at the top of one dictated letter, "that I am making much progress in my French." They had a running joke between them that she would one day teach Toussaint written English and he would teach her written French, but neither succeeded. So, in writing letters, when confidentiality is essential at his end, she has some French-speaker in the house (Hannah did not know the language either) translate as she dictates.

Mary Anna opened this particular letter by saying she is "very cross with myself my Dear Toussaint, for not having said adieu" before she hurried off, "but we will have the pleasure of seeing you in less than three weeks." Other family members had arrived at Catherine's house, undoubtedly to help maintain the vigil with Catherine. From home, Mary Anna deals first with the ordinary details of her household: "I hope to have the pleasure of William wearing the little vest you have sent him. He needed it. The pants are not too tight for him. The weather has begun to be a little better, but the nights are again very cold and the trees are retarded."

Then Mary Anna dwelt on the personal, the situation at Catherine Jones's home. "When one has a troubled soul," she said, speaking of the fever-stricken Mr. Jones, "it is easy to become agitated. As I was about to leave, Madame Pell cried and Mr. Jones had his arms over his eyes, and my heart was well served by arriving here [returning to her home in Rhinebeck]. I wandered around the garden where I walked with my little loving son. [In her mind's eye] I listened to [Mr. Jones's] words, I saw his gestures and his sad figure and my heart broke and I lifted my prayers to God for consolation.

"I implored Him to give me the strength to resign myself to his wishes. This is, my dear Toussaint, my sadnesses and my lonely promenades. Here I return to calm with my dear children whom I want to sparingly let see my sadness. How I think of you my good friend, a star for me of great consolation. Pray for me to the God you serve who pours forth into your soul the salutary balm which is so necessary for us. Love to Juliette. M.A.S."

There is no list of the many society families Toussaint served as hairdresser, but Eliza Hamilton, granddaughter of Elizabeth Schuyler Hamilton and Alexander Hamilton, certainly had hair dressed by Toussaint. It is likely the older women of the household did, too. This Eliza, in time, weds George Lee Schuyler, Mary Anna's second son.

Toussaint's personal popularity with the Schuyler family

stemmed from the fact that he reflected the very qualities the Schuylers admired. He was cheerful, trustworthy, refined, loving, religious, and considerate. The Schuylers had social prestige, yes, and strong family ties. Toussaint had the same, plus discretion.

General Philip and his wife, Catherine, had everything. Their family heritages dated back to the era when New York City was New Amsterdam. He owned land galore around the Albany area, farms, a fine New York town house, and had money, the best social connections, plus the friendship of the first president. (On March 4, 1781, George and Martha Washington were made godparents to the youngest Schuyler daughter, Catherine, later, Mrs. C. V. R. Cochran.) The Schuyler family was noisy, generally happy, harmonious, and religious. The general was a high-spirited, outgoing man even if his daughters, as young women, found him a little hard to take. His skills included those Washington admired: surveying, engineering, and hydrology. Schuyler became chairman of the Erie Canal project.

There was a great deal of easy affection within the family on the father's side. In letters he would refer to a daughter as "my amiable and beloved child." When New York City was the nation's capital (1789–1790) and Schuyler served there in the U.S. Senate, he always addressed his wife, in his letters to Albany, where they had their home, as "my dear love" and signed himself "most affectionately yours," or "ever yours affectionately." He made use of the wares from New York's busy seaport, sending oranges and other goods north, including parcels of lobsters and mackerel. (As most travel was by boat in those days, he tells his wife he has instructed the vessel's captain, Marsellis, that "if he had not a speedy passage" with the lobsters and mackerel, he is "to boil the former and salt the latter.")

Schuyler was a man who believed seven hours of sleep a night was sufficient for any adult, and according to daughter Catherine, before his family "had arisen, he attended to his private devotions." On other occasions he read prayers to his family and the servants. He was abstemious and a stickler about appearances. His children were always to be neatly dressed in case visitors arrived unexpectedly. He refused to listen to scandal and gossip. He "was the most forgiving of men who said that no one truly forgave a wrong who liked to recall it. He charged his children never to speak of their acts of kindness to others, nor of injuries [slights] received." Little wonder that Toussaint, who exemplified many of these same virtues, was so well received.

There was a distinct element to the welcome Toussaint received—it had to do with his color, and was based on class acceptance. The Schuylers were egalitarian in such matters, provided the individual black person was "a gentleman."

Catherine wrote that her father "was served by slaves, as were all men of that period." But Schuyler saw past their color. Catherine gives an account of Schuyler's relationship with a particular slave. "Being an observing man," she wrote of her father, "he was struck by the peculiar deportment of one [slave] in particular—a field hand—and upon inquiry found this man always took his meals alone, and never before he had washed his face and hands, and that all his habits were those of a person of some refinement. My father questioned him upon the subject and became perfectly satisfied that he was of high birth, undoubtedly a prince in his own country. [This was a man of] remarkable intelligence [whom Schuyler] took at once into the house, gave him an office near himself and the name of 'Prince.' Several apartments were allowed him, and the family and their friends treated him as an equal. Every New Year's Day he called upon everybody and was received with great cordiality."

Subsequently, the Schuylers had no difficulty in seeing the refined Toussaint's true worth or accepting him as something approaching a social equal, even though as a hairdresser he visited in order to serve. Many years later, Philip, Mary Anna's husband, undoubtedly summed up family feeling for Toussaint when he said of him, "I have met men who were Christians, and men who were gentleman, but I have only met one who was both. And he was black."

❖   ❖   ❖

Jean-Jacques Bérard, on arrival in New York City, was obviously wealthy and refined enough to compete at the same social level as the established Schuylers. In Manhattan in 1797–1799, the Bérard ménage, "formed at the time a gay and united family, with plenty of society and amusement. 'I remember,' said a lady who was acquainted with them, '[the teenaged] Toussaint among the slaves, dressed in a red jacket, full of spirit and very fond of dancing and music.' " (The red jacket was a favorite with the turn-of-the-century dandy. The famous miniatures painter, John Ramage, is noted at a party as "a handsome man of middle age [in] a scarlet coat with mother of pearl buttons.")

Jean-Jacques had brought sufficient funds for the little band of temporary exiles to live "in good style for more than a year." Unfortunately, as events developed, once in New York he did not seek the financial counsel of his new friends, the Schuylers. The general and his son-in-law, Van Rensselaer, had advised Madame du Pin when she was newly arrived to divide her money into three. One third purchased a farm between Troy and Schenectady, one third purchased its livestock, and the other third was kept for emergencies. When, in 1796, the French government restored to the La Tour du Pins their family estate, Bouilh, the family took the risk of further persecution in France and returned home—assets in hand. Bérard, by contrast, had all his New York assets in one fragile basket.

Bérard could move easily in this world of high society, plus he had another interest, also socially acceptable for a male: business. He'd shown himself sophisticated enough a manager to survive Saint Domingue's woes. Yet in New York, while fretting about the security and future of the Artibonite plantation, he'd undoubtedly scouted out investment opportunities. Because he was in international trade, the likelihood was he favored something in the shipping business, probably investing in an import-export shipping house.

❖   ❖   ❖

In France, meanwhile, by late 1798, the French Revolution had stalled. The Royalists felt their hand growing stronger, and the white planters in France were leading a counterattack to regain their property. The planters were pressing the government to stage a French military invasion to take Saint Domingue away from Toussaint-Louverture. The French government— Napoleon Bonaparte had not yet made his move to consolidate power in his hands—was not unsympathetic. For the next three years (1799–1802) this potential French invasion of Saint Domingue and its promised restoration of the planter aristocracy under the protection of French military might, kept hope alive among the ousted planters.

The absentee landlord planters in France, and those among Bérard's circle of friends in the United States, lobbied the French government relentlessly. Hopes were high. Not only did the French government now need Saint Domingue's revenues as much as the planters did, but Bonaparte considered Loverture a usurper.

❖   ❖   ❖

By 1798, the white half of the Bérard establishment in New York was reasonably well settled and in good cheer. The five black members bravely accepted their temporary new life, too.

The Saint Domingue Africans and mulattoes, like the whites, presumed this was a short-term exile until Saint Domingue quieted down, normalcy under the new order set in, and return was possible.

Just as the Bérards found their way into white society, the blacks in the household would have found friendly black and mulatto faces in the city, including some from Saint Domingue, for the exodus from the colony had been under way for almost a decade. Many planter families that landed in Baltimore, Philadelphia, and New York before the Bérards had their slaves and servants with them. Among the literate slaves and servants, a considerable number of letters flowed up and down the U.S. eastern seaboard in the same packets their masters and mistresses sent their letters to reestablish or maintain connections with their fellow exiles.

❖   ❖   ❖

Though Toussaint was initially unaware of it, black New York, free and slave, was a world of its own that existed at several levels. In the cellars, the African community had its own dancing clubs and drinking spots. At street level, free blacks were forming their associations for education and advancement, opening free schools for black children and trying to establish benevolent societies. Beyond the sidewalks, some free blacks operated their own businesses, mainly taverns and the like, though the majority of free Africans, as historian Christine Stansell notes, worked as "seamen, day laborers, waiters, barbers and whitewashers, generally in menial, ill-paid and casualized situations."

Among Toussaint's old and new black friends in New York was Jean-Baptiste Nelson. He was a "Negre creole" age thirty. He was freed in 1793 in Saint Domingue. Baptiste bought his freedom—paid in installments—from the widow Marie Antoinette Aubert in La Misère. There was nothing unusual about a slave taking ten to fifteen years to buy freedom, and Baptiste was still making payments when Toussaint was a young hair-dresser. Baptiste, who fled Saint Domingue for Cuba before making his way to New York, borrowed enough from Toussaint in 1805 to retire his debt to the widow.

In 1798 and 1799 then, the Bérard household, despite the deplorable winters that attacked the health of the tropics-raised Bossard sisters and their servants, had adjusted to its comfort-able circumstances. Jean-Jacques simply bided his time and waited for a propitious moment to return to the plantation.

❖   ❖   ❖

The exiles' history now was as much American as French. In 1799, George Washington died. The country was deeply moved; ordinary people expressed simple sentiments. Scratched with a quill pen on the final page of an early *Life of George Washington* by David Ramsay, M.D.—the protoype of the presidential best seller—a contemporary reader had written: "He was a good man."

Washington had had his difficulties with the French refugees and émigrés. There was the delicate time when the French Rev-olutionary government first sent its diplomatic representatives to New York. Washington, naturally, accepted their credentials. But George and Martha's levees included both these official agents of the Revolution and the New York–resident French ex-iles—the monarchists and aristocrats from the very families the Revolution had beheaded or forced into exile. Washington wrote to Hamilton complaining about the balancing act he had to perform to keep the warring French factions appeased.

In 1799, however, there was worse news for Bérard than the death of the American president. In the second half of the year "intelligence [news] from the island [Saint Domingue] grew more and more alarming, and M. Bérard thought it necessary to return to look after his affairs."

Prior to departing, Jean-Jacques told Toussaint that he "wished him to learn the hair-dressing business, and a Mr. Merchant, who dressed the hair of Madame Bérard, was engaged to teach him for $50." Toussaint began his apprenticeship shortly after, most likely in late 1799. The usual period of indenture for hairdressing in France was three years. Monsieur Merchant would have no reason to delay Toussaint's arrival at journeyman status and it could be that Pierre, a quick study, completed his apprenticeship in less than thirty-six months. The apprenticeship fee was to be paid on satisfactory completion of the apprenticeship, though it took a couple of years beyond that for Toussaint to retire the debt.

Jean-Jacques Bérard's greatest worry was clear enough. The plantation was at stake. In 1798, the year after he'd left the island, Louverture and yellow fever had finally driven the English troops out of Saint Domingue.

With Louverture now in control across the Saint Domingue colony, and with the huge Artibonite Valley plantations, previously protected by the British, being used by Louverture as patronage for his senior supporters, plantations were being seized and distributed among the victors. Louverture, who occasionally restored plantations to owners who appealed to him personally, took possession of forty plantations abandoned by their fled or dead owners. Others, senior members of Toussaint's successful army, were even more grasping in acquiring plantations.

Bérard's severest problem was that whatever the white planters' strengths in Paris, in the colony, under Louverture, whites had no leverage at all. Word had obviously reached Bérard in New York that L'Artibonite plantation had been seized, or was about to be. On expropriated plantations, the existing domestic former slaves—Zénobie and Ursule at L'Artibonite—were often initially permitted to remain and continue to work there. In Bérard's absence, day-to-day plantation management had been in the hands of Bérard's own foremen and supervisors, with Toussaint's grandmother, Zénobie, maintaining the chateau. Zénobie may have been Bérard's chief correspondent and the one to inform him of the seizure.

What made Bérard hurry back was that the only way he could regain his property would be through a successful personal appeal to Louverture—or, in time, through a successful French invasion that would oust Louverture and restore the properties to their owners. In New York, "Mr. Bérard, placing the property he had brought over to this country in the hands of two respectable merchants, took leave of his wife, as he thought for a short season."

Bérard sailed in hope, and arrived at Le Cap in late 1799 or early 1800, determined to see an end to the difficulties. It is not known if, once in the colony, he saw Zénobie. After some months there is no indication how long a period transpired but it would have been in 1800—"melancholy letters arrived from M. Bérard. His [L'Artibonite] property was irredeemably lost."

Jean-Jacques wrote to his wife: "Do not entertain any thoughts of returning home in the immediate future. As to our property, my dear Marie, I fear that we will be unable to control its destiny. We must wait to see whether it will be spared from destruction." (In one sense, this nonreturn to Saint Domingue was a temporary lifesaver. Had Louverture restored L'Artibonite to Bérard, and had the family and slaves returned, all the white Bérards and Bossards—and perhaps some of their black personal slaves—would have been slaughtered in 1804, when Haiti's Emperor Dessalines ordered death to all whites.)

As it happened, whoever had seized L'Artibonite was powerful enough not to have to relinquish it. L'Artibonite was too valuable a prize, a major property that had functioned all

through the troubles. More than that, though, it would be
Bérard's association with the British—his brother-in-law Gen-
eral Dessource served the British as military commander of the
St. Marc Regiment—that undoubtedly permanently soured
Bérard's reputation with Louverture, who had no reason to
trust the whites, and didn't.

After being absent, one estimates, for six or more months,
Bérard finally wrote to his wife, Marie Elisabeth, that "he must
return and make the most of what he had placed at New York."

Bérard might be anxious at this point, but he was not despairing. He knew many French exiles survived in the United
States by going into business, or running schools, or, like the La
Tour du Pins, farming. Bérard would know all the success stories. He would know how other refugees were managing to survive—primarily through teaching and land schemes. On the
education front, the seaboard Americans of some rank wanted
their children educated in the European manner, and certainly
wanted them to know French, the language of refinement.

For example, the exiled Baron and Baroness de Neuville
(he would one day return to New York as a diplomat) founded
a school and, when they returned to France, bequeathed it to
the newly widowed Victoire-Elisabeth Bancel de Confoulens.
(Not too far ahead, Toussaint would regularly visit the school to
cut the children's hair.)

She was another major character—named for two of Louis
XVI's aunts. At the time of the "Terror" she watched the severed head of her closest friend, the Princesse de Lamballe, carried through the streets on a pike surrounded by a cheering
mob. Like General Schuyler's favorite, Madame de La Tour du
Pin, Bancel was one more plucky French aristocrat. She'd dis-
guised herself as a baker's daughter in order to visit a prison to
see if her father, the King's close friend, was still alive. Finally,
fear for their lives forced the Bancel de Confoulens to flee to
America. In the United States, which he'd previously visited,

Bancel de Confoulens acted as an agent for the Duc d'Eprémesnil's Maine land scheme. For French aristocrats, the hope of building self-sufficient French farming colonies was a much-favored dream. But Eprémesnil died on the scaffold in Paris in 1794. Much later, the baron drowned in Casco Bay, Maine, leaving his widow destitute and with young children to raise.

Some of the French land schemes in the United States went forward, but finally faltered. One scheme was named for Schuyler's daughter, Angelica. Another, Asylum, with a three-story log cabin as its centerpiece, had been proposed as a place where Louis XVI and Marie Antoinette could live if they escaped with their lives. (They didn't.) These settlements, along with others like Black River and Castorland, became footnotes to both U.S. and French history.

Bérard would have to be resourceful. Though the plantation was lost, Jean-Jacques still had some money and some options still open to him, even if the opulent Bérard lifestyle would be no more. Then, in Saint Domingue, disaster truly struck. The letter from Bérard saying he "must return" was "followed by another, announcing his sudden death from pleurisy."

The year was 1801, and the grief that descended on the three white women and the five servants was the same any family would face when suddenly shocked into facing the death of a loved one. In New York, the Bossard sisters were marooned, leaderless, and closer to destitution than they realized. Still in her twenties and now twice widowed, Marie Elisabeth must have wondered what else fate could have in store for her. She was not long in finding out, for within a year (the traditional period of mourning), Madame Bérard was faced with the "failure of the firm in New York to whom her property was entrusted, [leaving] her destitute."

American traders with France did not have an enviable reputation. In 1788, the representative of a Bordeaux firm wrote to his New York counterpart: "the trading part of the United

States have lost every atom of their character and credit in Europe, so that if they want or wish to keep up a connexion with the Old World they must turn honest, 'from policy if not from principle.' "

The question the modern reader immediately asks is: Did the "two respectable merchants" to whom Bérard had temporarily entrusted his financial affairs see an opportunity and conspire to cheat the newly widowed Madame Bérard out of a significant sum of money?

The answer is probably no. A parallel disaster is the life of Elizabeth Ann Seton, which helps to explain why.

GLIMPSED, BUT NOT RECOGNIZED

THE FAILURE OF THE BUSINESS in which the Bérard money was invested highlights in turn a remarkable coincidence of two plaques on the exterior wall of St. Peter's Church, Barclay Street. Placed there in the twentieth century, one plaque commemorates Toussaint; the other marks the attendance at St. Peter's of the church's other famous parishioner, Saint Elizabeth Ann Bayley Seton.

There is nothing to suggest that Seton and Toussaint ever met, yet there is indication that Elizabeth Seton and Marie Elisabeth Bérard faced similar circumstances at the same time. Both were widowed as their husbands' financial standing disintegrated.

To keep the Seton-Toussaint chronology accurate, Elizabeth Seton first came to the parish on Ash Wednesday, in February

1805, and was received into the church the following month. Later, Bishop Carroll confirmed her, also in St. Peter's Church. It is during that period she would have seen Toussaint—if see him she did—without knowing who he was. Toussaint, Juliette, and Marie Bouquement would have been hard to miss in an otherwise generally all-white church. Despite a congregation upwards of twelve thousand parishioners, almost all white, the original St. Peter's was a small church holding no more than two hundred people.

Toussaint in private life was not yet prosperous enough that Father Matthew O'Brien, O. P., who welcomed Elizabeth into the church, would have approached Pierre to assist financially a newly converted widow with five young children to support.

Even without stretching coincidence into incredulity, however, what plummeted Elizabeth Seton's husband, William Magee Seton, into bankruptcy was the same set of transatlantic economic circumstances that likely left Marie Elisabeth Bérard destitute. Two years earlier, in 1798, as Louverture in Saint Domingue drove out the British and Bérard's plantation was placed at risk, the Seton family shipping firm's survival was already in doubt. The threat of war between France and the United States would mean the suspension of trade with French ports.

It is presumed that Bérard's money was invested in a New York shipping firm (imports, exports, and shipping were what he knew). The record implies that Marie Elisabeth was still gaining some income from this investment in the months following his death. Elizabeth Seton's own account explains what happened.

The prospective Franco-U.S. war meant waning prosperity for U.S. traders. The senior Seton died, and Elizabeth's husband, William Magee Seton, took over the family firm. The burden of recovery fell on William Magee, as Elizabeth called him, just as repairing L'Artibonite's fortunes fell on Bérard. Both men "must provide for the immediate family." Jean-Jacques Bérard, though childless, had the anxiety of helping his siblings in Paris.

Magee Seton did not have his father's business ability, and Elizabeth Seton wrote, "my poor William Magee has kept me constantly employed in copying his letters and assisting him to arrange his papers . . . I am tired of hopes and fears, the merchants are in such trouble through the Hamburg and London failures that I have to use every exertion to keep my poor William Magee alive. His present plan is [to relocate us] to the back woods where we shall not calculate 'dollars per load.' " The failures in Britain and Germany shook the entire transatlantic trade economy.

By December 1799, Jean-Jacques Bérard had left for Le Cap. In New York, it looked as though the young Seton might survive financially. Elizabeth wrote, "My Seton is well. His creditors in Europe have allowed him two years to settle the debt; but in that time nothing is coming in. Fortunately he seems to have made up his mind, and says little about his affairs. What he feels is another thing." Yet a year later, Seton's firm was told to either declare bankruptcy or he would go to prison. Magee Seton's was not the only shipping firm in trouble; all New York shipping houses were. Consequently, in whichever shipping company Bérard was invested, his fortunes would have followed Seton's into a similar bankruptcy from precisely the same causes.

Elizabeth Seton wrote: "How will it be with us? This is a nerve that shrinks from the touch, and 'Faith and Hope' are my only refuge." Marie Elisabeth Bérard undoubtedly expressed similar sentiments, though perhaps not as poetically. The day after Christmas 1800, Elizabeth wrote, "I have cause to sigh and weep from Monday to Saturday . . . I have this last week watched and attended the street door to keep out the sheriff's officers with as cheerful a countenance as ever you saw me with. And have given up my list to the commissioners of bankruptcy of all we possess, even to ours and the children's clothings." She was not yet widowed.

Like the pressure Elizabeth Seton was facing, biographer Hannah Lee notes that for Marie Elisabeth Bérard, "the constant [demand for payment] of debts unpaid was most distressing to her; but she had no means of paying them, and she could only beg applicants to wait, assuring them that she would eventually have ample means." "Ample means" was a mirage that never materialized. Madame Bérard equally had cause "to sigh and weep . . . Toussaint entered into all her feelings, and shared her perplexities; and though he had scarcely passed boyhood, he began a series of devoted services."

The "services" Toussaint was called upon to render to Marie Elisabeth took on a variety neither had imagined. He "was present when one day an old friend [of Marie Elisabeth's] called on her and presented her with [a bill] for $40, thinking her husband had left the money with her, and by no means divining her state of destitution. She assured him he should have his money, and requested him to wait a short time; she considered it peculiarly a debt of honor. When he went away, she said to Toussaint, 'Take these jewels and dispose of them for the most you can get.' "

Toussaint is now placed in a most awkward situation. He is a twenty-year-old black slave with jewels to pawn. This was New York City. Could a slave get a fair price? Could he avoid being accused of having stolen the jewels? He could go only to French-speaking pawnshops or jewelers. There are no answers to hand. We know only that he took the jewels "with aching heart"—a heart likely aching for more reasons than Madame Bérard's fall from affluence. For this could well be the moment at which Toussaint is starkly confronted by the true nature of the catastrophe that has struck the household with Jean-Jacques's death: There is no money.

❖   ❖   ❖

What is obvious from Elizabeth Seton's plight is that if the
Bérard household fails and bankruptcy is enforced, the slaves
could be seized and sold as negotiable assets.

Toussaint was bright and smart. He knew the four slaves
were vulnerable whether Madame Bérard intended it or not.
Only his freewoman aunt, Marie Bouquement, was safe. As a
commodity, which is how creditors would see him, Toussaint
was an intelligent male slave in good physical shape; Rosalie and
Hortense were marketable. Old Cabresse was probably too elderly for a purchaser to be interested.

However severe the icy chill that now enveloped Toussaint's
anxious heart, all that is known is what he said regarding Marie
Elisabeth: "It was a sad period for my poor mistress; but she believed—we all believed—she would recover her property in the
West Indies. She was rich in her own right, as well as her husband's, and we said, 'O madam! you will have enough.' But this
state of depression was hard indeed to one who had always lived
in luxury."

That's being very generous to Madame Bérard. She was, in
adversity, a pale shadow of the imaginative and hardworking
Frenchwomen like the couturière-turned-farmer Madame de
La Tour du Pin, and Victoire-Elisabeth Bancel de Confoulens.

He knows now the household is living on credit and mounting debts that Marie Elisabeth might never be able to repay. His
blood must have run cold many times as he faced up to the
fact—even if Marie Elisabeth did not—that he was the only immediate salvation the household had.

Worse, he was one of Madame Bérard's few assets. She had
her jewels—and her slaves.

Toussaint was an unusually sharp-minded young man who
operated out of necessity and circumstance on several levels at
once. As a slave-servant he had one set of duties and one face to

present. As a black man among other blacks, he was a slave and an astute young man supporting himself and others. Though he could not admit it, he could quickly work out that there was no immediate recourse, and might never be, to the fortunes that once existed in Saint Domingue. In moments like these, apprentice hairdresser Toussaint, though "scarcely past boyhood," no doubt immediately faced up to the significance of the Bérard household's precarious existence. (Being young and without cynicism, he may not have seen, as others might, that he was also a lone black male in a household of white and black women.)

Marie Elisabeth's two sisters make the first move. Madame Dessources and Ma'mselle Adélaïde confront the precariousness of their existence in New York City, and within months of Marie Elisabeth's plunge into destitution, and believing a French invasion of Saint Domingue now inevitable, they returned to Saint Domingue. There they could press their claims for the Dondon plantation. It was a thin hope—Madame Dessources was the widow of a general who vigorously fought against Louverture. Toussaint's aunt, Marie Bouquement, accompanied the sisters as their maid.

The return suited Marie, for she wanted to locate her daughter, Adèle. Bouquement's departure plunged Marie Elisabeth Bérard deeper into despondence.

Toussaint, meanwhile, was still confronted with Marie Elisabeth's $40 debt of honor. He solved the predicament his own way. Some time later, "he went to his mistress and placed in her hands two packets, one containing $40 and the other her own valuable jewels, upon which the sum was to have been raised. We may imagine what were her feelings on this occasion"—and Toussaint's: He had survived another day.

How had Toussaint raised the $40 (around $750 in today's money)? The record says he paid it from his savings and hairdresser's tips. "I had early resolved," he said, "never to go into debt." The precept had certainly paid off at this point. (Later, as a businessman, he did go into debt. As in normal business practice, some years he preferred to pay interest on his unpaid quarterly accounts and settle his bills annually.)

From this moment on the apprentice hairdresser must have turned into a veritable hairdressing prodigy, a whirlwind who probably turned no customer down, busy at all hours in the Merchant hairdressing establishment, plus hustling across New York to serve the least important Merchant clients in their homes. In this way, Toussaint's lifelong work habits were set early, out of sheer, icy necessity.

Once the two Bossard sisters and Marie Bouquement sail for Le Cap, Toussaint's burdens ease slightly. Though Marie Elisabeth is totally alone, Toussaint now has only five mouths to feed rather than eight.

How does he succeed? Magnificently. The record reveals that he undertakes these travails and carries these burdens with a smile on his lips and a twinkle in his eye (probably at his own audacity). Catherine Schuyler Church's daughter later writes, "You must not think that Toussaint was a grave, solemn man; he was full of spirit and animation." And if he was that way in his mature years, how much more so in his early twenties.

He had one certain ally as he carried these burdens.

Every morning at six A.M. he attended mass at St. Peter's Church. It was a practice that lasted for more than half a century. His other allies were in the circle of friends who offered encouragement and support, affection and good humor when they could offer little else. These are friends who lasted his lifetime. Some were people with whom he may have been acquainted in Saint Domingue, others were strangers to him before coming to New York.

Toussaint grew up overnight. He was the young man who,

until Bérard's death, had never had to make a decision in his life, they'd all been made for him. Now he had to be entirely a self-starter and self-sufficient. He had Zénobie's imperturbability as a model. He had to delicately pick his way through uncharted social, racial, and economic minefields. He was, after all, quietly in defiance of convention; he was, after all, still a slave. He could not dare to attract the wrong sort of attention to himself.

From 1801 onward, the young hairdresser not only had the household's money worries. As a young black man constantly walking New York's streets to serve his hairdressing clients, he also had to take great care for his personal safety, particularly of an evening—and much hairdressing was done in the late afternoon and early evening to prepare women for their social engagements that night. Kidnapping and the risk of being sold down South was an ever-present anxiety. There was always the possibility of an unprovoked attack, common against Africans.

Neither white Manhattan in general nor the the group charged with keeping the peace, the watch, was friendly toward the black male. Toussaint was a hairdresser, so was Louis Hart, a freed man when Pierre was still a slave. Hart lived on Water Street, only blocks from the Bérard home. Historian Shane White reports that Freedman Hart was standing outside his house when a white sailor began beating a black woman who lived in Hart's cellar. She fled inside. The sailor, Lewis Humphrey, tried to force open Hart's door using a knife. Hart protested and when Humphrey found out it was Hart's house, he struck him. Hart refused to fight and went into his house—which was later invaded when Humphrey returned with six shipmates. They broke into the cellar, beat both the woman and Hart, smashed his property, and stole some silver teaspoons.

The same year, 1801, with Bérard dead and Toussaint struggling to keep the household together, the three-man night watch in Greenwich Street accosted the freed black man Raphael Cooney, who lived adjacent to the Maritime Museum there. When the watch ordered him home, Cooney "insisted he already was, showed them his door, and reminded them it was not yet 10 p.m., city curfew time. He was a free man, he told the watch, and he would go into his home when he chose. The watch began to beat him mercilessly, not least around the kidneys."

Museum keeper William Waldron, a white, went to Cooney's rescue, but throughout the night Cooney "lost a lot of blood through his penis." Cooney's fate is not recorded.

The same writer notes something that even years later always kept Toussaint on his guard: "poor whites from the neighborhood attacked free blacks who, evidenced by their ownership of property, were managing to get ahead." Toussaint was industrious and gave every indication he would manage to get ahead, though life was indeed precarious.

❖   ❖   ❖

Toussaint's resourcefulness becomes a pleasure to witness. His imagination can almost be detected working overtime whenever there was a new crisis. And crises were never far away.

In 1802, the two Bossard sisters, now in Le Cap, were patiently waiting for the day to come when they could press their claims. This same year Toussaint completed his apprenticeship and Mr. Merchant, his mentor, wanted his money—the $50 apprenticeship fee. Merchant approached Marie Elisabeth for it, and Toussaint (deliberately, one presumes) overheard the conversation—he knew why Merchant was there. When his apprenticeship master asked for the money, "Toussaint heard [Madame Bérard] reply with faltering voice, 'it is not in my power to pay you. It must wait.' "

Toussaint again solved the problem. He followed Mr. Mer-

chant out of the house and entered into an agreement to pay
the sum himself, in installments. It took a year, but in 1803,
Toussaint "at length received an acquittal—he paid off the
debt—which he presented to his mistress. She was at first
alarmed, and said, 'O Toussaint, where can you have got all the
money, this money to pay my debts?'

" 'I have got some customers, Madame,' said he, 'they are
not very fashionable but Mr. Merchant is very good—he lets me
have them; and besides, I have all the money you gave me, my
New Years' presents—I have saved them all.' "

The reader already knows what Toussaint's contemporaries
scarcely understood: that beneath the Toussaint's calm and
cheerful exterior he was fighting for survival. And yet, one
senses, doing it with high spirits. He was pulling on every ounce
of his humor, energy, imagination, and deep reliance on his
faith to keep going. Yet he never turned inward. He faced out
and embraced the world as he found it. One other thing he
could not escape as he settled into his long daily round of hairdressing: His life was still dictated by the ebbing revolutionary
currents of the world into which he was born.

❖   ❖   ❖

The revolutionary turmoil that uprooted his French and Saint
Domingan generation is about to claim more Bérard family
members. In 1801, Toussaint-Louverture declared Saint Domingue a republic with himself governor. This display of power
further annoyed Napoleon. The colony's white planters' hopes
soared that year as Britain lifted its naval blockade of French
ships. France planned its long-awaited invasion.

Meanwhile, Marie Bouquement made contact with several
members of the immediate Toussaint family but could not locate
her daughter, Adèle. In Le Cap, where they were all lodging,

Toussaint's aunt also continued serving the needs of the two Bossard women. They were likely living off friends and money borrowed against the future return of their plantation. But Madame Dessources and Ma'mselle Adélaïde could not hold out. Their health, precarious, it was said, after years in the unhealthy New York climate, gave way. They became ill and were soon dead.

Madame Nicolas was now totally bereft. She begged Bouquement to return, promising they would all go back to San Domingo when the moment was propitious: "If it had not been for the last intelligence [news of an earlier delay in the French expedition]," writes Marie Elisabeth, "we [Marie Elisabeth, Toussaint, and the other slaves] should by this time have been at the Cape; as soon as the French troops arrive we shall return. If you are not well off, come back to me and we will all go to St. Domingue together. You know that you are a second mother to me. I shall never forget all that you have done for my poor sisters, and if efforts could have saved anyone, I should have them all. But God has so ordered it, and his will be done. Ah, Dear Memin [Marie Elisabeth's pet name for Bouquement], your religion will support you under all your sufferings—never abandon it! Write, or I will think you do not love me any longer. I am, as you used to call me, your Bonté." ("Bonté" in this context means "a little gift," "a little treasure.")

In February 1802, General Leclerc, Napoleon's brother-in-law, arrived at Le Cap with a fleet and twenty thousand troops. But Marie Elisabeth, undoubtedly stunned by her sisters' deaths, hesitated. Why is not known. Could she have realized it would be unwise to relocate until the French were actually victorious? That meanwhile, with Toussaint working, they were at least surviving? She may have received letters from her sisters setting before her the cold reality of Le Cap and Saint Domingue during those months.

Marie Bouquement was now the sole remaining link to
Marie Elisabeth's earlier life. Madame Bérard's world (like
Marie Bouquement's) had totally collapsed. Both were dis-
traught. Marie Elisabeth was desperate for something to cling to
and needed Bouquement for support. But Bouquement did not
yet budge. She was desperate in her search for her daughter.

All that was left to Madame Bérard was to live with what almost every white San Domingan planter, wherever exiled in the
1790s and early 1800s, still believed—that help was on the way.

Looking to Saint Domingue, where Leclerc tricked Louverture into captivity but nonetheless failed to overthrow the black
liberation, the colonial French confronted their worst nightmare. All hope of future plantations being returned was now
gone.

Matters worsened for Toussaint's extended family. Many
plantation blacks remained on the seized plantations. And this
was the case at L'Artibonite—at first. But in time the independent Zénobie and some of the others—not all—left for Port-au-
Prince apparently to try to survive independently. Pierre's
father and grandfather were still alive, for in one letter Zénobie
reports that his mother, Ursule, had had another child, but it
died. And Toussaint's grandmother adds: "Your father and
grandfather are jealous because you didn't send them any gifts."

For the Saint Domingans stuck in the United States, the
change in fortunes was precipitous. The exiled, formerly fabu-
lously wealthy planters now had to scrape along in America or
France as best they could. These former billionaires and multimillionaires were, more likely than not, facing destitution. On
their initial arrival, the Americans had supported many of them
out of tax money, but that benefice had ended. They had to
fend for themselves. Most were like refugee planter Gabriel
Nicolas, a broke charmer who barely supported himself in New
York as a musician.

Yet Nicolas is different. He stepped into received history, for he entered Toussaint's world—as a suitor for the Widow Bérard's hand.

Little is known of Gabriel Nicolas beyond this: Like most others in the formerly wealthy exiled plantation class, he had anticipated his land would be returned. As a skilled musician—a pianist and violinist—he found employment as best he could, which wasn't very often, playing in theater orchestras and at weddings and social functions. For whatever reason—loneliness, prudence, or propriety (she was after all a lone white woman living with a black man in her home)—Marie Elisabeth decided to accept Gabriel's suit.

In their wedding document issued at St. Peter's Church there is a hint of the longed-for previous times—an established home, a future that had promised only comfort (the bride, for this is a French legal document, reverted to her original family name):

I, the undersigned, have joined in marriage according to the rites of the Catholic Church, Gabriel Jean Baptiste Désiré Nicolas, citizen of the Isle of Saint Domingue from the Aquin Quarter, and now a resident of New York, a major in age and the legitimate son of Gabriel Jean Désiré Nicolas, former adviser to the Superior Council of Port-au-Prince, and Demoiselle Adélaïde Sophie de Lenois, citizens of the same quarter, and Demoiselle Marie Elisabeth Bossard, resident of the aforesaid Isle Saint Domingue and the quarter of Marmalade and a native of the Parish of Dondon, widow by her first marriage without children to Philippe Pierre Roudanes and in the second marriage, also without children, to Jean-Jacques Bérard, citizen of the quarter of Artibonite. The said Demoiselle Marie Elisabeth Bossard, a Major in age, being the legitimate daughter of the late Louis Bossard and the late Lady Marie Anne

Fleury, citizens of the Isle St. Domingue of the quarter of Marmalade.

> M. O'Brien,
> Unus ex pastoribus Sancti
> Petri ecclesiae
> 11th day of August 1802

Toussaint had not so much gained a new master as an extra mouth to feed.

𝓔uphémie Toussaint, age thirteen. She died the following
year from tuberculosis, which had also killed her mother, Rosalie,
Pierre Toussaint's sister. Euphémie was Pierre and
Juliette's legally adopted daughter.

*J*uliette Noël Toussaint, Pierre's wife,
also a member of a Saint Domingue (Haiti) family.

𝒜délaïde Marie Elisabeth Bérard (Madame Jean).
When her husband Jean-Jacques, Toussaint's master, died,
Pierre financially supported his widow until her death.
She freed Toussaint almost on her deathbed.

MINIATURE ON IVORY BY UNIDENTIFIED ARTIST; CA. 1800

COLLECTION OF THE NEW-YORK HISTORICAL SOCIETY

𝒫ierre Toussaint, age forty-six.

MINIATURE BY ANTHONY MEUCCI; CA. 1825

COLLECTION OF THE NEW-YORK HISTORICAL SOCIETY

$\mathcal{M}$ary Anna Sawyer (Mrs. Philip Jeremiah Schuyler).
If ever two friends were close, it was Toussaint and Mary Anna
Sawyer Schuyler. Over the decades she made the notes from
which her sister wrote the 1854 Toussaint biography.

OIL ON CANVAS BY GILBERT STUART; CA. 1825

COLLECTION OF THE NEW-YORK HISTORICAL SOCIETY

$\mathcal{P}$ierre Toussaint, photographed about 1851 or 1852, when he was in his early seventies. The picture was made by Nathaniel Fish Moore, whose sister, Sarah Ann Moore, was Toussaint's friend. Here Toussaint is looking across the page at his biographer, Hannah Lee.

ℋannah Farnham Sawyer Lee, Mary Anna's sister, was a prolific writer and bestselling author when she wrote her Toussaint "memoir." She also introduced Toussaint to the writings of the famous Unitarian preacher William Ellery Channing, which Pierre could quote from memory.

$\mathscr{D}$etailed information promoting the cause of the Venerable
Pierre Toussaint was contained in two volumes of findings submitted to
the Vatican in 1993. Also illustrated: headlines, a booklet, and signatures
in the Old Saint Peter's Church marriage register of the witnesses
of Pierre and Juliette's wedding, August 5, 1811, New York.

"$\mathscr{F}$REEDOM," 1802–1811

ONE WOULD HOPE, for Toussaint's sake, that when Monsieur Nicolas and Madame Bérard were joined in holy matrimony, the new husband would take over some of the young black man's economic burdens.

In fact, Nicolas's employment was, at best, irregular. The musician husband may have paid the rent on their first combined residence, No. 20 Reade Street, though even that seems unlikely. Two decades later Nicolas was still writing to Toussaint apologizing for not being able to pay what he owed him.

With the marriage, Toussaint's status altered, the slaves were no longer solely Marie Elisabeth's property. Legally, Nicolas was now co-owner. That didn't mean much change for Toussaint, for even Nicolas must have realized that the slave was held almost equally as high in his wife's affections as was Nicolas himself.

What degree of wedded bliss Marie Elisabeth anticipated in

her newly married state is hard to gauge. In two marriages she had never gotten pregnant, though she was still not too old to conceive. She was probably only seventeen when she wed her first husband, Roudanes, about twenty-one when she wed Bérard, and twenty-seven when she wed Nicolas.

In any event, in 1803, following the Bérard-Nicolas wedding, Toussaint wrote to Marie Bouquement urging her to return from Le Cap.

> Had you written through Monsieur Laferriere, you would have given me great pleasure as well as to Madame. She knows you are very worried and cry each day. She urges you to come here and I do the same.
>
> Oh, how happy I would be to see and to embrace you. I want you to believe that I love you very much, as does my sister; give many messages to our whole family. Tell me how the whole family is.
>
> Madame Nicolas's eye is still sore. All the servants in the house send their greetings. Mr. Aubrun [Father O'Brien, at St. Peter's] often asks me of you.

(The reason Father O'Brien's name was written as "Aubrun" is that, pronounced in French, O'Brien sounds remarkably like "aubrun.")

Marie Bouquement did return to New York. Her departure this time from Le Cap to the United States severed forever the New York Toussaints' physical connection to the island. She returned to the household as companion to Madame Nicolas, but probably held a job outside the house, too, in order to be financially independent. For Marie Elisabeth, a gradual decline now set in. It was enveloped by an all-encompassing despair—family gone, fortune gone, hope gone—but with an underlying physical ailment, for she began to lose her voice. It may have been cancer of the throat.

Toussaint by this time was fully occupied. He was determined to succeed in the profession he did not choose but one for which he displayed considerable talent.

Hairdressing, then as now, was highly competitive; there was no shortage of coiffeurs, peruke-makers, and hairdressers up and down the city. Any twenty blocks around Broadway would give Toussaint at least a dozen competitors. (One oddity is that throughout the entire Toussaint period Mr. Merchant's name does not appear in any of the available city directories. Perhaps Merchant was partner in an establishment that operated under a different name.)

Toussaint was at least fortunate that hairstyles had quieted down by the time he did his apprenticeship. Late-eighteenth-century hairstyles, when Merchant served his apprenticeship, had been a time of high and hilarious wigs. Their progenitor was the highly political and entertaining Georgiana, Duchess of Devonshire. She was depicted in cartoons of the period with miniature full-rigged galleys sailing amid the towering waves of her hair.

Hairstyles change rapidly as fashion shifts. In the Paris of 1789, as the Bastille was stormed, the Princess de Talleyrand wore a sizable wig. Within three years, by 1793, when the Terror began, the Princesse de Lamballe was all curls and ringlets. Her own. The poor Princesse de Lamballe—friend to Toussaint's friend and New York French school proprietor, Victoire-Elisabeth Bancel de Confoulens—had a hairstyle extremely well known to history. That's because the princess refused to take an oath against the monarchy. Consequently, she was sketched with her curls a few hours before her death. Physically thrown to the mob—the agents of the Terror—the princess died when she was almost literally torn apart. Contemporary reports note that immediately after her death, in a most macabre development, the mob had her hair redressed in its curls and "mounted on a pike for the Queen to see."

As the nobility fell into disfavor, "perukes [wigs] were discarded, the natural hair [permitted] to grow, and what were called 'crops' succeeded, with short hair curled over the head." Queen Marie Antoinette had a hairstyle of light curls similar to Princesse de Lamballe's, though without the ringlets. This simple but attractive style was the one in which Toussaint was trained. Envision portraits of the young Elizabeth Seton and her contemporaries, or any of the women of Jane Austen's early novels played on television, and this style immediately comes to mind.

"Through all these changes Toussaint continued to be [New York high society's] favorite. Pierre stood in high favor; no curls were as beautifully arranged as his." Toussaint himself welcomed shifting fashions in hair and clothing. In a display of wit he summed up fashion's shifts as a good thing for poor people. Fashion was "change, change and all to the good," he said, for "poor people who have to make a living." He probably spoke as much for those toiling throughout the entire fashion industry—cutting and sewing and fitting—as for himself.

To be a successful society coiffeur meant being a quarter-step ahead of the fashions, a trendsetter. But not too far ahead. Toussaint, fledgling yet fashionable, needed a "signature," something to make his ladies stand out in the crowd on significant social occasions. And soon he had one. He grew up in a country where flowers grew in profusion and mulatto and African women wore them in their hair. In New York, in the final moments of dressing a woman's hair for a levee or party, theater or ball, he invariably wove a fresh flower into his client's coif.

He took a special delight in selecting just the right blossom for both wearer and event. He loved blooms. Indeed, his friend Charles Phoenix, in rural New York, writes to him in mock formality about his fondness for flowers. "It will please [Mr. Toussaint] to hear we are never without bouquets, the wild flowers here are splendid and in great profusion."

Toussaint used his flowers to effect on his mistress before she married Nicolas. He said that when she was widowed, depressed, and in poor health, "sometimes when an invitation came I would succeed in persuading her to accept it. I would come in an evening to dress her hair, then I contrived a little surprise for her. When I finished, I would present her with the glass and say, 'Madame, see how you like it.' And how pleased she was! I had placed in it some beautiful flower—perhaps a japonica, perhaps a rose, remarkable for its rare species, which I had purchased at a greenhouse and concealed till the time arrived." Possibly it was on one of these outings, with a japonica in her hair, that Marie Elisabeth attracted Gabriel Nicolas.

Abetting Toussaint's hairdressing skills and success were his considerable personal assets, his charm and refinement, his sense of fun. "Some of the pleasantest hours I pass," commented one customer, "are in conversing with Toussaint while he is dressing my hair. I anticipate it as a daily recreation." He was elegant and he had style. He was witty yet refined. His French was superb (a plus for his American listeners wishing to perfect their spoken French) and his demeanor was pleasing. He was entertaining, musical, and funny. And discreet.

Discretion was of the essence. On one occasion, a nosy lady customer wanted information about some gossip going the rounds and said to him, "Do tell me, Toussaint, I'm sure you know all about it." "Madame," he replied with dignity though utmost respect, "Toussaint dresses hair. He is no news journal."

Toussaint the efficient hairdresser is captured in a contemporary novel published just before his death, and in a letter from a lady friend and former client then returned to France. Here is Toussaint as seen in Ben Shadow's 1853 novel *Echoes of a Belle*. Ben Shadow is certainly a nom de plume, and the writer was not likely a male:

> Alice was seated before her glass, a fashionable hairdresser
> had been sent for; and the illustrious Toussaint, with his good

tempered face, small earrings and white teeth, entered the room, his tall figure arrayed in a spotless apron. The curling tongs were heated, and there was a perfume of scorched paper as Toussaint commenced upon his operations. Oh, those cruel scissors, they had no mercy on the beautiful hair. What an execution! Alice shrank from the sight of her tortured head which, in a hundred "papillotes" [paper strips wrapped around ringlets before the curling iron was applied] seemed to stand upon end in every direction; whilst Luna held the brushes and heated the tongs, in silent amazement at this curious phenomenon.

But to Mrs. Vere (Alice's mother) Toussaint's sable face was a most refreshing sight. The elaborate "coiffeur" was completed, and Toussaint, enchanted with his "chef d'oeuvre de Valière." Alice thought herself a rival to Mrs. Tilton; she did not question the style; it was the fashion, and that was enough.

"Alice" in the novel could almost have been his friend Césarine Meetz (by then Mrs. Charles Moulton), who expressed similar shock at a "tortured head" when she wrote from Paris: "My Good Toussaint, How much I need you. Truly the French hairdressers don't have the least taste. They pull at and tug my hair and after having suffered with much patience for more than two hours, I look at myself in the mirror, hoping to find myself beautiful; but it's the contrary. I perceive a little face with donkey ears. I turn around to see if there's not some funny monkey behind me, but there's only the little hairdresser. Alas! It is therefore me, with a hairstyle." She attached a drawing and signed herself, "Césarine."

Hairdresser Toussaint had a depth to him and biographer Lee recognized it. She was an observant writer, a devout Unitarian, and a close friend of Unitarianism's founder, her pastor, the preacher Dr. William Ellery Channing. So she was no shallow critic where religion was concerned.

Lee wrote of Pierre, "He often quoted in his native language from the Sermon on the Mount, and the Beatitudes seemed to have found their way to his heart. His whole life was one of thought and observation." She introduced Toussaint to Channing's works, and soon he could quote from those at will, too.

Toussaint, hairdressing by day and by evening, came home at night to 20 Reade Street. There he faced the sickly Marie Elisabeth as she sank deeper. Her despair was legitimate; she was ill, and in desperate straits. For Saint Domingue's exiled whites, any lingering vestiges of hope that they would return disappeared in 1804. Dessalines, who had finally come to power as emperor in the internal struggles that followed Louverture's kidnapping, declared the colony, now Haiti, independent.

That final nightmare was the death of white planters' dreams. Their only recourse now—for the next half-century up to Toussaint's death, correspondence from France regularly alludes to it—was to pressure the French government to in turn pressure the Haitian government to pay restitution for the expropriated plantations.

As for Madame Nicolas's ill-health, Gabriel Nicolas is revealed as possibly a kindly man but certainly ineffective and no particular balm to Marie Elisabeth's need. Plus Nicolas must have felt some equivocation knowing it was Toussaint who read to her at her bedside, who brought in the treats for her that Nicolas could not afford, who shored up financially a household of which Gabriel was titular head.

More Caribbean blood was shed in 1804—this time in New York. Toussaint was affected when the handsome Nevis Island–born politician and American political leader Alexander Hamilton died in his duel with Aaron Burr. Toussaint knew the family well. Hamilton's widow, Elizabeth Schuyler Hamilton, erect in her open carriage for the funeral, and her little granddaughter Eliza, daughter of Hamilton's third son, James, were clients.

This same year, 1804, revealed another call on Toussaint's time and resources. Known as a Saint Domingan with a regular income—rare enough in New York—he was a new benefactor, as the needy, black and white, began to seek him out. He was a very easy touch and did what he could. Sometimes, in the early years, it wasn't very much. A fellow islander, though a white woman who may well have despised him back in the colony, wrote about herself in the third person as she appealed for aid:

> Persuaded that the misfortunes which afflict Madame le
> Duc, formerly a resident of Port-au-Prince, cannot be a matter
> of indifference to feeling hearts who learn that this unfortu-
> nate mother has the care of three young children, that she
> now lives in this city bereft of means to give them the necessi-
> ties of life, whose father was massacred by the negroes, she
> thinks that even though she keeps hidden the terrible details
> of her tragedy, you will be moved to help her according to
> your means.

Toussaint sent her $2, an amount with a twenty-first-century purchasing power of $40 to $50. The more dangerous call on Toussaint, however, came not from beggars and importuners but from the emergence almost annually of "the plague"—yellow fever. It had arrived in New York City the year before the Bérard family moved there.

❖   ❖   ❖

For centuries, whenever the cry "the plague! the plague!" went up, panic and fear gripped entire cities in the Western world. These sudden and virulent onsets of death were seen as other-wordly retribution. Malaria was believed to come from bad air—in Italian, *mala aria*—hovering over swamplands. Not until 1897 was it discovered that yellow fever and malaria were not the wrath of God but an effect of the natural life cycle of the mosquito. With "the plague" in town, those who could fled the cities. Yellow fever's slaughter was rampant, indiscriminate, and horrifying in scope.

In Toussaint's day all that was known were the horror stories from European cities, many of which had special plague houses, known as lazar houses (from Lazarus in the Gospels afflicted by sores). In Italy, a *lazaretto* was a dwelling where plague sufferers were forced to live.

Pestilences and plagues were not unknown in North America's earliest colonial days. A "great pestilence" swept through the Massachusetts Bay Colony in 1617. Europeans suffered worse. The plague in Italy four decades later killed off seventy percent of Genoa's population.

Yellow fever, common in Africa, was brought to the New World by slave traders, who regularly died of it. European sailors hated the Caribbean voyage because yellow fever would plague the ships. The sailors never knew the larvae of the yellow fever–carrying mosquito, *Aedes aegypti*, was flourishing to adulthood in their own water casks. As more and more whites died from yellow fever, the canard grew that the Africans were immune to it. (That belief, later labeled "scientific racism," was not disproven until 1928.)

Plague wasn't the leading cause of death. In America and Europe the more constant killer was tuberculosis. It took Toussaint's sister and his adopted daughter. Announcements of children's deaths from "consumption" (because the disease "consumed" the lungs) regularly punctuate the letters from Toussaint's European friends. Yellow fever, by contrast, has them worrying on his behalf.

There is some contention that the yellow fever mosquito brought about the 1803 Louisiana Purchase. It is said that Napoleon's plans for after Leclerc conquered Saint Domingue was for Leclerc to continue on to the Mississippi Valley (Mississippi and Louisiana) and occupy it as a major French settlement. Instead, yellow fever killed Leclerc and his troops. Napoleon presumed yellow fever lurked in the Mississippi Valley, too—a threat that prompted him to rid France of the vast region by selling it to the United States.

New York wasn't supposed to be unhealthy. In 1789, a leading physician, Dr. John Bard, wrote that "New York is justly esteemed one of the healthiest cities of the continent. Its vicinity to the ocean, surrounded by high and improved land with verdure and growing vegetables, with fragrant odors and buckwheat fields in blossom on the pleasant banks of the Jersey shore, two noble salt rivers, the salutary effects are confirmed in the complexion, health and vigor of its inhabitants."

Bard was only partially correct. By the late 1790s, at the first sign of yellow fever, wealthy folk like the Schuyler families would head immediately for their country estates. Elizabeth Seton's family moved to the seashore for healthy air; poorer people set up tents in the fields and farmland of Manhattan above Reade Street. The 1798 yellow fever epidemic, according to Elizabeth Seton's father, Dr. Richard Bayley, a noted physician and surgeon, was "of the most deadly kind, more like the plague." It spread desolation along the entire east coast. For Elizabeth and the extended Seton family, escape meant eighteen crowded into a five-room beach house.

The following year, as the Bérards and Toussaints arrived, was even worse. It lasted throughout the summer and into the fall. And though the Seton family fled to her father-in-law's country home near Bloomingdale, New York, her son, William, still contracted the disease, but recovered. In 1800, Elizabeth Seton writes of the poor, yellow fever–infected Irish immigrants on Staten Island, whose misery was "past all description." Two years later Dr. Bayley himself died of the disease.

No one knew who might succumb and who might be spared.

It was deadly, but not deadly enough to scare off Toussaint. "One lady mentions that when the yellow fever prevailed in New York, by degrees Maiden Lane was almost wholly deserted, and almost every house in it closed. One poor woman, prostrated by the terrible disorder, remained there with little or no attendance, till Toussaint, day by day, came through the lonely street, crossed the barricades, entered the deserted house where she lay, and performed the nameless offices of a nurse, fearlessly exposing himself to the contagion."

Later, when he was married, Toussaint continued to take these risks. During one epidemic Toussaint discovered that "a man was left wholly alone. He was a stranger, but Toussaint took him to his house, nursed him, watched over him, and restored him to health. This stranger was a white man." In nursing yellow fever victims, Toussaint had the example of doctors like Elizabeth Seton's father, and the succession of pastors at St. Peter's.

Finally, in 1808, after a decade of annual plagues, a New York State–appointed Streets Commission ordered the redesign of the New York street system to allow the "free and abundant" flow of air. The redesign of New York City probably led to the incidental filling in of many of the shallow man-made pools enjoyed by the *Aedes aegypti* as breeding grounds. Combating the plague may have been deliberate in its planning and accidental in its success.

Toussaint's works of mercy stemmed from his work with the St. Peter's parish Benevolent Society. He was notably active as its fund-raiser, collector, and distributor. When fellow parishioner M. Du Berceau wrote to Toussaint he obviously anticipated that Pierre would tap the more affluent parishioners for funds, too: "Do me the service, my dear Toussaint," wrote Du Berceau, "of recommending to the Society, Madame Hayes who lives at No. 82 Wooster Street, in the court-yard. What is most necessary to her is some firewood. This poor woman is suffering greatly from consumption. If you wish to stop at my house, I shall re-mit to you my subscription."

That Toussaint tried to live the beatitudes is obvious from the earliest records and correspondence. He went where needed, including to prison. There is no clue as to what had be-fallen his friend or acquaintance L. Emmerling, who wrote from Bellevue Prison: "My dear Toussaint, it is to you, consoler of the unfortunate, that I appeal, to beg you, to plead with you to come to see me in this sad place. I have written to many per-sons, but in vain! I beg you to come here and see me. Take a car-riage. I will pay the fare. God will repay you for this kindness which I ask of you. I have many things to tell you. I beg you, do not fail me. I await you today or tomorrow, or even later. Your unhappy friend, L. Emmerling."

❖   ❖   ❖

As 1806 turned into 1807, the condition of the long-sorrowing and long-suffering Madame Nicolas worsened. She developed a throat affliction, lost her voice, and was reduced to writing notes by hand. Whatever she requested, Toussaint tried to obtain. De-spite his exhausting days "from the markets he'd bring fruits she would have known as a girl." Whatever expense he went to, Marie Elisabeth consoled herself by assuring Toussaint he would be fully repaid from her property in San Domingo once it was recovered. Toussaint "had no such belief."

Marie Elisabeth, unable to talk, barely able to walk, and mainly confined to her bed, gradually lost ground. That she had specific maladies there is no doubt, yet she suffered equally from losing her sisters, from homesickness, and from the crush-ing lack of hope. Marie Elisabeth Bossard Roudanes Bérard Nicolas lost the will to live. On July 2, 1807, just in time for In-dependence Day, she formally granted Toussaint his freedom.

There is a hint in Hannah Lee's account that Nicolas may have played the key role in encouraging Marie Elisabeth's decision to give Toussaint his freedom. Lee wrote: "Probably the subject never occurred to her." (One senses in the quotation that Hannah Lee is repeating something Toussaint told her. And that he may have said it with a touch of asperity, or even a little bitterness.) Marie Bouquement's daughter, Adèle, though never located, was given her freedom on the same day as Toussaint. Rosalie, Toussaint's sister, also a slave in the Bérard-Nicolas household, was not. (When Nicolas inherited his wife's slaves, he did not free them. He kept Rosalie four more years in bondage until, on May 21, 1811, Toussaint was able to buy her freedom.) This is how Toussaint was freed:

> I, the undersigned, Elizabeth Bossard, wife of Monsieur Gabriel Nicolas, declare with the consent of Mr. Nicolas, my husband, that my intention is that Pierre Toussaint my slave shall be and live free of all servitude and I consent that he shall enjoy liberty like any other freed-man, that this present act be given all the public authenticity that it may have. Made at New York, July 2, 1807.

Witnesses who signed the Extract of the Minutes of the Chancellor of the French Commissariat in New York include both Nicolases, Father O'Brien, and his good friend Jean Sorbieu. (The important detail here is that Toussaint was granted his freedom as a French citizen according to French law. Freed, Toussaint was not an American, he was French. Equally, by birth, he was now a Haitian citizen, too.)

Not much later, within hours or days, it is hard to tell, Madame Nicolas asked Toussaint to summon the priest. She made her confession, received communion, and died. Much later, Toussaint would remark, "I knew her full of life and gayety, richly dressed and entering into amusements with animation." Of her dying, he said, "now the scene was so changed, and it was so sad to me. I only asked to make her comfortable, and I bless God she never knew a want."

As a much younger man, he had watched the approaching death from tuberculosis of the first Madame Bérard. He could recall his and Rosalie's futile attempts to help her breathe. Now the second Madame Bérard, though named Nicolas, also slipped away. Still only in his twenties, there is a new depth to Toussaint. From his childhood and young adulthood experiences of death and dying, from the bloodshed he had witnessed during Haiti's violent path to independence, from nursing plague victims, came his "wonderful capacity in sickness; how often he smoothed the pillow and administered relief to disease. He was constantly summoned as a watcher, and gave his services to the poor without money or price. One of his friends said that 'his pity for the suffering seemed to partake of the character of the Saviour's tenderness at the tomb of Lazarus.'

"When he visited his friends in sorrow, his words were few; he felt too deeply to express by language his sympathy. Once he said, 'I have been to see poor Madam Cruger.' [She had lost a member of her family, possibly her husband.] 'And what did you say to her?' said a friend. 'Nothing,' he replied, 'I could only take her hand and weep with her, and then I went away. There was nothing to be said.' He felt that, in the first moment of stunning grief, God alone could speak to her."

Many good people have sat with the sick and cared for the dying; others, equally selfless, have nursed plague victims by bringing them to their own homes and risking contagion. Still more have given time and money to help the poor, the unemployed, the distressed, and the exiled. A few people visit prisons and console the incarcerated. Good servants have cared for their employers to the end. Kindly men and women have saved the face of the proud and the vain, and not sought their undoing. Countless people have helped the desperate and the destitute in person without depriving them of one iota of their dignity.

What begins to distinguish Toussaint as we watch him move from his twenties to his thirties, however, was not that he did any one of these things but that he did them all.

In 1807, now a freeman himself, he redoubled his efforts at saving enough to purchase the two freedoms that mattered most to him—those of his sister, Rosalie, and a young Saint Domingan girl he had met, Mary Rose Juliette Gaston. She was a member of the extended Noël family of Baltimore, as was Rosalie's prospective husband, Jean. It took Toussaint four years, until 1811, to save the money to purchase both Rosalie's and Juliette's freedom.

These were highly sensitive matters to Toussaint. What he welcomed was that as a free woman, Rosalie was free also to marry whomever she chose.

The matter of purchasing his future wife Juliette's freedom was more delicate. And it was executed quite surreptitiously. For both their sakes, his own and Juliette's, Toussaint did not want it to be known that he had bought a young woman's freedom in order to marry her. It smacked of bride purchase. Indeed, it was such a well-kept secret that no one knew of it until after Toussaint's death. Going through the records still available to her at that time, his biographer Hannah Lee apparently discovered the papers, now lost, that recorded his purchase of Juliette's freedom.

His sister, Rosalie Toussaint, wed Jean Noël in St. Peter's on May 27, 1811. Pierre and Juliette were married three months later, on August 5.

The Toussaint wedding was like a wartime marriage, for in 1811 war with the British was in the air due to the constant British-U.S. disagreements over shipping rights and other slights. With any declaration of war, a British invasion of New York was a distinct possibility. In February 1812, President

James Madison persuaded Congress to declare war, which it did in June not knowing, due to the slowness of communications, that the British had already agreed to Madison's requests.

In those days, San Domingan weddings had dozens of witnesses, and the main witnesses at the August 5 Toussaint wedding celebration included men who were Toussaint friends for life, no matter how geographically near or far their later whereabouts. There was Jean Sorbieu, who would soon return to France, first to Rouen and then to Paris, and Jerome Villagrand, who remained for many years in New York before moving to Virginia. Other signatories included Gabriel Nicolas, John Benjamin, Donatien Cilardy, and Bernard Etienne. The new pastor, the Jesuit priest Father Anthony Kohlmann, not wishing to fill pages of the parish register, simply noted "and others, witnesses who have signed."

The new couple had combined interests but came from slightly different worlds. Juliette Toussaint had close family and friends living in Baltimore, to which she occasionally traveled to stay with her cousin Fanny Montpensier. The widowed Madame Montpensier was friends with or possibly related to one of the founding sisters of the first U.S. Roman Catholic religious congregation for black women, the Oblate Sisters of Providence. In New York City, too, Juliette, though a fun-loving and devoted member of her husband's wide range of friends, had developed her own circle. A frequent destination was Brooklyn—just a short ferry ride from lower Manhattan—where she had family and friends.

The newlywed Toussaints at first occupied two rooms at the top of 20 Reade Street. Nicolas, after his wife's death, stayed on in the house, living on the main floor, where his cook also had a room. At no point, however, with Toussaint free, wed, and in economic fact the man of the house, did Nicolas seem inclined to leave. Not until 1817, when Toussaint decided to rent his own home—he signed a lease with Abraham Bloodgood for 105

Reade Street—did Nicolas move on. Nicolas left New York City for somewhere in the South and returned north only once for a visit, a trip probably financed by Toussaint. The French San Domingan remained in regular contact with Pierre and always remarked in his letters how indebted he was to him. Given Toussaint's generosity, there is no reason to doubt Nicolas's remarks.

This decade witnessed that other marriage which profoundly affected Toussaint's life, the 1806 wedding in Boston of Philip Jeremiah Schuyler and Mary Anna Sawyer.

Through the Schuylers and his hairdressing talent, Toussaint had now met his closest white friend, Mary Anna Schuyler. And because of her, and her sister, we know as much as we do of Toussaint's story.

ELEVEN

JULIETTE AND PIERRE

PIERRE TOUSSAINT and Rose Mary Juliette Gaston Toussaint shared a common heritage. They were African Caribbeans from San Domingue, solid in the Catholic faith common to the French Antilles. From the moment of their wedding in 1811, in St. Peter's Church on Barclay Street—he was twenty-nine, she was sixteen—Pierre and Juliette were partners in the charitable acts of good works they separately and jointly undertook.

Their faith-filled, cheerful, helpful characters were formed and maintained by the fact that they were dutiful, trusting, and prayerful. On the top-floor landing between their bedrooms was a prie-dieu, a crucifix, "and many beautiful emblems of the Catholic faith, gifts to Toussaint which he carefully treasured." Toussaint's mature adult life and actions were anchored by and in his and Juliette's forty years together, and in their mutual faith.

With his marriage, Toussaint was starting a new family just

as, through the aftereffects of revolution, he was losing another.
The final letters from Grandmother Zénobie and his mother,
Ursule, appear to have been written shortly after the marriage.
There is a letter from his sister, Marie-Louise Pacaud, the year
before Pierre was married. Marie-Louise had arrived in New
Orleans from Cuba and wrote to say their mother and grand-
mother were living in Haiti in great misery (*grande misère*), but
Marie doesn't say where.

Marie-Louise is not doing particularly well. She apparently
is companion to a woman, but there is no evidence of self-pity
in her letter—she seems to share her brother's stoicism. She has
been ill with swollen legs and hopes the swelling will dissipate
with time. She asks Toussaint to embrace their sister Rosalie for
her and says she is without news of "Antoine," most likely her
husband. His whereabouts are an indication of how far Saint
Domingans fled the continued turmoil on the island—the last
she heard of Antoine, she writes, he was in Portugal. "God
knows what he's been doing since he stayed with his brother
and William in La Trinité [Cuba]."

Marie-Louise tells Pierre she knows people who will be traveling to New York from New Orleans and hopes to send news
through them. In the meantime if Pierre could send her a
medium-sized quilt, she will send him the money for it.

Toussaint never ceased from having friends or acquaintances who returned to Haiti continue the search for his mother
and grandmother—and his cousin Adèle, Marie Bouquement's
daughter. Toussaint never knew exactly when his grandmother
and mother died. Marie-Louise, meanwhile, writes that she
would not dream of returning to Haiti, "a country of disorder
and tyranny where there is continued fighting."

Toussaint provided for Adèle in his will should she surface,
but like so many who remained in Haiti, she was gone without
trace. (A decade after Marie-Louise's letter, there is one from his

cousin Auguste in Cap Haïtien, dated 1822. He wrote without news to Toussaint, saying, "I desire, Monsieur, that you be happier than we in your search on this matter.")

Marie Bouquement died at the end of August 1812. Of the nine from the Bérard household who had come to New York, all four whites and now the first black were dead. Old Cabresse was still alive; Hortense had left for work elsewhere and is not subsequently mentioned. Pierre is free, as is Rosalie, though her health is not good. Bouquement was buried in "the Catholic ground" on Mulberry Street (Old St. Patrick's Cathedral) on August 30. Toussaint paid the $15 bill. She was fifty-six.

By this time, Pierre was doing quite well financially, though at 105 Reade Street Juliette and Pierre took in lodgers to help with the expenses. Receipts in Pierre's papers touch on simple everyday incidentals that reflect his relative prosperity, though he doesn't always appear to have rushed to pay those bills when they arrived. He showered his new bride with little gifts. When he settled a nine pounds, nine shillings, and sixpence bill with Frederic William Dannenburg (for necessities that include new strings for his violin), he'd bought Juliette a necklace with a cross, as well as some coffee-colored silk dress material. He earned every cent the hard way. He walked, stood, cut, curled, talked politely, listened with interest, left not too hurriedly, then went to the next appointment to repeat the process.

Too soon, Pierre had another funeral to pay for: Rosalie's. In the years immediately following her marriage to Jean Noël, Rosalie was periodically abandoned by her husband. He disappears from history shortly after Rosalie becomes pregnant. It is possible she was living in Baltimore, or Wilmington, Delaware, and not New York until, extremely sick, Juliette and Pierre brought her into their home. Rosalie, who was only thirty, died from tuberculosis early in 1816, six months or less after the birth of her daughter, Euphémie.

Toussaint himself named the child. She was born on September 16, the feast day of St. Euphémie, a fourth-century martyr reputedly burned alive after having her teeth knocked out with a hammer. (Her shrine at Chalcedon became a pilgrimage site, and she was a cult figure in the Middle Ages. But by the time her little Afro-Caribbean namesake was christened, the saint's luster had faded as a focus of devotion.) Juliette brought the sickly six-month-old infant and her mother into her own home. Dr. Berger, who was by this time attending Rosalie, "did not give much encouragement" that Euphémie, also threatened by tuberculosis, would survive. "But Toussaint," wrote Hannah Lee, "who was always sanguine, fully believed her life would be granted to them. Every day he took the feeble little creature in his arms, carried her to the park, to the Battery, to every airy and pleasant spot where the fresh breezes sent invigorating influence, hoping to strengthen her frame and enable her lungs to gain a freer respiration."

Euphémie became one of the many joys among the sadnesses in the early years of Pierre and Juliette's married life. Love, fresh air, and good fortune brought the little girl into a secure childhood. Euphémie naturally provided Toussaint with deep emotional satisfactions. He and Juliette had longed for a child, and though Juliette was pregnant at least once, in 1819, it was not to be. Euphémie filled the void. As Euphémie passed out of infancy, a teacher, Mrs. Ruckel, lived in the Reade Street house for a while and ran her one-room school there.

If Toussaint had a free day, it was Sunday, though some women, planning a glittering Sunday soiree, might call on him even then. Otherwise, he was always in demand.

> Mrs King requests Mr. Toussaint to call on her at No. 56 Bond St. at 6 o'clock tomorrow afternoon to dress her for Miss Ming's ball.

Dear Toussaint, [wrote his friend Sarah Anne Moore] I
have been very sick, but am getting well enough to begin to
think of making myself look handsome again. Will you come
this afternoon at 6 p.m. or half past to cut and curl my hair so
that I may be fit to show myself in the parlour tomorrow.

[Mrs. E. Wainwright wants Pierre Toussaint] at four to cut
the children's hair. 59 Bleecker St.

Mesdemoiselles Haywood, Cruger, Yates, Battelle, Scar-
borough, Hosack, Sanford, Packard, Hamilton, d'Wolf, Jackson, Irving and Drake prient Toussaint d'avoir la bonté de
venir de bonne heure.

It was perhaps during his visit to Louise Bancel's school to dress
the students' hair, that he found time to give them some dancing instruction. And as an aid to getting it right, he would leave
them the steps on a note: "en avant 4 en arrière, & chasses &
déchasse sans rigidon/balance vos Dames a vos place & un tour
de main. . . ."

He was coiffeur on call at all hours to young men and
women alike. On special occasions he apparently served as valet
as well as hairdresser to young "chevaliers," as Toussaint referred to them. "Mrs. S. Jones will thank Toussaint to call tomorrow if he is disengaged, to cut the children's hair. She also
wishes Toussaint to dress her son Monday evening for the Ball."
This Mrs. Jones is Mary Anna's stepdaughter.

❖   ❖   ❖

Pierre and Juliette were enjoyable characters. The record that
remains has frequent references to the good times had with the
Toussaints. In 1835, their friend Madame McDowell, now wid-

owed and living in Paris, wrote, "I miss being with you because we could really laugh together."

The couple had many merry moments, and were not above playing kindly pranks on others. There was an impoverished Frenchman who thought very highly of himself and his social connections. He would boast to Pierre about the wealthy friends he had who kept him well fed. Juliette and Pierre enjoyed their private joke—it was they who were sending the meals around.

On another occasion one can almost see and hear Pierre and Juliette laughing together during the transaction. Juliette is considering buying a mourning shawl to wear and the playful exchange between them could be that of a modern husband and wife in a twenty-first-century department store.

"How do you like this for mourning," said she to Toussaint.

"Very pretty," he replied.

"I think," she said, "it is handsome enough for church."

"Oh yes, very good for that."

"Don't you think it will do to wear if it rains?"

"Oh certainly."

"I think it will do sometimes to wear to market, don't you?"

"Very nice," he replied, "pray take it, Juliette. It is good for mourning, for church, for rain, and for market. It is a very nice shawl."

Needless to say, she bought it. And they probably had a good laugh together each time she wore it.

The good-humored relationship and Pierre's deep love for Juliette come out in his letters. On one occasion when Juliette was down in Baltimore staying with Fanny Montpensier, Toussaint wrote teasingly: "Present my compliments to Miss Fanny and tell her that I hope she will not set you too many bad examples. I know that, though she is very devout, she is *un peu méchante* [a little wicked]." Toussaint hopes that Juliette will return from Baltimore with Fanny's "devotion, but not her *méchanceté* [her wickedness]." Fanny, however, delightfully wicked, was a faithful friend to the end. The last surviving letter to Toussaint, in January 1853, prior to his death in June that year, is from Fanny.

A decade later when Juliette is with Fanny, Madame Toussaint was taken seriously ill with "a villainous attack" (it was feared she had cholera). In his letters at that time, Toussaint candidly expressed his deep love for her, told her she should remain as long as she needed, and that George Schuyler (Mary Anna's son) was astounded that Toussaint was able to manage living on his own. "I love my wife," wrote Toussaint in closing his letters. "My dear wife, I send you a thousand embraces. . . . Adieu my dear friend, I embrace you with all my heart, your faithful Pierre Toussaint."

Juliette was quick to help Toussaint with his needs, and yet, though much younger, she did it with a keen perspective on the shared equality of their relationship. In her marriage to Toussaint, she knew that with him she had a right to a will of her own. That is quite a comment when one accepts that she and Pierre were wed two centuries ago, when wives, like children, were expected to be seen rather than heard. Juliette was quite clear about their relationship. She said she would yield to Toussaint's will on occasion, but only because she was "not obliged" to do it. She had a choice.

This was not simple forbearance or agreeableness on Toussaint's part. Juliette, like Zénobie, came from the African matriarchal heritage. Toussaint would have no reason, and no prior examples in his own family, to consider Juliette as anything less than equal.

Juliette's days are almost as fully occupied as Toussaint's, for she is busy, and not just from housekeeping and marketing, though marketing apparently was a specialty—friends, knowing Juliette's skills as a shrewd bargainer at the market stall, occasionally asked her to market for them. A note from Louis Binsse asks Juliette to get him oysters for a party he's planning, and not to pay more than a sum he specified. Her cousin Fanny Montpensier in Baltimore has Juliette shopping in New York for her and for the nuns at the Oblate convent. Juliette was able to purchase most things at a better price than was available in Baltimore.

Madame Toussaint also had the daily requirements of the Toussaint lodgers to cater to. These invariably were middle-class or upper class whites who fitted into the more refined category of "paying guests." Lodging meant full board—three meals a day—plus laundry (then known as "taking care of the linens"). Juliette also coped daily with the comings and goings of Euphémie's little friends attending Mrs. Ruckel's one-room school, though by this time Juliette likely had daily help—the Toussaints could afford it.

More commitments were ahead. In 1809, Elizabeth Seton, as Mother Seton, founded the first community of American women religious, the Sisters of Charity, in Emmitsburg, Maryland. By 1816, the first of her sisters, at the request of Father Powers at St. Peter's, were in New York to open an orphanage, which they did the following year. (St. Peter's was always ahead of things. In 1800, the parish had opened a free school.) The new institution was for white orphans only. It became a popular charity among the French and American society women in the Toussaint circle, particularly for his friend Madame P. LaRue. When she left for France, Toussaint took over her role as major fund-raiser and collector.

However, in typical Toussaint fashion, because there was no facility for black children, he and Juliette were already taking abandoned or orphaned African-American boys into their home. These boys they raised at their own expense while seeing to it they had a rudimentary education. Toussaint worked hard to place them in jobs. One or two may have been apprenticed in the hairdressing shop on Church Street. But the bulk of the daily responsibility of caring for these boys fell on Juliette.

Being abandoned, some of these young charges could be unruly. "Bill" seems to have been one of them. "Dear Uncle," noted Euphémie, "O how near poor Mr. Gentil's [her piano teacher] son came to being hurt by a broom Bill threw with such force that it stuck in the door. 'Tis true there is a Lord to protect children as well as grown persons. His mother had him in her arms and if she had been one step nearer the door her child might have been killed. I think when Bill is out of the way no person will be sorry."

Of others in the house, Euphémie remarks, "I think our little boarder is very nice. I think he is an old head on young shoulders." Perhaps he, too, was one of the African boys the Toussaints took in, for soon Euphémie writes that "he must have been very hungry for there was a table set for him and he ate most everything on it."

The boys were troublesome. The Peter Euphémie refers to in this letter sounds like a young lad Toussaint was willing to apprentice at his Church Street shop. Peter has obviously run away and broken his apprenticeship, and Toussaint is seeking his return. Peter is black, causing Toussaint to be doubly worried about the boy's safety because of the risk of his being kidnapped.

Euphémie is a very perceptive young miss. "Dear Uncle," she writes, "I do not think that the advertisement you put in the paper will do you any good, for I think Peter is able to say he came from another part of the world. He is so used to running he cannot walk. He has run away from that sweep master. I think that a trade is very good for him, he has grown very much indeed. He does not seem to be ashamed. Did you notice that

when you asked him his name he said it was Peter—as much as
to say he did not know?"

Not all the Toussaints' lodgers are satisfactory, either. In
1827, Euphémie writes to Toussaint: "Dear Uncle, I take the liberty of asking what you are going to do with the people in the
front room. They will not pay until you send Mr. Quirk after
them. I am glad for you that you have got Mr. Lafont, for I believe he is a very clever gentleman. You will be sure of your
money to have it when it is due. When the room is fixed it will
be a little different from the way in which it was kept by that
horrible set who lived in it before." (There was an evangelizing
element to the Toussaints' lives. When Monsieur Lafont finally
died in the Toussaint home, a friend wrote from Paris, "if he
had not been in your house, no one would have talked to him
about God, and he would have died without knowing." Another
friend writes and thanks Toussaint for bringing her son back to
his Catholicism during the time the young man stayed with
Juliette and Pierre.)

Was Mrs. Martial similarly a troublesome former resident?
Euphémie writes that "Mrs. Martial, I think you are too good to
give her up. If I had the power to do as I wanted toward her she
would not have such a good person to deal with for I think she
is very mean to treat us that way."

The adopted daughter and the aunt had a lovely relationship. Juliette encouraged Euphémie in household skills as well
as schoolwork. The child's love is more freely expressed—still in
the somewhat restrained language of the day—when she writes
to her aunt than in her letters to Toussaint. "Dear Aunt, as this
is your birthday [July 6] I thought I would like to write you a
letter but I have nothing much to say except that I [send] you
much joy and hope you live to see many returns of this day and
every one more happy than the last. Adieu dear Aunt, your affectionate niece, E. Toussaint." Three weeks later she writes,
"when I get older I will embroider a frock for you."

As a couple, the Toussaints freely offered hospitality to a wide variety of travelers, not infrequently impoverished priests or seminarians requiring accommodation while en route to somewhere else. Those taken in and nursed in their home ranged from strangers with yellow fever to a priest suffering from a common scourge of the day, "ship fever"—typhus.

In the 1820s, Juliette often directed her efforts into helping the newly founded Oblate Sisters of Providence. The Toussaints' charitable acts were as immediate outside the home as inside. Pierre's friend Marie Navarre wrote from Paris in 1835, "you take on the role of the priest. You are such a religious man, a man of compassion, risking your life taking care of others." Referring to one poor and abandoned woman and the risks Toussaint took during the epidemics of "cholera and yellow fever," Navarre comments, "you were the one who helped her with her religious duties before she died."

A group of "French people of color" wrote to Toussaint that "you go beyond excellent morals and religious duties." The Toussaints found money for stranded friends in the Caribbean, helped poor seminarians continue their studies, responded to beggars, to friends, and even passing acquaintances down on their luck. Goods—tobacco was used like a currency in those days—were sent to aid family, former colleagues, and supplicants alike in the Caribbean Islands.

On a lighter note, Juliette was famed for her gumbo. Their correspondents in France and New Orleans across forty years frequently request gumbo, or write to Juliette to thank her for sending it. When the herbs were in season, Juliette would carefully package crocks of gumbo and Toussaint would see them onto a *paquebot* for Le Havre en route to the dinner tables of friends in Paris.

The newly widowed—the memory of Madame Bérard was strong—could always be sure of his help. His correspondents' candor is remarkable. An American friend in France, in a letter to Toussaint, pours out all the intimacies of her heart toward her husband, "I am so deeply in love with him, with his soul. I love him with all the force of my soul, and if I talk to you like this," she tells Toussaint, "it is because I deeply, deeply trust you."

Occasionally, men, in this most reserved and proper of times, do the same, though in a more restrained way. In New York, an acquaintance, possibly a neighbor, who thanks Toussaint "for your liberality toward my wife—I hope God recompenses you," also asks Toussaint not to consider him an "ingrate, and excuse me from my past follies." (Toussaint knew what the writer's follies were; history has no record.) Juliette and Pierre's correspondents, some demanding, some chatty, some seeking favors, some commanding "do this, do this"—because the writer was in France and needed something in America—loved this couple.

The Toussaints seem to never have lost a friend.

There is not a great deal of correspondence from their black friends, but in what exists (see Chapter 15) there is usually a strong undercurrent of merriment and good humor. From Baltimore, when Madame Sanitte Dousson wrote a letter to Juliette, with whom she'd stayed in New York, her husband, Joseph, appended a note to Toussaint: "I am very flattered by the civilities you and your dear spouse extended to my wife, and the friendly letters I have received. She affirms me in the opinion I have formed of your character from public rapport and personal knowledge, not forgetting your lively singing voice."

It is obvious the Doussons are among the Toussaints' close black friends. And that among his friends his violin playing and merrymaking continued long after it was no longer evident to his white friends. Years later, white friends recall Toussaint's entertaining ways in the days when they were still children and he played his violin for their songs and taught them dance steps.

❖   ❖   ❖

Toussaint's devotion to his church was complete. Its needs were his duties. Besides being an active member of St. Peter's parish's social welfare committee, he belonged to the Blessed Sacrament Society, committed to regular Holy Communion and parish support.

Juliette and Pierre tenderly cared for each other during illnesses, and as letters from their friends in France reveal, each had bouts of serious sickness. Juliette undoubtedly understood Pierre's loneliness and longing for his birth family members. In America, she had family, and in later years her mother, Claudine Gaston, lived with them. He loved Euphémie deeply, but he had other familial feelings. His extended family was Mary Anna's family and he regarded little William Schuyler, her firstborn, as the son he never had. (Mary Anna's husband, Philip, may have had a greater influence in these matters than the record suggests, and been a strong factor in the welcome Toussaint always received at the Schuylers' family circle. Hannah Lee, in one of her novels, has a hero and abolitionist named Philip Schuyler.)

In the following glimpses—one an extract from an 1893 article, the other a letter Toussaint himself wrote—we see Toussaint completely at ease with children. Depending on the company, he could hold back just a little with some adults. In the letter, Toussaint is shown as almost madcap in correspondence with those he loved.

Emma Cary, writing in *Ave Maria* magazine late in the nineteenth century, provides a secondhand reminiscence of Toussaint with children—and with adults. Cary quotes a woman who, as a child, had known Toussaint.

> Why, Toussaint was a household word with us, and is still so. [Families well known in the history of New York] often talk

of him today. He came every day to our mother's house to dress my mother's hair, and our hair too.

My sister and I loved him, and there was nothing I would not confide to him. It was like the confessional to talk to Toussaint, you were so sure of his secrecy. And no matter how freely we confided in him, he never swerved from his respectful demeanor. He always stood when he talked to us. "Do sit down, Toussaint," someone said to him one day. "Madam, I can not," he replied.

And he was gay and amusing, too, and when we were little girls he would dance for us and show us very gracefully how our parents had danced when they were young. He had taught himself many things; he had good taste and an excellent memory. He would quote whole pages of Bossuet and Massillon—Massillon was his favorite author. If Toussaint had been an educated man he would have been illustrious, for he had a genius. But his great influence lay in his perfect Christian character, his exquisite charity and consideration for others, his tender compassion for all.

When Toussaint himself puts pen to paper (in French) his merriment bursts through. The background is this:

William Schuyler, Philip and Mary Anna's firstborn, was so loved by Pierre that Toussaint's first, and quite substantial, will was made out almost exclusively for this William's benefit, once Juliette died. (William died young while staying at his aunt Hannah's home in Boston.) At the time of this letter William is well, and is perhaps about seventeen or eighteen years old.

William has obviously previously and playfully chided Toussaint for all his highborn friends in Paris. William has singled out for particular notice Toussaint's friend and faithful correspondent Loïsa, Comtesse de Boesteind. Loïsa is cousin to the Baron de Tascher, a relative of Josephine, Napoleon Bonaparte's wife.

Now Toussaint replies in kind to William: "Sir, I received your charming letter, which truly gave me the greatest pleasure in the world, and I well know you are a young man *comme il faut*. Yes, dear sir, I count myself the happiest of mortals when I receive letters from Madame the Countess of Boesteind. I am equally proud when I receive a letter from William Count Schuyler, for I think and I am certain that you have the sentiments of a true count. Thus, if you ever marry, and I have the pleasure of receiving a note from your wife, I will think it is from the Countess de Schuyler."

This idea catches on among Toussaint's friends, and before long, from Philadelphia, comes a letter from Marie Rose Binsse who addresses Toussaint himself as *"mon cher comte"* (my dear count). The letter tells Pierre she has bought two gourds of gumbo that she is sending up to him with an American lady. She reminds him that this is October, and that if he really wants good gumbo he should buy it in August. She keeps up the *mon cher comte* joke in all her subsequent letters. (And the gumbo is a success—in France: Marie Navarre is soon writing back to Toussaint to thank him for it.)

A certain drollery marks the underlying good-humored chaffing Toussaint gives and receives in correspondence with close friends. Jerome Villagrand teases Toussaint and wonders if Pierre can "spare a little time from devotions and duties" to write. His friend C. Phoenix and his daughters Evaline and Mrs. Janeway regularly have fun when they write to him. The three-some left the city after the 1835 fire and moved to the country-side of Little Sodus, New York. Phoenix cheerfully twits Pierre: "My good friend Toussaint, what has become of your prophecy? Can you tell me who it was said that Madame Janeway and Madamoiselle Evaline could not stay in the country six weeks? You see that that time has passed, and yet, here we are, and very *happy* too, I assure you. We are pleased, beyond our expectations. I do not believe we should have taken any more pleasure in New York, though of course it is of a different kind. I know that Mr. Toussaint is a personage of great taste. It will please him to hear that we are never without bouquets, the wild flowers here are splendid and in great profusion."

The daughters in a letter write humorously of their doings—"you will laugh when you hear of your two ladies turning into farmers, never the less it is true, only imagine it Toussaint [we] have a farm of nearly a hundred acres." They also send Juliette a caged bird. Given that Juliette later sends two canaries down to Baltimore, there appears to be an east coast trade in songbirds as well as gumbo.

Toussaint was as constantly in demand as that other hairdresser, Beaumarchais's Figaro. Absent friends would ask him to get in the painters or decorators, to ensure their New York home was prepared for their return. Acquaintances, returning temporarily or permanently from France or the Caribbean, would write and beg him to find accommodation for them—and then complain bitterly about New York rental prices when he could not find them something cheaper. All this of a man working a seventy- to eighty-hour week. French friends would have Toussaint scurrying to the French consulate in New York to acquire for them copies of marriage certificates and other documents suddenly desperately needed in Paris or Le Havre or Rouen.

They would implore him to find news of missing relatives, pass on letters, and even get involved in settling family disputes. In transnational transactions he handled their money for them. The level of trust everyone had in Toussaint's judgment, the expectation of assistance they unfailingly relied on, the candor as they discussed their intimate problems with him, the regular references to their mutual Catholic faith are constant hallmarks in the correspondence.

Toussaint had an active Christian life, and a jolly social life, within and beyond daily pressures. He kept up with the political and social news his French friends relied on him to deliver. He and Juliette and Euphémie were theater-, concert-, and operagoers. And he was certain to get tickets for Euphémie and himself when the circus was in town.

They gave every appearance of being settled. Financially, they were certainly secure. Yet in the year 1815, when they took Euphémie into their lives, Toussaint received a letter from Paris that for years tempted him to pick up and move to France. There he would not only be reunited with the Bérard family and his friends who had left New York to return home, but he and Juliette and Euphémie would be truly free.

For France offered its black citizens what America withheld: equality.

TWELVE

$\mathscr{A}$URORE—AND 1822

IN OCTOBER 1815, a Madame Brochet, a Frenchwoman visiting New York and staying in the City Hotel on Broad Way, asked the hotel to find her a French-speaking hairdresser. Toussaint was summoned. Madame Brochet, who had been in the city for some time, told Toussaint she was lonely in New York, for she spoke no English. Toussaint told her there were "many agreeable French families in New York." "Yes," she said, "she had letters to a number of them," but none could fill the place occupied by her dear friend in Paris, Aurore Bérard.

Toussaint, who was both astonished and delighted to hear the name, pressed Madame Brochet for details—and supplied some of his own until they were convinced it was the same Aurore Bérard, his godmother. "Toussaint hastened back to communicate this delightful surprise to his faithful Juliette. The lady was soon to leave the city and return to Paris." Toussaint wrote to Aurore but, by some confusion, when he carried his letter to Madame Brochet to deliver to his godmother, he learned the Frenchwoman had already sailed. Toussaint pined over the lost opportunity, but very early in the following year a letter dated November 27, 1815, addressed, "A Monsieur Toussaint, Coiffeur," arrived at the Reade Street house.

Madame Brochet had obviously told Toussaint of Aurore's distressed circumstances and poor health. He in turn had told the Frenchwoman he would be happy to have Aurore come to New York and live with him and Juliette. Meanwhile, in their first communication, Juliette sent Pierre's godmother a selection of fashionable kerchiefs.

The letter from Aurore, thirty-nine, detailed how she had survived by running the tobacco kiosk she owned in the Faubourg St. Germain and that she lived nearby at No. 10, Rue de Tournon. (Rue de Tournon today is a handsome street with the Luxembourg Palace at one end and easy access to the Church of Saint-Sulpice at the other. Mainly a residential area, as in times past, there are stores and amenities, including neighborhood cafés.)

The old, fragile letter, folded and worn from being read again and again, expresses the mix of sorrow and joy that has become a familiar rhythm in Pierre's life:

> Madame Brochet, on her return to this city fifteen days since, has given me news of you, my dear godson. I, as well as my brothers and sisters, am truly grateful for the zeal you manifested in wishing to learn something of us, and for the attachment which you still feel for us all. After the information that Madame Brochet gave me, I cannot doubt that you will be glad to receive a letter from me.
>
> I write to you with pleasure, and I have felt much in learning that you are prosperous in your affairs, and very happy. As for us, my dear Toussaint, we have never quitted Paris. Our situation is not happy. The Revolution deprived us of all our

property. My father was one of the victims of that unhappy period. After being confined six weeks in prison, and under constant inspection by the government in their own place near Paris, both he and my mother died of grief. My brothers and sisters are married, but I am not, and am obliged to make exertions to live which have impaired my health, which is now very poor. Were it not for that, I might be tempted to accomplish the voyage you desire; but I am no less appreciative of the offers you made through Madame Brochet, and I thank you sincerely. It is consoling to me amidst all my troubles that there exists one being who is so much attached to me as you are.

It was when Aurore wrote "I wish we could live in the same town that I might give you details by word of mouth of my family" that his godmother may have sown the seed that bedazzled and tantalized Toussaint for a decade and a half—the idea of moving to Paris with Euphémie and Juliette.

(The letter took even longer than usual to reach Toussaint. "It's not easy for me to correspond," she wrote him, "as I don't know anyone in Le Havre." Toussaint's friends in Paris needed to find someone who was traveling to Le Havre, the major departure point for the United States. That person would see the letter aboard ship. Aurore later sent her letters through Sorbieu, who knew people in Le Havre, including, by 1822, Toussaint's friend Madame Larue. At that time, New York–Le Havre was a forty-two-day trip, and eastbound was the faster voyage. The alternative method for mail delivery, as also happened with many of Toussaint's correspondents, was to locate a friend, or a friend of a friend traveling to America who would take the letter along. Toussaint lived in America's major port; he had few problems sending his letters. He simply had to wait for a *paquebot* to France. His niece, Euphémie, wrote to him on one occasion telling him the *paquebot* was due to leave and she had letters she'd like to send.)

In the same letter Aurore wanted to know more about "your wife, I know you have no children. Do you know anything related to Saint Domingue? What has become of all our possessions, and our ancient servants. Tell me all you know about them. Have you any of your former companions in your city? My nurse, Madelaine and your mother, are they still living? Tell me everything you know."

On one level, the advent of godmother Aurore into his adult life completely unsettled Toussaint. On another level, of course, he simply had to carry on with his day-to-day life. Yet from 1815 on he was always speculating on his departure for Paris. Sometimes there was even an approximate departure date set. But always, seemingly at the last minute—meaning six months ahead of time on one occasion—the idea was scotched. There was a major reason for carefully weighing the decision. His friends, as will be seen, warned him that he couldn't hope to be as financially successful and secure in France as he was in New York. Toussaint, in time, developed a different strategy. No matter how long it took, he would work industriously until he built up sufficient monies to survive in France without having to work.

This chapter, then, has two themes: the consequences of Aurore's letter contrasted with Toussaint day-to-day life in 1822, a typical year. At this point Toussaint's correspondents begin to flesh out for today's readers key facets of Pierre's character. In their hundreds of letters, these friends and relations, colleagues and beggars provide needed additional cross-hatching and shading to Hannah Lee's portrait.

Aurore's almost dominating presence in the adult Toussaint's life is a reminder of a time when, two centuries ago, most particularly in Catholic Europe and its colonies, godparents had an intimate relationship to their godchild. That has been diluted in modern times when for most Westerners being a godparent amounts to little more than a onetime guest appearance at the church, and an annual Christmas card with a check in it.

The closest one gets to the Bérard-Toussaint traditions today is glimpsed in *The Godfather* movies and in the immigrant communities—not least in the families from Hispanic lands and Caribbean islands.

In the eighteenth and nineteenth centuries, the godparent was local, loving, and highly responsible for the spiritual welfare of the child. And constantly involved in it.

For example, it may have been young Aurore Bérard, only five years older than her godchild (she was nine when he was four), who back in Saint Domingue helped him memorize his first prayers and early school lessons. When little Pierre went to mass in St. Marc, it may well have been Aurore who later, in her own childlike version, described to him what was happening on the altar and why. In fact, if there was anything prim about Toussaint, and there's not much trace of it, he might have copied it from Aurore. Even in her letters she remains a bit bossy and pursed-lipped. Aurore's main role in Pierre's early life was that their special relationship undoubtedly enhanced his position within the Bérard family. He was something more than Ursule's child and Zénobie's grandchild.

To fit Aurore into the greater circle of Toussaint's friends in France means reintroducing those friends. In 1818, Jean Sorbieu, Toussaint's best man, a former Saint Domingue planter, returned to France as the first of more than a dozen of Toussaint's close friends to return home. This came following the restoration of the monarchy after Napoleon's defeat at Waterloo and his exiles to Elba and, finally, St. Helena. Napoleon's likes and dislikes provided Toussaint with some customers, too. These included the Neuville family, who fled Bonaparte's wrath and founded the school in New York that the Bancel de Confoulens took over when the Neuvilles returned to France with Napoleon's exile. (Then Neuville was sent back to the United States as the French ambassador.)

Sorbieu initially settled in Rouen before moving permanently to Paris. With the exceptions of Sorbieu, who was apparently comfortable financially, one attraction in France for some of Toussaint's friends was jobs—places in the royal court and its various offshoots.

Sorbieu's wife, Cotonie, for example, held a full-time position many other women would have envied—as lady-in-waiting to the Princesse de Sambole. Nonetheless, after an absence of so many years, some returnees were sorry they'd left New York. Not because they didn't find positions but because France, and they themselves, had changed so much in their absence. Deschamps Lagnel, commenting to Toussaint about their mutual friends, said, "All, as many as we are, do not have anything to be pleased about in coming to France. I will leave off saying any more." (Lagnel is despondent for other reasons, including the loss of his daughter, for "my dear Celeste is no more. I lost her after an illness of four months to a complaint of the chest [tuberculosis], an illness too common here in Paris.") The Lagnel family was closely connected to potential sources of royal patronage, but even that connection didn't bring all the brothers the positions they hoped for.

These royalist sympathizers in Toussaint's circle, once in Paris, generally lived in and around the Faubourg St. Germain, just south of the River Seine. And they were an extended family—when the Lagnels' widowed mother returned to France from New York shortly after her sons, Sorbieu soon paid a call and informed Toussaint. Through Sorbieu, Pierre's godmother, Aurore, was drawn into the circle, and what occupies the circle—and many early Sorbieu and Bérard letters to Toussaint—is the question of "the move to Paris."

There is some suggestion in Sorbieu's letters that he and Aurore did not exactly see eye to eye on the advisability of Toussaint moving to France. Early on, Crotonie Sorbieu accused her husband of thwarting Toussaint's plans. Sorbieu told Toussaint, "I was speaking with your godmother" (Aurore had visited the

Sorbieus in Rouen with two of her nieces) and "your project fell like a bomb here. My wife reproached me for wrecking it."

Sorbieu professed innocence, but Toussaint's best man was actually looking out for Toussaint's best interests. Sorbieu had already taken Aurore's measure. More, he weighed the widespread charitable and self-effacing service work Toussaint was doing in New York against Toussaint's projected move and his "motive of being useful to [Aurore]." Sorbieu praised Toussaint's consideration toward his godmother, but writes, "I do not permit myself to give you advice on this subject for the reason you are so useful to so many people in the country where you are that it would be a misfortune for the many you would abandon." He was, in fact, warning Toussaint off.

There is no denying what Sorbieu understood—and Toussaint, too, surely grasped—that Pierre was doing extremely well financially from an entrée to a type of New York clientele he could never replicate in Paris. Sorbieu told Toussaint "that the same craft you follow in New York with much success, as I have said, presumes you have the means to earn your living and to conserve what you already have." Sorbieu was strongly hinting that Toussaint probably would not have such success in Paris.

Even so, in 1819, Toussaint announced plans for an early departure from New York. Sorbieu maintained his stance: "you are more useful where you are." And even Aurore, gradually bending to Sorbieu's influence, one suspects, wrote in a March 26 letter that same year, "I do not permit myself to give you advice. I let M. Sorbieu, who knows your affairs, direct you." In all this one senses Toussaint is nostalgic perhaps for a familial time in Saint Domingue that may have existed only in his memory. Contemplating Paris, he was being driven both by his heart and his head. His heart had the impulsive advantage when he mused, but he was essentially hardheaded and in control whenever it was decision-making time.

In May, Sorbieu himself wrote to help Toussaint calculate

what his earnings might be in Paris vis-à-vis Manhattan. Ever implicit in Sorbieu's missives was the idea that Toussaint ought to seriously think twice before moving.

The following year Catherine Cruger joined those who were advising Toussaint to stay where he was. Aurore writes: "I have talked about you for a long time with Madame Cruger and of the desire you have to come to France. If we consult only our pleasure in seeing you again, we would tell you to leave immediately. But your happiness is what concerns us and we tremble about giving you advice. According to Madame Cruger, living is more expensive here than in your city where you have many customers a month. Here one hardly dresses one's hair, only for concert balls, and the chambermaids dress their mistresses' hair in private life.

"You have practically a fixed income," warns Aurore, who is in desperate financial straits, "here we do not know if you will have. Put yourself in our place and you will see how delicate it is to advise you. If I had a fortune I would not hesitate to tell you to leave because I would be assured that whatever happened to you you would never be unhappy. But alas, my position is such that I can have no joy. I have lost all my fortune. The business funds of the tobacco shop that I have do not belong to me. I cannot yet reimburse anything. After having managed the shop by myself, my health, already ruined, was destroyed. They forced me to put someone else there who does not run it like me. Finally, they reduced the shop's revenue to me, which caused me to want to sell it. The present time, unfortunately, is not a good time to sell."

His godmother told Toussaint that if she could be certain he was coming to Paris, he could take over the tobacco shop from her and Juliette could run it and receive the eight hundred francs Aurore paid her employee. "But I always feared that would not be to your taste. At this moment, I cannot stop my steps to sell it. If the shop is not sold by the time I receive your response, I will delay selling and await your letter." Despite this inducement, Aurore was now at pains to ensure that any decision be Toussaint's, not hers. She is not urging him to come: "All this is only an idea, not a wish of mine for you to do it. Envision the thing and you may want to try your luck [with the tobacco shop]. But My Dear Toussaint, you earn enough in New York that you can put something aside each year for your old age when comes the rest that is necessary. I speak to you as someone who loves you well. You will see what Mrs. Cruger writes to you; friendship will direct her pen."

Sorbieu invariably softens his apparent opposition, slightly, writing quite sincerely how delighted he would be to be able to see and converse with Pierre in person. At one point Sorbieu assures Pierre that in Paris his own sister (Jean Sorbieu was still in Rouen) and Pierre's large circle of friends would welcome him to the city and see him settled. But Sorbieu remained uneasy and Pierre sensibly hesitated. (The Sorbieu family at this point left Rouen and moved to the capital, probably because the Princesse de Sambole, whom Cotonie Sorbieu served, moved to the royal court.)

Year after year Toussaint was going to Paris and didn't. Sorbieu was probably at the heart of the indecision. There were many solid reasons besides the wish to be reunited with Aurore and his friends for Toussaint to consider the move. The strongest was Euphémie's future.

New York in the 1820s, signaling rising hostility against black people and Catholics, offered no social inducement to remain. The Toussaint's daughter, and to some extent Pierre and Juliette themselves, were always vulnerable to being assaulted or, far worse, kidnapped, shipped south, and sold to a plantation.

"So tenderly guarded was little Euphémie," writes Hannah Lee, "that he never suffered her to go out in the streets alone." She never went anywhere without the most secure adult supervision, and that usually meant Juliette. (Not that Paris was totally safe. Beneath the general calm there were periodic threats against the royal family, and an occasional assassination.)

Even Sorbieu writes, "there is no tranquility in France at this point. Another plot has been discovered against the royal family." Whether, with these frightening tidbits, he was attempting to further scare Toussaint away from a move to France one cannot say.

So much for Toussaint's contemplated change. What awaited him if he stayed put?

As 1822 opened he was already forty and would turn forty-one in November. He had his at-home clients and his Church Street hairdressing establishment. Those were constants, yet the city and America were changing all around him. By 1822, "Old New York" was giving way to new New York's shifting location uptown.

In the city, the new fashionable address of note was Hudson Square. Designed on the style of the gated London addresses, Hudson Square had its fenced park with fine houses all around. This is where Philip and Mary Anna Schuyler had their new town home. In 1822, these addresses are in some contrast to the ever-spreading slum areas, noticeably the notorious Five Points south on Mulberry Street, barely blocks from St. Patrick's Cathedral (today's Old St. Patrick's).

Churches are on the move, too. Christ Church on Ann Street was unused once the Episcopal parish moved north to follow its congregation. Shortly after, the Catholics bought the empty church for a new Catholic parish with the same name. At Toussaint's church, St. Peter's, the Catholic community was bursting at the seams. Pastor Kohlmann reported he had some sixteen thousand parishioners, primarily Irish. By 1822 there were barely five hundred slaves left in Manhattan (though they were still as numerous as ever in the New York and New Jersey farming regions), though the black population numbers escalated to more than ten thousand.

"Old America" of the original colonies saw a new America opening up westward. "Old America seems to be breaking up and moving westward," wrote the European Morris Birbeck. Trading America was turning into manufacturing America (without losing a beat in the growth of its maritime commerce). Steel was replacing wood, steam engines replacing sails, the new frontiers were Ohio and farther west.

Those who could, fled. As each new state joined the union (Indiana, 1816; Illinois, 1818) its population soared (Indiana's increased almost sixfold from 24,000 to 147,000 between 1810 and 1820). Nearly half a million European immigrants swept in during the 1820s and they were all landing in New York City. The growth and potential for still more growth was phenomenal: In 1822, the Hudson and Lake Champlain Canal was just about finished and the Erie Canal, which would ensure New York's preeminence, would open in another three years. That all meant the land speculators were having a bonanza, but the shrewdest and wealthiest Americans, those with the sharpest vision, understood where the real money was to be made in American real estate: New York.

Rents were rising and though food was uncommonly cheap (even by Baltimore's standards, which is why Fanny Montpensier was always inveigling Juliette to send victuals south), wages were almost stagnant. A worker paid ninety cents a day in 1800 was earning only a dollar in the 1820s—simply because there were more people than jobs. The laborer and his family, if they lived in a ground-floor room, had "sand on the floor" that "did duty as a carpet," wrote J. B. McMaster, "no glass on his table, no stove, no matches and rarely tasted fresh meat as often as once a week." He wore "leathern breeches, checked shirt and red flannel jacket."

Speculation had gripped the real estate market. Like everything connected with finance in New York throughout the nineteenth century, these developments took place in a regular and frequent business cycle of boom and bust. John Jacob Astor led the way in the booming early 1820s, and what Astor did plays directly into what Toussaint began to mimic in a most minor way. In 1822, Astor redeveloped Richmond Hill (the mansion extolled by Abigail Adams). Astor moved the building to another site, opening it as a place of public entertainment. The newly cleared land he sold off for development—and further fueled the housing boom. Toussaint, a keen listener in the houses of New York's great and influential, both as he dressed hair and as he took his leave, would hear all the stories as they unfolded. And he was smart enough to know that the wealthy knew what they were doing. And so, in the years ahead, Toussaint, in a very small way, began to do the same.

He occasionally bought a property and also invested in banks and insurance companies. Some of these things he did openly and in his own name. His closest acquaintances were quite aware of his activities. However, because he was a black man in an antipathetic New York, some of his real estate was held for him by George Lee Schuyler, Mary Anna's son.

Toussaint had a monopoly on the society homes he visited to dress hair. The normal method of payment for a daily visit was through an annual contract. Three decades earlier, in 1789, one New York hairdresser charged two thousands pounds a year to his top clients for a weekly visit. Presuming Toussaint had the same type of contract, six contract clients attended on almost a daily schedule could have meant a guaranteed annual income for Toussaint of $60,000–$80,000 a year in today's money—today, such an income for a family of three would place him in the lower half of the middle class. But Toussaint also had his hairdresser's shop and additional, noncontract clients, who sent notes whenever they needed his services. In the 1820s, it is reasonable to estimate Toussaint was doing very well, and by the early 1830s, extremely well. And he was earning every penny of it the hard way, through constant personal service.

It was through seeing Toussaint in this context of financial security that his French friends urged him not to quit New York. This was certainly uppermost in the mind of his closest white and Catholic friend, Madame P. Larue, when she writes in 1822 from Le Havre: "It's my turn to speak to you of others that I have seen in Paris. I will begin with those who interest you the most, the good Madame Cruger. I did not find her as well as they told me she would be. She was very tired. I found Ma'm-selle Angelica grown and beautiful, and the oldest son [Edward] a very pretty boy. They are in a charming situation, having a very beautiful garden.

"We spoke of you, as you must imagine," continues Larue, "and we are sorry not to see you. Nevertheless, with regards to you, Madame Cruger thinks, like me, that it is much better you stay in New York than come to France. You are loved and known and, without flattering you, are so considered by all honest people there. Here [in Paris] you would need a good deal of time before acquiring this same reputation, which is everything in life, and [that reputation enables] you through your occupation to earn well. Here they dress their hair very little because their chambermaids all know how to arrange hair. It is only for the grand occasions one needs a coiffeur."

Toussaint was in a booming city, frankly secure amidst economic turmoil, admired, and with a seven-year-old daughter to care for. His life was full. In terms of his church work, 1822 was significant because Toussaint took on a major burden: fund-raising for the Sisters of Charity orphanage, previously handled by the industrious Madame Larue.

That year his friend Jean Baptiste, whom he'd assisted with money to close out his freedom purchase, wrote in March from Haiti to say that another friend had spotted Toussaint's mother,

Ursule, in Port-au-Prince. "I have not seen her myself," Jean Baptiste wrote from Les Cayes, a long and difficult distance from Port-au-Prince, "but I have written immediately to tell you." It was the last such sighting, and led Toussaint no further. His correspondent also informed him that Lady Marie Anne Fleury, mother of the three Bossard sisters, had died in Les Cayes. How, as a white woman, she had survived the 1804 slaughter is not known. Equally intriguing, given that Haiti was now a black republic, was the information from Toussaint's friend Chardinette Chardin in Cap Haïtien (as many then spelled the former Le Cap Francois), that "Mr. Jean Phillipe Bérard is at this moment chef de Battaillon of the St. Marc regiment . . ."

Was this young man one of Jean-Jacques Bérard's nephews? Was Haiti using white mercenaries as senior officers? Madame Chardin had written to the commandant to introduce herself and seek more details, but there is no further information in Toussaint's papers.

Other letters rely more on Toussaint being at the beck and call of all his friends. Marie, a friend in Le Cap, writes in April 1822, "I beg you to render me a service. Verify that a payment has been received by my sister. See if you can find a ship free to send flour. She needs 100 gourdes for passage. I can do nothing, but if you could render me this service I would be much obliged to you."

In Haiti Toussaint's cousin Auguste had gone into business for himself. He sought to make Toussaint a major supplier of everything from "silver headed horsewhips for the young chevaliers" to "silk, and good quality cheese and salt pork." Auguste provides Toussaint with a list of the prices of goods in Haiti so Pierre can gauge the price differential between Port-au-Prince and Manhattan. In return, Auguste wants to send Toussaint "shipments of palm oil, coffee, copper and other commodities that we can sell without loss." It was an interesting joint venture.

The entrepreneurial Toussaint occasionally did import barrels of fruits or other goods from Haiti. Ships' bills of lading for freight forwarded to Toussaint are among his papers.

Closer to home, in Long Island, Jean Sorbieu's wife's cousin, the Veuve (Widow) Goudain, writes to Pierre complaining that she was losing her lodgers, that "to be a mother is to resign yourself to unhappiness." This note comes not long after Toussaint has negotiated a twelve-month contract with his own new lodger, G. S. Nexsen. Toussaint, "in consideration of the sum of $16 per quarter hath granted unto the said G. S. Nexsen all sight and privilege to the front room on the first floor of the house No. 105 Reed Street and also a garret bed-room in the same, from the first day of May 1822 until the first day of May, 1823."

In the spring of 1822, yellow fever once again struck the city. And the year ended with a business downturn. Toussaint's friends, knowing his penchant to nurse the sick during the plague, write in alarm asking if he and his family are safe. (One writes to Juliette, anxious because she had not heard from her.) From Paris, Aurore writes: "Mr. Sorbieu, who is now regularly here, is worried—I am, too—about you. Yellow fever has made such great ravages in New York we fear for you. We long for your news." Yellow fever and Toussaint's risk-taking are part of the Toussaint family's reality. At home, Euphémie writes to Toussaint to ask if he will "take me out in the summer providing there is no yellow fever to prevent us."

Biographer Lee described his works: "It must not be supposed that Toussaint's charity consisted merely in bestowing money; he felt the moral greatness of doing good, of giving counsel to the weak and courage to the timid, of reclaiming the vicious, and above all, of comforting the sick and sorrowful."

Otherwise, day in and day out, as before, he walked the streets of rapidly changing Old New York, from one hairdressing appointment to another, in the homes of clients practically immune from the business cycle. And as he plodded these streets of a cold, rainy, miserable November day on his way to his next appointment, Toussaint had time to muse about France.

Yet as he entered a house, and shook the rain from his hat and cloak, he knew from his French friends that if New York's winter weather was poor, winter in Paris was even worse.

THIRTEEN

An Interlude

IT IS STILL THE 1820s. We have aisle seats in the theater of Toussaint's life. The stage, from backdrop to footlights, is crowded with Pierre's friends and relations.

In effect, Juliette and Euphémie, even more so than Toussaint himself, would want the world of today, looking at Pierre's life, to know that whatever is known of him is the gift of Toussaint's two friends, the Sawyer sisters, Mary Anna Sawyer Schuyler and Hannah Farnham Sawyer Lee. Without their words, records, and insights, and the letters preserved by these two sisters, Toussaint and his name would simply have been swallowed up in the mists of time. His wife and daughter would also want Pierre to make the introductions.

Onstage, Toussaint steps forward. He is in his early forties, smiling, composed, and quietly enjoying himself. He is tall for the times, five-foot-nine according to the forensic anthropology team that later examined his remains. It is Toussaint's white women friends who, comparing Toussaint to the average, invariably refer to him as "tall." Alongside other men of that era, Toussaint would be the same height as Ben Franklin at a time when the average male on the east coast of America was about five-foot-five. It was a world of shorter, often slim city men who became squat with age. True, there were striding plantation-bred giants like Washington and Jefferson, but Madison and Monroe were both five-foot-four.

The city directory of 1821 is the first to list Toussaint, as "Toussaint, Peter, hairdresser" at 105 Reed Street. (The street was sometimes spelled "Reade," sometimes "Reed.")

There are two existing Pierre Toussaint portraits, both of which are formal. One is a December 1827 miniature on ivory, made when he was forty-six. Then there is a photograph made by Nathaniel Fish Moore, president (1842–1849) of Columbia College (later Columbia University). It was done at a sitting about 1850–1851, when Toussaint was seventy or seventy-one. The picture may have been made in Toussaint's home, for he is seated in an ornamented chair. In the late 1840s, Pierre's deceased elderly friend Louis C. Binsse left him just such a chair as a token of admiration.

As these were the days of glass-plate photography, where the sitter had to remain quite still for several seconds, Toussaint is obviously concentrating on doing that. Yet there seems to be a slight hint of merriment to his eyes as he does so.

The 1827 miniature was done as a Christmas gift for his wife. It caused much excitement in the household. Euphémie told him: "I must write to Mrs. [Cesarine] Moulton to tell her about your having your miniature taken. I know that it will please her and make her laugh." And Euphémie had immediately done so. Portraits of Juliette and Euphémie were done shortly afterward. (All the portraits are in the safekeeping of the New-York Historical Society.)

Both Toussaint depictions show an attractive subject. He is a handsome man, and very dark, pure African. In the miniature he looks directly at us, confident and assured, yes, yet with a charming wistfulness in his eyes. His hair is close-cropped, and he has a very short brush beard that parallels the line of his chin. His nose is straight, fairly pointed, and broadens quite widely at the nostrils. His shoulders are back, his posture erect. Though there is a suggestion of wistfulness in his eyes, the over-all effect is of a man who looks the world squarely in the eye. Given the formality of the moment, Toussaint is depicted as a person both intelligent and knowing.

In both portraits he is extremely well dressed, normal for a formal sitting. In the miniature he wears a starched, turned-up, low collar. (This is distinct from the high collars of the day that nearly touched a man's ear; a low collar did not reach the jaw-line.) He wears some form of jewel on a slender neck chain, and there is a patterned silk, perhaps the edge of a scarf, protruding from the white linen vest—itself nearly masked by a day coat with broad lapels and large buttons. He appears as the success-ful businessman he is.

The Moore photograph of thirty years later reveals a man with a strong, slightly rounded face that narrows slightly to a firm jawline. His hair, now white and allowed to curl a little, has receded considerably, and side whiskers have replaced the beard. His face is not particularly lined. The eyes that now peer out from under his eyebrows in a head tilted forward slightly by age are those of a man who has seen much, suffered much, un-blinkingly. He is stooped at the shoulders, yet there is a deter-mination not present in the earlier picture.

In Moore's photograph Toussaint wears a starched white stock or shirt-front with a well-tailored coat. It could be a velvet evening jacket for there are turned-back, silk-lined cuffs. If in the first portrait Toussaint looks like a competent, caring lawyer, in the second he appears as a wise judge.

The Moore photograph is part of an intriguing story and a

two-way confirmation. Until Toussaint's remains were exhumed in 1990 as part of the canonization application proceedings, it was always believed that the Benjamin Fish Moore picture was of Toussaint, but there was no proof. The Metropolitan Forensic Anthropology Team from Lehman College, City University of New York, provided the proof. The computer match-up of the photograph with photographs of Toussaint's skull was conclusive. (However, the anthropological examination was not able to help with Toussaint's approximate birth year. Dr. James V. Taylor explained that age is the most difficult thing to assess from remains; Toussaint's were described as those of a man "over 65.")

Toussaint was not unaware of photography. He would periodically meet "Little Philip" Schuyler (Mary Anna's grandson) at his school to walk him home, and one day took Philip to the "daguerreotype studio" to have his picture made. (Toussaint so loved Philip, wrote Philip's sister, Georgiana Schuyler Brandt, that he was the one who took Philip to his first day of school: "walked the little boy with his white hand in the black hand. They were great friends and companions, Philip often writes from the cottage to him.")

The formal portraits to one side, the descriptive words of Toussaint's friends in their many letters paint a portrait of a cheerful countenance, of an energetic and imaginative man, fun and reassuring to be with. But never frivolous and, indeed, a man already starting to offer to friends, and to those who appealed to him for help, the wise counsel that would mark his later years. It is that man who now takes his bow from the stage, to the thunderous applause of those tightly surrounding him.

❖   ❖   ❖

Toussaint does not remain center stage. To the crowd's delight, he first brings forward Madame Juliette Toussaint, and next, their daughter, Euphémie.

Juliette, confident and with a broad, beaming smile, is in her mid-twenties. She is slightly lighter skinned than Pierre. Judging from her portrait, she is a solid, good-looking woman with a round face, large intelligent eyes, and evidence of humor flitting about her lips. Around her head she wears an artfully wrapped colorful kerchief. It is the type of kerchief that, by the end of this decade and beyond, her cousin Fanny will beg her to send down in abundance to Baltimore. There they can be sold to aid the soon-to-be-founded Oblates Sisters of Providence, the first congregation of black women religious.

Her dress is white, worn with a belt high up her chest, just below the bust—the height of fashion for the times. The belt has an ornamented buckle. Her pendant earrings have a pearl or similar stone close to the ear, with a larger multifaceted stone below it. She wears a series of gold chains around her neck. A longer chain, possibly with a cross or a medal on it, disappears into the lace-trimmed neckline of her dress, which has leg-of-mutton sleeves. The dress itself is worn off the shoulders, showing her to be firm-breasted and solidly built.

She is not a large woman but one of very pleasing appearance. From France a letter is read from Cesarine: "I hope that my good Juliette carries herself well. Tell her that I think of her very often and that I wish I could have one of her good creams or puddings or calalou [a spicy vegetable dish]." Those on the stage applaud knowingly.

As Madame Toussaint gracefully steps back into the crowd, the shy Euphémie is encouraged forward. She is just a teenager, probably thirteen, with a narrow face and large eyes, inquisitive but slightly wary. She is of slight build and carries a small woven basket of blooms and greenery. Euphémie, too, has drop earrings, and a single-strand beaded or pearl necklace. Her neckline, as on her mother's dress on which it was probably patterned, is lace-trimmed, though far more demurely cut. The white puffed sleeves at the shoulder give way to decorated lace sleeves down to the wrist. Her dress is belted, but not as high as Juliette's.

Cesarine's letter states: "Without doubt Euphémie studies her piano very much, and you must pass many afternoons with great enjoyment." Euphémie smiles briefly and retreats to Juliette's side. The knowing crowd applauds appropriately—many of them having enjoyed Euphémie's entertainments.

To Juliette's delight, Toussaint now takes the hands of Mary Anna Sawyer Schuyler and Hannah Farnham Sawyer Lee, walks them forward, then retires.

❖   ❖   ❖

Hannah Farnham and Mary Anna are the children of Dr. Micajah Sawyer, and his wife, Sybil Farnham Sawyer of Newburyport, Massachusetts. Both of their parents were the children of doctors. Hannah, born in 1780, was the sixth of eight children; Mary Anna, born six years later, the last. Only four survived into adulthood, the girls and two brothers, William (born 1771) and Thomas (1783). The Sawyer family is close, religious, witty, capable of self-criticism and of gently criticizing others.

Micajah Sawyer's activities go some way to explaining why the sisters, from their writing, appear self-assured as well as good-natured and humorous. Newburyport saw itself as Boston's rival, and Dr. Sawyer was one of its leading citizens. As a doctor, he never treated people according to their ability to pay, and served the poor willingly. He was a Whig who had served throughout the American Revolution on the Committee of Safety and Correspondence. As a businessman, he was an incorporator of the Newburyport Turnpike Company, but he had broader interests—as a charter member of the American Academy of Arts and Sciences, the Massachusetts Medical Society, and the local humane society. He writes openly and affectionately in his letters to his daughters.

The sisters were well schooled, though details of their education are unknown. Congressman John Quincy Adams found the Sawyers "a very agreeable" family and described Hannah and Mary Anna as "two uncommonly handsome daughters." Their parents gave elegant parties that Adams said exceeded the best in Washington, D.C.

The portrait painter Gilbert Stuart, newly arrived in Boston, was commissioned to paint the sisters' portraits. Hannah's great-great-great-grandson Thomas A. Paine describes them:

"Hannah is a study in red and black. Her face is a classic oval. Her dark hair is curled around the forehead and piled high with a comb. Her dark eyes sparkle, her full red lips and the color of her cheeks betray an almost mischievous mirth, and her low-cut black velvet dress abundantly reveals other charms, veiled behind lace, enhanced by a loosely wrapped, brilliant red shawl. Though swag-draped Roman columns in the 'Grand Manner' form the background, and though Hannah herself would have called the effect Grecian, to me there is almost a Spanish, even Goya-like quality to this portrait of poised, spirited young womanhood."

Paine finds that the portrait of Mary Anna "reveals a more girlish and delicate young woman with pert dark eyes, elaborate curls of dark hair, and the same full lips, a slightly aquiline nose, all together forming an impish expression. She is wrapped in a shawl and has a lace collar about the neck. The dress is light. The background is plain. She looks delicate and smaller than Hannah."

Portraits of both women in their later years show them more similar to each other in appearance even though the familiarity is obvious in the earlier depictions.

Only George Lee Schuyler, Mary Anna's youngest child, lived into old age. He married Alexander Hamilton's granddaughter, his cousin Eliza, and was a successful businessman and yachtsman. He gave the America's Cup to the New York

Yacht Club. As a young man George would write delightedly to
Toussaint and at length about steamboat trips on the Mississippi. One steamboat in which the family had a major financial
interest was being given speed trials to attract attention—commercial attention that is—to its capabilities. While George extolled the pleasures of such inland voyages, his mother, Mary
Anna, though she occasionally went along, was slightly less en-
thusiastic.

Her granddaughter Georgiana Schuyler Brandt (George's
daughter), in the 1920s, in a scrawling, barely decipherable
hand, left a scattering of notes that refer to Toussaint. "My
grandmother," she said, "thought him [Toussaint] so exceptional that she made notes of some of his conversation with her.
These notes of hers form the basis of [Hannah's] work." It is
from Georgiana that we know that George Lee (her father) held
real estate for Toussaint when blacks were forbidden ownership.

Georgiana also emphasizes that among her grandmother's
approachable and kindly characteristics was that grandnieces
regarded Mary Anna as a wise person whose judgment was always sound. She had a reputation with her grandnieces as a
person worth consulting, though sometimes she would give advice while at others she would say, "you must make up your own
mind."

Mary Anna's personality is seen, too, in the exchange of letters with her parents and siblings. These letters are mutually
charming, good-natured, and openly affectionate (she apparently carried those same characteristics into her relationship
with Pierre). She is an entertaining and perceptive writer. In
one letter to her parents she mentions attending a "smart ball
given by Colonel De Voes, who you will remember as John's old
master. He is not as pompous, vain and ostentatious as his servant, but very good natured." There's also a suggestion of wit of
the "girl-talk" variety in the correspondence with friends her
own age as when her correspondent remarks, on a mutual

friend's decision to wed, "she has consented to become subject to that odious, dear sweet creature, man."

Mary Anna is politically astute, too. In 1807, President Jefferson asked Congress for an Embargo Act in retaliation for the press-ganging of American seamen into the British fleet. The act embargoed all ships from leaving U.S. ports. The result was economic disaster, ruinous to hundreds of businesses, with vessels rotting at anchor at the wharves. Mary Anna comments to her parents, "this embargo business has occasioned a great deal of distress in New York to the poor and labourers who are cut off from all means of earning a subsistence. Those who considered themselves, & were considered by others as rich men, have become bankrupts—so much for our wise administration."

She is enlightened, especially on matters of religion. In a letter to Toussaint from Europe in the 1840s, she says, "My dear Toussaint, I go to the Catholic churches, and they are all grand and ancient. I always remember my own *St. Pierre* [Mary Anna's emphasis], and often kneel and pray with my whole heart. Ah! Dear Toussaint, God is everywhere! I see him in your church, in mine, in the broad waste, and the full city. May we meet in peace and joy. I am ever your friend, M.A.S."

As the correspondence in the chapters ahead shows, it was not simply Mary Anna Schuyler who saw elements of saintliness in Toussaint. She was speaking for many with her letter. And as she makes her bow and retreats into the crowd on stage, those gathered fully understand.

Now alone in the limelight is Hannah Lee, who had the larger challenge: to capture Toussaint on the printed page. This she undertook to do obviously at Mary Anna's request, when the ailing Mary Anna knew she could never attempt it herself.

Hannah and George, settled in splendid circumstances in Boston, had six children, three of whom died in childhood. Mary Anna and Hannah named their children for each other's families—Mary Anna had a George Lee; Hannah had a Mary

Anna, and the two families were close and intertwined for three generations. Hannah was thirty-five and pregnant with her last child when George, who had just been elected a state representative, died in his sleep. He was forty-one.

Mary Anna and Hannah's older brother William had been leading an adventurous life but had never married. He now invited his widowed sister and her children to live with him in his magnificent house at 87 Mount Vernon Street, Boston. Secure in that environment—once she'd recovered from the shock of her husband's death and an illness—Hannah decided on a course that in time produced the book on Toussaint.

Her descendant Thomas Paine wrote, "for Hannah Farnham Lee widowhood was ultimately a good thing. Without a husband to define her identity and confine her to the conventional norms of feminine conduct, and with an adoring brother to settle all her cares, she was free to grow and make her own mark. She found contentment without having to find a new husband." In her fifties, with most of her children now on their own, Hannah decided to become an author. Over the next fifteen years she wrote more than a dozen books, including *Three Experiments in Living* (1837), described by Paine as "a clarion call of American feminism to come," which was probably America's first best-seller written by a woman (thirty editions and 125,000 sales at a time when the U.S. population was a mere 15 million). It was dedicated "to the female community."

Lee's literary output ranged from romantic fiction to Christian morality tales to art history. She was a wise and successful author when, at seventy-three, she started work on the Toussaint memoir. Mary Anna's notes were augmented by her last two meetings with Toussaint (whom she had undoubtedly met many times during regular visits to Mary Anna's New York City home) after her sister's 1852 funeral. Her *Memoir of Pierre Toussaint, Born a Slave in St. Domingo* is now etched into history.

For all that she wrote one and a half centuries ago and

aimed at the audience of her time, Lee genuinely tried to capture the entirety of the man—and mainly achieved this in terms understandable today. Yet this memoir, in which Pierre Toussaint is seen as black and Catholic on Hannah Lee's terms, exposes both Lee's strengths and limitations.

The issue is clear: What she wrote, coupled with letters to Toussaint from his friends, plus one or two jottings by others who remembered him, is all that we know about Toussaint.

She was elderly and energetic (and would live a further twelve years, to eighty-five) when she sat down to write her memoir of Toussaint. It was a considerable undertaking. Handwritten in manuscript, it is polished, poignant, and precise in detail and style, though there are possible errors in a couple of key dates (see the Appendix).

Yet more than once, as she probes Toussaint's deeper emotions, she understandably ends on a note that jars the twenty-first-century reader. Lee's lapses, if that's what they are, matter because she is the essential starting point for everyone today who attempts to understand Toussaint.

Her memoir, though generally balanced, nonetheless was influenced by Harriet Beecher Stowe's *Uncle Tom's Cabin, or, The Life of the Lowly,* Hannah's own lack of access to Toussaint's black friends (which she acknowledges), and Toussaint's own likely reticence in discussing certain topics—especially with white American women.

The timing of Stowe's work was unfortunate for Toussaint, and for Hannah, appearing as it did just two years before Pierre's death.

Uncle Tom's Cabin was incredibly influential—there had never been a book like it. In its own way it thrust slavery, through fiction, four-square into the face of white Americans in a manner they had not previously experienced and, as it happened, could not easily resist.

The story was initially serialized in the New York abolitionist press with people desperate for each succeeding installment. Designed as an abolitionist tract, it succeeded in its aims, and it raised tremendous sympathy for the slaves. Read as a white account of the feelings and likely actions of a black slave, however, *Uncle Tom's Cabin* portrays Africans as whites saw, or wanted to see, them. The characterization "Uncle Tom" became a pejorative to describe a particular type of African American: servile and capable of sacrificing his family's interests to those of his white master.

Toussaint was the first black to be stuck with the label, not because he deserved it but because he was the first prominent black New Yorker to die following *Uncle Tom's Cabin*'s appearance. The label was used for him in a New York newspaper obituary only days after his death. And it was used again in nineteenth- and twentieth-century articles.

Biographer Lee occasionally tends toward Stowe's sentimentality and stereotyping, yet one senses to her credit her attempt not to. For example, Toussaint is depicted by Lee as always being cool, calm, and collected. She mentions that he admits to a quick temper but that he had the strength to control it—"that he was born with it, and was obliged to bear it about with him." Pierre's friend Jerome Villagrand offers a deeper insight. In a letter to Toussaint describing his granddaughters, Villagrand says of one, "she is a little hot-head, but a heart par excellence. She resembles you, my dear Toussaint."

That was from someone who'd known Toussaint for thirty years: "a little hot-head, but a heart par excellence." When Toussaint was among his French intimates and confidants, or his fellow blacks, and had no need for discretion, what was he a hothead about? Was he simply impatient, was it that he didn't suffer fools gladly, or was he inclined to erupt over trivialities? Or was he hotheaded about his lot in having to support the Bérard household? Was he hotheaded about the way blacks were treated? About slavery? Among white French friends who treated him as an equal, Toussaint may have spoken volubly, one surmises, against many things he would not air with white Americans, and from them receive nods of concurrence.

Lee sometimes puts in Toussaint's mouth a type of nineteenth-century "Southern plantation black-speak." That's probably a Harriet Beecher Stowe-ism. Despite Toussaint's known deficiencies in spoken English, this "black-speak" does not ring true in the mouth of a person whose first language was French. At other times in the memoir, Toussaint's quoted voice is as crisp as Hannah Lee's own.

Here she discusses Toussaint at the moment he has taken full responsibility for the white household, and crams into one miniature paragraph an entire catalogue of stereotypes: "Belonging to a race proverbially full of glee, and while on the island among his sable brethren, first in dance and song, he now scrupulously rejected all temptation for spending money, and devoted his time to his mistress. We presume few remember him in his early manhood. Then he was tall and well made, with the flexibility of limb which belongs to his race." Such descriptions fix Toussaint in history's ledger in a particular way.

Lee sees issues of color in some of Toussaint's decisions when the more likely issue was a difference in social class. One example comes when Toussaint does not sit down to have afternoon chocolate with visiting white American and French friends. Even today a butler (and Toussaint was in the service trade, he was a hairdresser) would not sit at the table with his employer. Lee does note that many pale faces (her word) were visitors to Pierre and Juliette's home.

In matters like this, Toussaint's reality is always more complex than Lee acknowledges. Not because she was simplistic or diffident, but because she was writing in her time. Where his white American friends (as distinct from his white French friends) are concerned, Toussaint is very sensitive to the degrees of social segregation that the white American world insisted on.

One white American friend, obviously a Protestant, asked Toussaint if he could arrange for her Catholic French visitor to accompany Pierre to mass at St. Peter's, where he had a pew. Toussaint obliged, but seated the white Frenchwoman in the pew of a white woman, rather than his own. When the Frenchwoman asked why she had not joined Toussaint in his pew (for in France she could have done so without anyone commenting), Toussaint told her, "Oh Madame, it would not be proper."

He was explaining to a foreign visitor the governing American social code, not expressing a personal opinion or preference. With his "it would not be proper" he was bowing, as he had to, to prevailing American prejudices—prejudices that did not in fact exist inside his own household. Prejudices that did not exist in France.

When Toussaint's godmother, Aurore Bérard, describes to Pierre the benefits of his moving to France with his family, one advantage she writes of is that "you will be treated as an equal." (How that must have resounded in his heart. Echoes, surely, of Grandmother Zénobie's tales on her return from living briefly as a freewoman in France.)

Even so, Aurore means Toussaint would be equal in matters of race, not social class.

❖   ❖   ❖

At times, biographer Lee interprets the nuances of Toussaint's attitudes and behavior with great acuity. Like her sister, she is a practicing and deeply religious Protestant. Here Lee tries to explain Toussaint's Saint Francis–like insight into, and compassion toward, human suffering. The narrative is at the point when Madame Bérard is severely depressed—probably "clinically depressed" in today's understanding—and no wonder. Her husband and sisters have died; she is bereft of family. She is penniless and dependent on the skills of a slave hairdresser for her everyday survival.

Lee writes: "It appeared his great study to shield her from despondency. In his constant and uniform system there was something far beyond the devotion of an affectionate slave; it seemed to partake of a knowledge of the human mind, an intuitive perception of the wants of the soul, which arose from his finely organized nature." (Mary Anna would have learned of Toussaint's ministries to Marie Elisabeth when she married into the Schuylers' New York milieu.)

Biographer Lee tends to see Toussaint's loyalty to Marie Elisabeth Bérard in terms of his being a slave content with accepting his lot. Yet Lee cannot know that. "When Toussaint first came to this country the free negroes and some of the Quakers tried to persuade him to leave his mistress." (One presumes this is after Jean-Jacques Bérard has died and it has become known this black slave has undertaken his mistress's support.) "They told him that a man's freedom was his own right. 'Mine,' he said, 'belongs to my mistress.' "

Toussaint was correct here on two counts. First is the obvious one: to walk away from Marie Elisabeth Bérard would not have made him a free man, it would have made him a fugitive slave. More tellingly, he had no claim on American citizenship. Once legally freed, he was automatically a French citizen. He was born in a French colony, owned by a French family, and was freed (as already noted) under French law (in 1807). His freedom really did belong to his mistress. The laws of the United States could not free him. Toussaint was French property. And he knew where he stood on these matters.

Again is it only fair to note that Hannah Lee worked at considerable disadvantage. She was working essentially from someone else's notes (Mary Anna's) of events that had taken place decades, even a half century, earlier. Hannah could not speak

French, therefore her conversations with Toussaint were perforce limited to his ability as a conversationalist in English, which was not remarkable.

Lee links Toussaint's compassion to his faith. She speculates on where his being black and a slave fits into it. Toussaint, she writes, "knew exactly what was due to others and himself, while his heart overflowed with that Christian kindness which far surpasses mere worldly politeness." Her description, quite lovely in its way, coincides with that of his friends in their correspondence, revealing Toussaint as a man who seriously, daily, attempted to fulfill God's will as he understood it.

Toussaint was, she continues, "observant of all the forms of the Roman Catholic Church; through winter and summer he missed no matin prayers, but his heart was never narrowed by any feeling as to sect or color. He never felt degraded by being a black man, or even a slave; for he considered himself as much an object of divine protection as any other human being."

While Lee's perceptions here are sharp, and her nineteenth-century writing precise, it seems quite unlikely Toussaint "never felt degraded by being a black man, or a slave." To the contrary, his sensibilities, his sense of decency and dignity would have been constantly stung in and around the streets of New York—and perhaps in some parlors of New York's wealthy, and most certainly in the portico of St. Patrick's Cathedral itself, when he and Juliette and Old Cabresse were refused seats. It might be more accurate to state of Toussaint that he was strong enough of character and fortitude to never give the appearance of feeling degraded. His dignity in the face of the way Africans were treated in the society, and in the way slaves were regarded, comes from the fact that there was nothing servile about him.

Lee continues that Toussaint "understood the greatness of the part allotted him; that he was to serve God and his fellowmen, and so fulfill the duties of the situation in which he was placed. There was something truly noble and great in the view that he took of his own nature and responsibilities." These are very strong assertions from one who was an observer and not an intimate. His many friends, reading such a statement, would have nodded their heads in agreement. Those who knew him best would have strongly demurred, however, if Lee was implying he accepted his slavery "situation" unconditionally and in perpetuity.

And this is where that major issue in Lee's biography is now joined: Lee infers Toussaint accepted his slavery. Stacked against this: Toussaint did not accept his sister Rosalie's slavery and wanted her a free woman before she wed. He did not accept his wife-to-be Juliette's slavery, nor the slavery of those whose freedom he helped redeem. He himself would not have wed unless freed. But it was not an issue—he had been freed.

Lee's reason for Toussaint's acceptance of his bondage, beyond his Christian fatalism, was that "He was born and brought up in St. Domingo at a period that can never return. In the large circle around him there were no speculations upon freedom or human liberty, and on those subjects his mind appears to have been perfectly at rest." In fact, whatever Toussaint felt, these probably were not issues he discussed with either Hannah or Mary Anna. "When he resided in New York," Hannah wrote, "he still preserved the same tranquil, contented state of mind [as on the Saint Domingue plantation], yet that he considered emancipation a blessing he provided by gradually accumulating a sum to purchase his sister's freedom. But he does not appear to have entertained any inordinate desire for his own freedom. He was fulfilling his duty in the situation in which his Heavenly Father chose to place him, and that idea gave him peace and serenity. When his mistress on her death-bed presented him his liberty, he most gratefully received it, and we fully believe he would not have suffered any earthly power to wrest it from him."

The phrase—"but he does not appear to have entertained

any inordinate desire for his own freedom"—is a chilling statement, and one that must be countered. For it is the essence of "Uncle Tomism."

May we, rather, believe that the reason Toussaint did not attempt to buy his freedom was related directly to his concepts of what was meet and just: that he believed he had earned his freedom and had no reason to buy it. More strongly, that for reasons of precedent Toussaint was adamant in a deeply held (if unstated) conviction that just as Zénobie had her freedom from the Bérards and Marie Bouquement had hers from the Bossard sisters for services rendered, so he believed he was *entitled*—genuinely *entitled*—to his freedom from Marie Elisabeth Bérard.

Lee's reading of Toussaint's character on this point is that he was adamant to the point of obduracy and proved this precisely by remaining a slave rather than stooping to purchase his liberty. The strongest support for this contention is in an 1810 letter from his sister Marie-Louise shortly after she arrived in New Orleans from Cuba. Marie-Louise obviously has not been in touch with Toussaint for quite a while. She asks Pierre if he has been given his liberty yet—by which time he had been free for almost three years.

The point, of course, is that she has been given hers, and her question presumes his freedom will likewise be given to him. It was a family tradition. Toussaint had every reason and expectation that he would be given his.

Marie Elisabeth Bérard was grossly negligent in not granting freedom to Toussaint far earlier.

Lee describes Toussaint as "unlettered." She means not that he was illiterate but, in the style of the day, that he had not been prepared as a scholar by academics. If she is correct, it means that outside the Bérard chateau schoolroom Toussant was self-taught. There's little to go on. His handwriting is excellent; his few surviving letters are succinct or witty and written with ease, not labored. Given the sheer volume of his correspondence, the letters he wrote regularly to people of all classes seem to have come easily to him. No one writing back gives any indication they are writing to a person of a lesser level of education or intellectual interests or attainment. With only two notable exceptions, their handwriting is not superior to his. (The exceptions are people writing in the most beautiful "copperplate" style imaginable.)

There is no definite answer on his education, only a strong feeling that back on the Bérard L'Artibonite plantation, Zénobie would have seen to it that Toussaint received every educational advantage she could have obtained for him. And she was in a position to press hard on his behalf.

Lee admits she has only half the picture. She agrees that when she speaks of Toussaint's "friends, we do not include people of his own color, though most gladly we would procure their testimony were it in our power. That he was a fast and true friend among them we know, but our walks have not led us among them."

Lee made no attempt to seek them out, and that is not a criticism of her scholarship. Many of his early black friends were dead, or had moved away from New York City. There existed no easy means by which a white woman writer could enter this world at short notice.

The only friends she can talk about are "those to whose houses he daily resorted—people in New York of the highest class in rank, cultivation, and wealth. It was by such he was sought and honored long after his labors as a hairdresser had diminished." (In great measure, when it comes to seeing Toussaint through the eyes of his black friends, all Toussaint biographers, black or white, are in the same delicate situation, though it is terrain not completely bleak or barren.)

What Lee does hope is that Toussaint's example will lead his fellow Negroes to follow in his footsteps. If that sentiment at first blush sounds gratuitous or racist, it isn't. For Lee boldly states that Toussaint is a model white men also should emulate.

And with that final observation, Hannah Lee, on stage, applauded loudly by Toussaint, bows her head in acknowledgment of the plaudits deservedly offered for the stellar work she undertook. It is a work that, in major measure and given the limitations of the time, she satisfactorily delivered.

Toussaint accompanies Lee back into the stage crowd as he is absorbed once more by his family and friends. Now, holding his hand, however, is another observer whose preserved comments also reveal Toussaint: his most persistent correspondent, young Euphémie herself.

FOURTEEN

"DEAR UNCLE"

FOR FOURTEEN YEARS, Euphémie was the center of the Toussaint household and Pierre and Juliette's lives. She called him "uncle," which Toussaint was. Yet he loved her like a daughter, which Euphémie also was—legally, by adoption. In her letters to Juliette, Euphémie occasionally signs herself "your daughter," though in her letters to Toussaint, Euphémie always refers to Juliette as "my aunt."

Every Friday, from the age of seven in 1823, until her death at fourteen in 1829, Euphémie wrote weekly letters to Toussaint. She addressed him either as "Dear Uncle," or "Cher Oncle." These letters, almost 180 years later, provide modest though invaluable insights into the life, piety, and interests of the Toussaint household.

Why letters when Pierre, Juliette, and Euphémie all lived in the same household? There were two reasons. Of an evening, when most families gather, Toussaint himself was invariably gone from home to work in the homes of others. Of a morning he was up early for daily mass, and may have seen Euphémie briefly on his return. But then he'd be off to his shop until it was time to start his house calls.

Weekends might be little different—extremely busy on Saturdays, right into the mid-evening, returning home only after Euphémie was in bed. Most Sundays they probably attended church together in the Toussaint pew at St. Peter's. Some Sundays—even at Easter—he was not with them but on call for coiffeur duties. Those Sundays he probably attended a very early mass.

Euphémie's weekly letters were a way for Toussaint to maintain a special fatherly relationship with his daughter, track her week, and note her progress in English and composition. After the age of eleven her letters were almost identically written in English and French so he could see how her French was coming along, too. After he read Euphémie's weekly letter, Toussaint often answered her requests verbally through Juliette; other times he sent little notes to Euphémie. That does not mean that father and daughter never talked—on occasion he was home early enough that she proudly made his coffee for him—rather, Toussaint developed a system for monitoring Euphémie's behavior and progress even when he was not present.

Her phrase "Dear Uncle" not only opens her letters, but she sometimes drops it into the middle of them, too. The correspondence reveals the role Juliette and Pierre's friends play in helping shape Euphémie. Mary Anna Schuyler sends suitable little books of inspiration—most of Euphémie's reading matter would be the instructional and "morality tale reader" of the day.

She often mentions the fables or secular morality tales she has read that week (and in the same long sentence is equally likely to remind him of his promise that they're going to the theater or circus): "Dear Uncle, When you see Mrs. Schuyler will you tell her please I am very much obliged to her for that little book she was so kind to send me. I have read it through and it is a very good and religious book." Or, "Dear Uncle, Will you be so kind as to buy me two books, the title of one is *The Good-Natured Boy*, the other is *Cock Robin*."

In total, Euphémie's correspondence makes the reader privy to a household that regularly visited friends (with trips to Brooklyn, probably to Juliette's family); was musical; attended the theater, opera, circus, and concerts in people's homes; and was very devout. Prayer and reliance on God were part of everyday practice and commentary.

Euphémie was musical, she played the piano and the violin and sang, and she kept "Cher Oncle" up to date on her musical accomplishments through the comments of her tutor, Mr. Gentil, on her performances—and through her regular requests for new pieces of music. She was pious. On one occasion she writes in French, "I will be so content if I am able to serve God and follow him always so that after our deaths, in glory, we will be with Him in Heaven."

Euphémie wrote her "Dear Uncle" letters with a quill, the stiff, feathered plume plucked from a bird's tail. Quills didn't stay sharp or firm for very long, and she regularly asked for new ones. When she was older, her request was for "a new penknife." ("Penknife," to shape one's quill points, is how the word for a small pocketknife originated.)

Euphémie lived in a world of early deaths, and was quite conscious of it. As she marks her birthday each year it is a little chilling to see her write of hopes that she might live yet one more year. The little girl also saw, possibly through her parents' eyes initially, the evidence of hard lives all around her, particularly when the breadwinner died. Toussaint could be that dead breadwinner, and quite early Euphémie is conscious of this fact. She was sympathetic to the demands on her uncle, promising that when she turns thirteen it will be "my turn to work for you."

Death and sadness are regular components in her commentary. But she is still a little girl, too, and does French homework at the bottom of the same letter as she notes, "Dear Uncle, I have heard that Mr. Welsh is dead. I pitty his poor children but some of them are to small to feal it yet I pitty them. Dear Uncle, I am very much obliged to you for letting me go to the party on Monday. Adieu Dear Uncle. J'ai gagné il a gagné ils ont ils gagnèrent [I won, he lose, they have, they won]."

❖   ❖   ❖

New York is a work-or-don't-eat city, and people scramble to survive. Among them are the little chimney sweeps who climbed into fireplaces and cleaned the flues, a filthy job that drastically shortened their life expectancy as it undermined their health through lung diseases and testicular cancer. That the usually caring younger Euphémie could be unfeeling or a little bit snobbish was something she later recognized in herself. And it showed in an incident concerning a chimney sweep. In 1827, Euphémie pondered an incident that occurred just before her friend Madame Soulis returned to France. Euphémie is now about to write to her: "Dear Uncle, I will ask her if she remembers when I got quite angry with her for giving tea to a little [chimney] sweep because he had a cold. I told her that she ought to break that cup. And she asked me if I did not think the little sweep was flesh and blood like anybody else."

Several themes run through Euphémie's letters. She regularly petitions Toussaint for simple entertainments and needs, and when she doesn't receive them she nags him politely, as a child can, until she gets them (while assuring him she will ask for nothing else for a long time). She is observant and not above being a social critic, which suggests that at home either Pierre or Juliette, and possibly both, were not above criticizing errant behavior in others.

She can also be extremely strong-headed (just as Toussaint himself admitted he once used to be). As a ten-year-old she was so furious with Toussaint on one occasion that she refused to wish him a happy birthday. But two days later, serious and contrite, she regretted her meanness: "I am very sorry that to please you I did not wish you a happy birthday as I had not a clear heart to wish it to you. I feel very angry with myself to think that I had occasion to make you angry. Dear Uncle, will you be so kind as to forgive me this once and wait until Newyears and then I hope I will be able to wish you a happy Newyears and feel happy myself."

On New Year's Eve, 1825, she did precisely that. "I wish you a happy Newyear and many happy returns. Dear Uncle, will you be so kind as to accept this small gift. It is not much but it is as much as I can give this time. I hope that Newyear I shall be able to give you something worth speaking of, not only as respects giving, but my Reading, Writing, Music. It is true the time is past when I might have improved myself to greater advantage but I can't recall it." (As an interesting aside, Euphémie spells the feast day, Newycars. "Newycars" or "Newyork" as one word were not uncommon usage at the time. A reminder of that eighteenth-century style can be seen today in the title of the late-eighteenth-century-founded New-York Historical Society.)

Toussaint was very pleased with this particular letter and, through Juliette, told Euphémie so. But there's a greater value than mere historical footnote to this outburst from Euphémie and her subsequent contrition. Pierre and Juliette are teaching Euphémie right from wrong. In her apologies one hears the moral echo of her parents' voices.

Euphémie provides, too, a clearer picture of Toussaint's religious sources of strength. As a nine-year-old she asks for a New Testament. In today's context this is actually quite remarkable. Throughout the nineteenth and twentieth centuries, up to the reforms of the Vatican II (1962–1965), Catholics were specifically discouraged from reading the Scriptures. Lay Catholics were considered incapable of handling the New or Old Testaments unless under the express guidance of a priest. Such was obviously not the case among eighteenth- and nineteenth-century French Catholics of the educated class.

From Euphémie, therefore, comes confirmation that Toussaint's Scriptural devotion was by no means limited to his early education. Through her it is obvious Toussaint's attachment to the New Testament was lifelong and regular. It was because "Dear Uncle" read the New Testament that the young Euphémie decided she must, too.

❖   ❖   ❖

Sometimes she was a little moralist, at others a little fatalist. The following excerpts are more or less in chronological order.

As an eight-year-old she writes, in August 1824: "I will be very glad when summer is out and winter comes so that I can play in the snow and make balls. I think all last week has been very cold indeed. It is very singular that when summer comes I do not like it, nor winter neither, I wish when summer comes it would snow. Yet we know we must be pleased with everything God does for us in this world. You know He does it all for the best." And she closes with her own little philosophical observation: "Something more I think is very singular. That when this is Monday we wish it was Sunday." And ten days later "Dear Uncle, Oh what hot weather, almost suffocating, but God has sent us a little rain which I hope will make it a little cooler."

Intermingled with all of this is the little girl Euphémie. In one of her early letters she writes, "Dear Uncle, I am in my ninth year it is time for me to be good. Dear Uncle, do tell me how must I pass a whole week well, for when ever I begin the week well I always end it bad." But soon she has forgotten that, and on December 19 writes: "Dear Uncle, now for Christmas and all its pleasures." The following year she promised, "Dear Uncle, I am determined to begin next week to be a good girl. I want to ask you if I can invite two or three girls to see me in the course of a few days as it will be my doll's birthday and you promised to buy me some calico for curtains for my doll's bed but I would rather you would get me only enough for a frock. No more favors at present."

And two weeks later, "Dear Uncle, I want to know if you will not take me to the circus or the theater next week or week after next. I believe you have forgot your promise but I have not forgot. And to the museum if I am good." Two years later, at age eleven, she's expressing her immediate wishes, but not without the Toussaint family sense of what—or rather, who— was proper. "Dear Uncle, O will you be so kind as to let me go and see that young lady, the same which I have once before asked your permission to visit. Dear Uncle, do grant me this favor and I will not ask for another in a great while. My Aunt knows her godmother. She is a very respectable woman and her mother likewise."

Euphémie knows she is an orphan, and each St. Euphémie's Day she visits the home established by Mother Seton the year after Euphémie was born. The orphanage visits were not intended by Toussaint to be a grim reminder. Helping orphans was part of one's work as a Christian. When the Sisters began the New York home in 1817 with five orphans, it was in a little house on Prince Street opposite St. Peter's Church. When Father Power became pastor, the orphanage was one of his priorities and, encouraged by Bishop Du Bois, he raised money to see the premises expanded. As Toussaint was deeply involved in that work, so was tag-along Euphémie. On one early occasion she asked, "Uncle, what are orphans?" He explained they were children with no father or mother, to which Euphémie countered, "but have they no uncle?" Toussaint was deeply touched by her remark.

When Euphémie was preparing for her first communion, she wrote, "Dear Uncle, after I have made my first communion,

I would like to have all the little orphans to come and drink tea with me. I dare say they would be very glad to come and they do not often have an opportunity of having a good tea with some little delicacies." As a twelve-year-old, she wrote, "Dear Uncle, When we were at the orphan asylum how glad they seemed to be when they saw the cakes. There was a dear little girl there, I do not believe she was but three years old. She was a very nice little thing. I should be very glad to have them all come here and take tea some afternoon."

In English she soon writes, "Oh how happy I feel to think that I am so near to make my first communion. Dear Uncle, my conscience is so clear I hope it will always be the same. We do not deserve the goodness of God but he is so good that he pardons all our sins. We are his children. He loves us and we ought to love him." She writes, "Dear Uncle, I have begun to know how we must serve God. I hope it will finish well and that I may always remember my duty towards God." In her "Cher Oncle" letter in French that week she expands a little on her beliefs: "it is a very good thing to know how to serve God, in order after our deaths to live with joy and glory with him in Heaven."

At this time New York erupted in another outburst of anti-Catholic agitation. Euphémie was horrified, and perhaps a little fearful. "Dear Uncle, O what a shameful thing it is to have any body insult our God. I should like to know where these people expect to go when they die. I certainly think they will go to no other place than Hell, and burn there in fire and brimstone. I hope that God will preserve me and all my family [from] such sin." Then his niece reminded him he promised to give her a sewing kit and sampler so she could cross-stitch the Lord's Prayer.

Euphémie revealed that Toussaint was not completely tied to Manhattan. "Dear Uncle, I think you have forgotten your promise," she wrote to him on July 28, 1825. "The week is almost out and you said that you would go to Brooklyn with me and my aunt. If you would I should be very glad. Adieu Dear Uncle. Euphémie Toussaint."

There are indications he traveled to Baltimore, and may have been to Albany or Boston—all seaports readily served from Lower Manhattan. More tantalizing, there are two Euphémie letters that suggest Toussaint had been to London. It is extremely difficult to know what to make of them. The journey did not take place. It would be out of character for Toussaint to cross the Atlantic and not visit Paris—he had so many reasons for going to France. In letters to Toussaint from all his adult friends, there is no reference to any London trip. Could it have been a ruse by Pierre and Juliette that permitted Toussaint to occasionally travel somewhere, or to meet some obligation requiring absence, without involving Euphémie in the details? That appears most likely.

In July 1825, Euphémie wrote, "Dear Uncle, I heard that you was going to London to see the Queen, but I did not believe it. I believe it would be good to you and my aunt to go in the country for a month, and I should like to go in the country, likewise."

In August of 1826, a year after she first mentions it, Euphémie is welcoming him back. "Dear Uncle, I have heard that you have arrived from London and I am pleased and hope to see you." Quite mysterious. Yet as with most parents, Pierre and Juliette do keep some things from Euphémie. For example, at some point in 1824, according to Aurore, Toussaint was very ill—she refers to "your frightful sickness, fortunately you have not felt the after effects." Euphémie never mentions it.

Euphémie has at least three attributes of a growing child: an observant eye and a critic's skill combined with a young girl's wishes and delights. On January 14, 1826, during a time when fundamentalists were forecasting the end of the world, Euphémie wrote to Toussaint, very sensibly, "Dear Uncle, I have heard that an Angel appeared to a watchman and told him that the City of Newyork was to be destroyed by an earthquake on the 19th of this month. Some people say that the Angel appeared with music, but I do not believe it all, though it has terrified some people very much and I know a lady and her husband that it has made sick."

Euphémie's skepticism was borne out a week later when she supplied her own analysis of the nonevent: "I am very glad I was not frightened at the report concerning the earthquake. I think they wanted to get people out of the city that they might have a chance to steal but God did not permit them to succeed in their wickedness." Again, her social eye and wit were brought to bear in her reaction to the events of the day. She was scandalized at the news of a man who tried to poison an entire family. "God kept them from dying. I think the man ought to be hunged. The world is coming to an end every day more and more."

She was equally scandalized—and on her moral high horse—at the sight of a "drunken man being carried to the Bridewell on a cart. What a disgrace." But then the Toussaints' friend Madame Larue sends her sugar plums in a beautiful box from Paris and she's busy writing a "thank you" note to France. Her social commentator skills are soon exercised again, however: "I do not know what this world is coming to for there was found in the street yesterday morning no less than three dead men. One supposed to have been murdered. One died in a fit, and as to the other I have not heard the cause of his death. I pray to God morning and night that such a thing may never happen to you, for then I do not know what would become of poor me."

The national festival is coming: "Dear Uncle, we have not quite a month and a half before the Fourth of July. I have heard that this is the 50th year of independence and that we will have a greater parade than usual. I hope that we will have better weather to go and see the tents than we had last year. It rained all day on the third, but luckily it was clear on the Fourth." And two weeks later she is asking, "Dear Uncle, will you be so kind as to let me have two or three young misses to spend the afternoon on the Fourth of July. I do not wish to make any ceremony at all. Oh how glad I am to see Mrs. Cruger again in Newyork and now I would like to see Caroline Sorbieu and her brother." Alas, it wasn't a spectacular Fourth. "Dear Uncle, O what a handsome uniform I saw on the Fourth of July. But as it rained they had no fireworks at the City Hall except a few rockets."

The family frequently attends the theater, and in 1826, Euphémie asks Toussaint to take her to see *Richard III*. Later she asks to see *Cinderella*, as she has read the book several times.

That same year, Euphémie hears that "the Italian opera singers have arrived and you said that when they came you would go to the theatre and I hope I shall be able to go. I have heard that they cannot speak any other language than Italian." The Italian singers later sang also in St. Patrick's Cathedral. And caused an uproar. Author Arthur Sheehan unfolds the story this way: The Garcia Singers opera troupe was brought to New York by two promoters, Dominick Lynch, Jr., and Lorenzo Da Ponte. Lynch was a relative unknown, but Da Ponte was legendary—a priest in disrepute who wrote the librettos for Mozart's *Le Nozze di Figaro* and *Don Giovanni*. As Da Ponte he had been a royal favorite in Vienna, but his life had hit a vortex and, in desperation, he had made his way to New York.

There, in a bookstore on Broadway, Da Ponte was discovered "hungry and destitute by Clement Clarke Moore, author of *The Night Before Christmas*." Moore took Da Ponte into his home and pulled together sufficient people interested in learning Italian that Da Ponte could earn a precarious living teaching it. It was Da Ponte who convinced Garcia to make the trip to Manhattan where Maria Felicita Garcia, the daughter, starred in the production. Problems arose only when the Garcia singers sang in St. Patrick's Cathedral. It was a benefit performance for the

Sisters of Charity orphanage. The St. Patrick's choir was so out-raged—no reason was given—that the members quit en masse.

Da Ponte's urging had brought much good to the Garcias, for Maria Felicita Garcia was subsequently wed in St. Peter's Church and as Madame Malibran became a famed New York singer and actress. Monsieur Malibran was personally well known within Toussaint's New York French circle. The new Madame Malibran's ambitious intention of capturing Paris's heart as she had captured New York's brought slightly tart letters to Tous-saint from the Larues and Sorbieus.

Madame Larue notes, "I knew already, My Dear Toussaint, the news of the future marriage of M. Malibran and Mlle Gar-cia but I didn't know it was to happen so soon. I am astonished that it can take place on Maundy Thursday in the church. That's something they would not do in France. One cannot even be married in Lent without the dispensation of the arch-bishop." The Sorbieus write that "Madame Malibran might not receive the reputation in Paris she has achieved in New York for there are many fine actresses to give her competition here." (Euphémie delivers the coup de grâce in a comment that as a singer Madame Malibran is only on a par with some of her friends.)

Toussaint's French friends were Catholic—most of them would have been in St. Patrick's on the Garcia singers' day—and in many subtle ways the friends' lives added to Euphémie's so-lidity in faith and morals. "When we were at Mrs. Bancel's on Sunday we went half way through the garden. How beautiful it is and we saw that little chapel." She is absorbing her Christian-ity, too, from the services she attends, "Dear Uncle, Oh what a large funeral poor Mr. Stanton had and Mr. [Father] Power preached to show us and tell us what we are. We think we are a grate [sic] deal but we are nothing. We are made out of dirt and will return to it again. Dear Uncle, please excuse me this week for having so short a letter." (It was customary in those days to refer to Catholic priests as Mister, "Mr. Power" rather than "Father Power," the pastor of St. Peter's Church.)

One constant in Euphémie's life, as in Toussaint's, was music. She takes great pains with her advancement in piano and violin, and she sings. Her first tutor is Césarine Meetz, whose father, Raymond, obliged to flee Bonaparte's France, became Toussaint's friend. Meetz taught music to members of the French nobility, possibly even members of the French royal family. It was Meetz who, in 1822, when Euphémie was six, sold Toussaint Euphémie's first piano, a serviceable though unornamented piece that cost Toussaint $50.

The piano took some considerable punishment from Euphémie's young visitors. "Dear Uncle, Theodore has broken two cords of my piano. I wish to know if his father is going to get it repaired. Will you be so kind as to ask Miss Meetz for a piece [of music] called Tom and Jerry," she asks. Soon Euphémie is practicing "The Caliph of Baghdad," and making her way through Telemaque and a twenty-five-page overture. Musically, Euphémie is apparently confident and competent.

During one "afternoon" or "evening," when she is obviously playing for guests at the Toussaint home or the home of one of Pierre or Juliette's friends, she notes she was "frightened and trembled like a leaf and I said to myself if I was to make any mistakes in this I would be very sorry. But I had the good fortune not to make many." She is also quite astute at these musical evenings: "I was very much pleased at Mrs. Waldron's party. Miss Plate sung very beautifully with the guitar, though I think she sung rather too low. But she is very bashful indeed." After another musical party she remarked to her uncle, who apparently was present, "how well that lady sung Home Sweet Home. I wish I could sing it as well. Miss Salle was so very modest that she could not sing at all. I think her mother is very foolish not to accustom her to sing in public."

The following year, in February, Euphémie attended the

wedding of Miss Césarine Meetz to Mr. Charles Moulton with whom she will move to Paris—and from where she and her father, Raymond, will remain faithful Toussaint correspondents.

At eleven Euphémie is teaching music herself: "my little scholar improves very fast. She knows all the notes the sol and fa key both. She seems to wish to play pieces soon but I cannot let her until she plays the solfage well and perfect." Her scholar surfaces again in a later letter. Euphémie is either making a tart remark about the scholar (Mary) and Mary's mother, or she is laughing, as Juliette and Pierre so often did, at people's foibles. "Dear Uncle, I understand from my scholar Mary that she will get her piano next week. She says her mother has been to look at it and it is very large and beautiful. It has been a long time coming! I should laugh if with all their show they want to make [about it], their piano would not be a good one. That would be no more than they deserve. I suppose that is the reason they did not want our piano, because it is not ornamented enough." Euphémie has a new one, for the Meetzes are returning to Paris.

In 1826, Raymond Meetz had invited Euphémie to visit his home where, she writes, "I saw a most beautiful piano at Mr. Meetz. He plaid [played] on it when we were there. It had a drum and a tambourine. One minute it went so loud you might hear it from the corner of the street, the next minute so low you could hardly hear it in the room." Later, when the Meetzes return to France following Cesarine's wedding, Euphémie inherits the piano.

Euphémie thanks her uncle for buying it and promises to learn "very fast and well that I may give you the same satisfaction for having spent your money on it." (That same year marks the brief return of another musician into their lives, Gabriel Nicolas. The journey may have been subsidized by Toussaint. This is, as far as is known, his final meeting with Toussaint, though they continued to correspond.)

The Meetzes as a family illustrate the enlightened racial attitudes of the French compared to the continued bigotry general in the United States (though not among the Toussaints' white American friends). Euphémie wrote this letter to Toussaint following Césarine's wedding: "O how sorry I was you [were] not there to see Miss Meetz married. She looked so sweet and beautiful like an angel but what I think was so good was she should come and kiss my aunt and me before all the company. I believe nobody would do it but her." What a magnificent statement by Césarine. The point would not have been lost among the many Americans present at what was otherwise a high-society French wedding.

Soon Euphémie is "learning a most beautiful variation with [her new instructor] Mr. Gentil and he says next week he will accompany me with the flute. We are sorry to lose that amiable Mrs. Moulton [Césarine]. O how sorry I am." A few weeks later, Euphémie has organized a musical gathering for a group of the Toussaints' friends. The young girl basks in Toussaint's compliments and adds, "I am pleased that Mrs. Moulton says the same because she does not flatter like a great many other ladies. I think she is more than a lady." In May, Euphémie writes, "We are losing the amiable Mrs. Moulton, although I know she will return soon." By May 27, "we are certainly going to lose Mrs. Moulton for good. Her poor mother is in great trouble to think she is going. Dear Uncle, I understand you [were] quite pleased with my writing. I hope that you will always say the same thing."

She learns that the Toussaint family friends, the Sorbieus in Paris, have been struck with a great tragedy, "that poor Mrs. Sorbieu is dead. O how sorry I am for her children." The mood immediately shifts as she adds, "I want to tell you these few words in secret, that what I will give my aunt on her birthday I'm afraid will be very little." In a later letter she wants a sampler to embroider for her aunt. Euphémie tells him about her dreams ("Dear Uncle, do tell what makes people dream so often"), her progress in reading, "both French and English." Before long, Euphémie learns that now "poor Mr. Sorbieu is very ill. I should be very sorry for his son and daughter if they were to lose him. And, Dear Uncle, I have not heard you speak of Mrs. Larue in a great while. I should like to know how she is." (Sorbieu had a stroke. His children continued to write to Toussaint on his behalf.)

"Dear Uncle, O how pleased I am that you have received a letter from Mrs. Moulton. What a queer thing she is to put that elegant picture in the middle of her letter." A year later, when Césarine plans a return visit to New York, Euphémie zeroes in on the veneration accorded godparents in their culture at that time. "Dear Uncle, Mrs. Morange is quite vexed to think Mrs. Moulton should write to tell all her friends [that she is returning] and not to her which is her God-mother. It is not treating a God-mother well by any means."

The Toussaint family's musical life continues to include outings: "Dear Uncle, Thank you for taking me to the opera. I was very much pleased particularly with the music and the singing. There [were] a great many French ladies there and Mrs. Binsse was there with all her scholars. Dear Uncle, will you please get me a lead pencil as I am very much in want of one to draw patterns." A couple of weeks later they went to the musical theater: "Dear Uncle, the music was beautiful. Mrs. Alexander is my favorite. I think she is a beautiful actress, so light and easy. In fact I think she is everybody's favorite really. Dear Uncle I believe there is a vessel arrived from France. I would like to write to Mrs. Larue." (As a ship from France would take several days to unload, load, and turn around, Euphémie is letting Toussaint know he'll have to get her letters to France down to the *paquebot*.)

As a thirteen-year-old, her theatrical tastes had matured. It is at this point Toussaint takes her to see *Richard III*. The more grown-up Euphémie shows through in both her sentiments and her writing style. "Dear Uncle, do you know if there is a six o'clock Mass on Sunday. If there is I should be very much pleased to go if you would let me." "Dear Uncle. So poor Mr. Malau is dead [she had seen him during a visit earlier to the Bancels' home]. I believe he has suffered a great deal so it is better that he should be in the other world than this for he will not suffer there. He will be with God and have eternal happiness."

The domestic tragedies in the Toussaints' closely knit French circle continued. "O what a great loss we have met in losing Mr. Bancel for he was a very good man. [Bancel had drowned in Maine.] He was good to every body. The Bishop [New York's French-born John Du Bois] preached a great deal about his death. It is a great pity that the Bishop cannot speak English better for he made a beautiful sermon. I pity poor Mrs. Bancel for she has nobody to support her now." (This is the point at which Mrs. Bancel [Victoire-Elisabeth] took over the de Neuvilles' school.)

Euphémie doesn't forget. Six months later she is writing to Toussaint, "Dear Uncle, can you tell me if you please how Mrs. Bancel is for I have not heard anything from her in a great while." She also lets him know that his clock "strikes wrong but I think it is no use to have it fixed for it will never strike well." As the end of the year approaches, her letters include a long one for Toussaint to forward to Césarine, and she hopes, too, to soon see Toussaint's close friend, Catherine Cruger and her daughter.

Time and again Euphémie is a mirror on the family's religious sensibilities. "I am very thankful that you say how much pleased you are with my letter the week before last. I know if I ask God in my prayer he will make me good." She now is only two years from death when she writes, "he will recompense us by having us with him. We may not live long but our names will be written in Heaven."

Her maturing voice, her sense of self, and the knowledge of Pierre and Juliette Toussaint's love for her are ever more evident in letters such as this: "Dear Uncle, give me leave to tell you as well as my pen will permit me, or rather as well as my in-experience is capable of directing it, how truly sensible I am of all your favors. My prayers morning and night are offered up to Heaven for your preservation. Nor are you ever in the day ab-sent from my thoughts."

Early in the New Year of 1829, Juliette "mentioned her fears" to her husband that fourteen-year-old Euphémie was "threatened with consumptive [tubercular] complaints. He could not believe it, he could not listen to it. But alas! It soon be-came too evident." Biographer Hannah Lee, drawing from her sister Mary Anna's recollections, and possibly Toussaint's, too, continues that once he was convinced, "then there was no rest for Toussaint night or day."

In his anxiety, Toussaint the unflappable, the capable, the great consoler, started to fall apart. "He required the unremit-ting consolations of his friends to soothe and calm his mind. He hung over the darling of his affections with an intensity of feel-ing that threatened his own life. The good Father Powers de-voted himself to uncle and niece." Euphémie was not told of her condition.

He is far from alone in grief. The ailing Jean Sorbieu writes to Toussaint to report the death of his son, Eugene, from "cere-bral fever. Adieu my dear Toussaint, pray to God for me, for us all."

As Toussaint had nursed countless others, not least the sec-ond Madame Bérard, he now sat on Euphémie's bed, "handing her articles beyond her reach" and amusing her. Friends filled her rooms with gifts and treats, but Euphémie had little ap-petite. She'd say, " 'I make uncle eat all these up, but I keep the flowers to look at.' It was her delight to rest in her uncle's arms, to tell him how much she loved him, and what she would do for him when she got well."

Toussaint must have prayed almost constantly. Of his friends' kindnesses and concerns he would say, "I thank God for all his goodness." As Euphémie "wasted away, without any painful struggles, he said one day, 'God is good; *we* know that here on earth, but my Euphémie will know it first *there*.' " He pointed upwards.

Then she was dead.

She died on May 11, 1829. With her death, letters poured in from France and elsewhere. From the Lagnels and Larues, from the Baillys and de Boesteinds. From the American South. Toussaint heard from Gabriel Nicolas, "no one knows better than I how much you were attached to her. However, as you say very truly, we must resign ourselves to the will of God. I am sorry that Juliette has been ill and hope that your next letter will speak of her re-established health." (The impoverished Gabriel Nicolas is more than a little embarrassed at having to add, "not that I do not think of you, or that I love you less, but I was troubled because I was not able to send you anything.")

These letters help today not only in displaying the writers' compassion and love for Toussaint in his loss, but they fix Toussaint in the New York social firmament.

Catherine Cruger wrote, "my tears have flowed with yours; but I could not weep for *her*, I wept for *you*. When we resign to the Eternal Father a child as pure as the heavens to which she returns we ought not to weep." Cruger then clearly reveals the stratum of society within which Toussaint was an extremely well respected member: "Her short life has been full of happiness . . . raised in the wealthiest and most elevated classes, the most gentle virtues and affections have surrounded her from her cradle . . . if death had struck you instead of her," says the practical Catherine, "to what dangers might she have been exposed? May the consciousness of the duty you have so faithfully discharged mitigate this bitter sorrow."

Mary Anna Schuyler wrote in similar terms, and added, "the remembrance of your beloved Euphémia presses upon my heart."

(The onslaught of sadness, however, was not done. Early the next year, twenty-two-year-old William Schuyler, the young man Toussaint loved as a son, died. Now it was his turn to console Mary Anna. Juliette, Pierre, and Mary Anna, like Jean Sorbieu, were swallowed up in their sorrows.)

For a long while Toussaint could only say to those who came to comfort him, " 'My poor Euphémie is gone,' and as his lips uttered these words, he covered his face with his hands. He grew thin, avoided society, and refused to be comforted. But his mind was too pious and rational to indulge long in this excess of sorrow. He listened to high and holy consolations, and found resignation in the prayers of his church. Those who witnessed his struggles to command himself at this time and perform his daily duties have spoken of him with reverence."

Toussaint was too solid in his beliefs and compassion to remain mired forever in his woe. His "deep affliction" drove him harder than ever to "benefit others. When funds were wanting—and he had insufficient—he would use his influence in promoting fairs and, in individual cases, raffles; disposing of elegant and superfluous articles at a just price when their owners were reduced to poverty. His ingenuity in contriving means of assistance to others was remarkable." He had always been a one-man employment agency, finding people for jobs, and jobs for people. This flair apparently flourished further.

In some of Euphémie's final "Dear Uncle" letters, knowing as we do that she is nearing death, we are touched by the great poignancy of her remarks. In almost the last letter preserved, Euphémie writes, "How pleased I feel to think New Year is so near although I do not know who will live to see it." She did, and returned to an earlier theme. "Dear Uncle, I am very thankful you [were] so much pleased with my letter the week before last. I know if I ask God in my prayers he is too good to his children to refuse what we ask. He made us to serve him respectfully and will recompense us in Heaven. We may not live long but our names will last."

The pious, friendly, sometimes studious young Euphémie shines through nearly two centuries to leave an image of a slightly earnest yet normal and fun-filled girl. The image brings a smile to the face. It is the lingering image, from almost two centuries ago, of a kind and curious and perceptive God-loving teenager. In Euphémie one sees reflected Pierre and Juliette's merits.

She wrote: "We may not live long but our names will last."

Euphémie, this young, nineteenth-century African-American girl, spoke presciently. She could not know that almost two hundred years after she penned those words, her name would be part of the received history of the Catholic Church in the United States.

FIFTEEN

HOSTILE CITY, RACIST CHURCH

THE FIRST DECADE OF THE 1800s opened with 5,867 blacks in Manhattan, about 10 percent of the population. Almost half the blacks (43 percent) were slaves. The decade would close with 9,000 blacks in New York City, only 16.2 percent of them slaves. Even so, despite the drop in percentages, as one historian noted, "the idea of [New York] being a benevolent slave society was a chimera, a self-deceiving myth propagated by New Yorkers in a vain attempt to distinguish themselves from the evil they perceived to exist in the South."

And in that city, as Shane White wrote covering the 1770–1810 period, " 'French Negroes' [Saint Domingans] maintained a high profile. They came from a society where violent resistance to slavery was almost a commonplace." There is no evidence of violent public or private resistance from Toussaint, and this is one curtain it would be useful to sweep aside—the one drawn between Toussaint's white world and the regular conversations he had with his black friends. The curtain does flutter slightly open momentarily, in one or two letters. Other than that Toussaint's silence is almost total.

As a slave and a free man, Toussaint survived and then flourished in a servant role in a racist society. To some extent, he survived on society's terms, as all Americans must whatever one's race, class, job, or role. Yet the record suggests he operated to a greater extent on his own terms than his white friends may have recognized. This independence of spirit is reflected in the letters from Toussaint's black correspondents.

There are empty passages in the conversation that surrounds Toussaint's life. That's not surprising. Even with a more complete written record, however, some conversations are never recorded—those of the bigots and racists for whom Toussaint would have been a topic. Racism is both a public and a silent language. Silent racism is the fleeting glance, an almost imperceptible nod, a barely detectable attitude, a certain body language—the message is semaphored and received.

Toussaint would have understood this in a manner his 1854 biographer could not.

What is true for the bigot is true for the victim, the object of racism, bigotry, or class ridicule. Group victims also have a silent language, their own telegraph systems, their own codes. This code includes a highly refined code of conduct when obliged to be in the presence of the bigot one cannot challenge. One is not privy to Toussaint's exchanges in this silent language but some of the violent events in the streets of New York and incidents in his own life provide clues to it.

Was Toussaint a member of a black or black Catholic cognoscenti that watched out for one another, quietly but concertedly? Quite likely. One glimpses that when Juliette's friend Fanny Montpensier writes to Toussaint from Baltimore about that city's increasing hostilities toward blacks. There was something deeper in his discussions of black and race issues than his white world knew about. Alerted by a lifetime of dangers, there were constant messages, warnings, and alerts whispered around the black grapevine. Even from their earliest days in New York, slaves of the Bérard household knew the risks.

In 1801, Toussaint was barely out of his apprenticeship when his fellow black and mulatto San Domingans protested as Madame Jeanne Mathusine Droibillan Volunbrun attempted to illegally ship twenty slaves to southern states. Accounts report that "a group of 'French negroes' gathered outside her Eagle Street house," a crowd that swelled to hundreds and became "the city's first full-blown black riot." Was the "hotheaded" twenty-two-year-old Toussaint one of that crowd of "French Negroes"? One certainly would like to think so, but it seems unlikely—he was probably at work. Was he with them in spirit? One hopes so, but there is no proof. If he was with them in spirit it was a conviction he would likely have withheld from his white friends or biographer.

Even two decades later, freemen like Toussaint were still at risk from kidnapping and "blackbirders," bounty hunters returning runaway southern slaves to their owners. In the 1820s, only quick-witted action—again due to word likely spread rapidly on the black grapevine—saved from slavery three free black men who had gotten drunk in a tavern and were hastily taken aboard a ship for the South. Such luck did not follow Thomas Jones, a free black employed by a lawyer. In 1828, blackbirders seized Jones and falsely testified in court that the freeman was a runaway. The judge accepted their testimony. Jones was quickly sold into slavery and despite newspaper stories reporting the harrowing events he could not be traced to be rescued.

Except in old age, Toussaint—fit, handsome, and educated—would have fetched a fine price anywhere.

This was a racism different in degree from the twenty-first-century black-white divide. Racism in the United States today is socially and politically (and legally) unacceptable, yet it remains endemic. Today's periodic headlines of black men chained to trucks and dragged to their deaths, of indiscriminate and vicious violence, remain a tragic part of a continuing, barely subterranean bigotry. Think of it in these terms: *The Philadelphia Encyclopedia,* published in 1797, the year Toussaint arrived in the United States, contained a definition of "Negro" that was a scurrilous list of accusations and stereotyping with no moderating language in between. That scurrilous list would not be aired in public today, but there's no doubt such ideas still exist in some sections of society.

But even in Toussaint's time, there were nuances to the dreadful reality. A young black friend writing to Toussaint from the Caribbean could provide this contrast: "They are surprised in the Colonies at the enthusiasm with which I speak of the United States, because in general the men of our race here suppose that all people of color are treated like cattle there." Had Toussaint's correspondent gone to the farms of rural New York and New Jersey, or the plantations of the American South, he would have been giving fellow blacks in the colonies a very different account.

The black community in New York had a tradition of trying to make itself heard. When the British invaded the United States during the War of 1812, some African Americans took out a *New York Evening Post* advertisement and urged blacks to head to Brooklyn Heights to build fortifications. "Under New York's liberal laws we dwell in safety and pursue our honest callings," the advertisement stated, "none daring to molest us whatever his complexion and circumstances."

Such a statement, historian Shane White notes, was written more from hope than from accuracy—part of the blacks' bid to convince white New Yorkers of their worth. Even so, White acknowledges that New York blacks were never simply swept along by white wishes or whims, or the "currents of repression and discrimination" that whites stirred up. "This activism should not surprise," adds White, for New York blacks had "established an opposition to slavery few if any states could equal." There is no evidence that it was an activism to which Toussaint subscribed. In his maturity he acted on an individual basis, never with the group. An example of that was the help he gave his friend Louis Benoît as Benoît "escaped" to Canada.

❖ ❖ ❖

Benoît reveals the tenor of the times. He was married to a white woman, and because of constant harassment had to flee to Canada. Benoît, a fellow San Domingan, wrote from Montreal of the pleasure he took, in Canada, of being able to promenade with his wife and children without "a party of American scum [*"la crapulle ameriquin"*] walking around me and calling, 'look at the n——— with a white woman' " (*"un dem niger avec une femme blanche"*). With his little family, wrote Benoît, he could take his pleasure in the public gardens, the circus, or the theater without being relegated to a place for Negroes only "as in the grand world of New York."

The Benoît letter says of Toussaint only that Pierre is a good friend. The incident of Benoît resettling in Montreal says much about what Toussaint lived through, though little about Pierre's response, except that he helped where he could. In Benoît's case, Toussaint apparently helped him fiddle some items through Canadian customs by understating their value.

Some blacks saw Toussaint as a person always willing to help; others as a friend delightful to be with. *Vos compatriotes les Gens de Couleur Français* [Your compatriots the French Free People of Color] wrote to Toussaint. "Knowing your good heart and humanity," the black and mulatto committee members of the Brothers United mutual insurance project stated, "we have taken the liberty of addressing you on a matter of religious and moral obligation.

"The Holy Scriptures demand, and God said to give aid to those who need aiding. Your compatriots, the French Free People of Color, see their unhappy position in this country as one without prospects. Necessity obliges them to form a mutual benefit society as security against illness and death." They sought divine guidance from God and permission from Toussaint to enroll him as "an honorary member." Whether this was a tribute or a device that would enable them to use Toussaint's name in attesting to the worth of the society is not known. What is certain is that Toussaint held on to their appeal until he died. Similarly, he kept in his box of correspondence the invitation extended to him and his family to attend the "annual exhibition of Colored Pupils School No. 2."

With black friends as with white friends, it is Toussaint the man of faith who stands out most clearly. As a black friend in Port-au-Prince wrote in a letter already quoted earlier in part, "nothing can touch my heart more than to receive your benedictions—the benedictions of a religious man. I have known many men and observed them closely. But I have never seen one that deserved as you do the name of a religious man. I have always followed your counsels, but now more than ever, for there are few like you."

❖   ❖   ❖

By 1820, a New York City–based Colonization Society, a back-to-Africa movement, was created at a time when black New Yorkers in general were faced with antipathy and declining job opportunities. Black Catholics like Toussaint had members of their extended postexodus San Domingue family in Cuba, Martinique, and elsewhere in the French, English, or Dutch West Indies. They had less personal identification with Africa than with the Antilles.

On New York's streets the growing antagonism toward the blacks came from the burgeoning population of job-seeking Irish-Catholics, who saw the blacks as a threat to their own employment in the menial trades. And it was this same looming Irish-Catholic presence that, on the other sweep of its pendulum, generated public anti-Catholicism.

The early 1800s were not hospitable to Catholics, and as the century developed the bigotry grew worse. By 1815 there was a Protestant revival so strong it closed New York's theaters—bad news for French refugee musicians like Gabriel Nicolas, the mainstays of the New York orchestra pits. In the eyes of these same revivalists, writes historian Christine Stansell, "a Catholic was not a Christian but a superstitious heathen, and no accommodation with this priest-ridden lot—short of conversion—was possible." She adds that the theater-banning New York City Tract Society, which "represented the rising commercial and industrial bourgeoisie, was an impulse toward self-definition, a need to avow one's own class aspirations." Their evangelicalism gave coherence to an as yet ill-defined group in the city—middling and newly wealthy people.

American society was anti-Catholic and anti-black, and the U.S. Catholic Church was antiblack and pro-slavery. Toussaint had little reason to feel welcome on those accounts. Further, there was no Catholic accommodation with black Catholic slaves except in the most patronizing terms—to see them married in order to save their souls. Slavery itself was endorsed by Catholic bishops. Black people might have the same souls as whites, but not the same rights. Historian Cyprian Davis indicates this and much else in his remark that "slavery marked the American Catholic Church in a way no other American institution would."

Amazing then, the extent to which the Catholic African

Caribbeans and Catholic African Americans, slave and free, cut through the bigotry in their church and still found freedom in the faith itself. Yet they did. For Toussaint and his black friends their deeply held belief and Catholic practice was a constant. As Madame Bérard wrote to Marie Bouquement, who could not find her daughter, "Ah dear Memin, your religion will support you under all your Sufferings—never abandon it!" And none of them did. And though the words were addressed to Marie, the phrase "your religion will support you" was the one Toussaint lived by. How Toussaint's white and black friends regarded him as a Catholic was consistent and admiration-filled. His reputation was solid. In France, because of what she heard from his friends there, his godmother, Aurore Bérard, could write, "the assurance that everyone expresses of your religious character gives me great pleasure."

In the wider world, Toussaint would have known through St. Peter's Church that in 1807 Pope Pius VII canonized Benedict the Moor. Benedict (1526–1589), a slave in Messina, Italy, was the first of three sixteenth-century-born men associated with blacks and/or slavery who were canonized. His canonization, writes Davis, casts light on the sociopolitical element in saint-making. It was "not only for [Benedict's] sanctity, but because his canonization was a statement regarding the evils of the slave trade." Benedict is the patron saint of African Americans.

Leo XIII's canonization in 1888 of St. Peter Claver (1580–1654) and John XXIII's canonization of St. Martin de Porres (1579–1639) almost eighty years later served similar dual purposes. St. Peter Claver, Spanish-born son of a farmer, and a Jesuit, labored his adult life in Cartagena, Colombia, South America's major slave trade center. He became patron of the mission to blacks at the moment in the late nineteenth century when some religious orders were beginning to turn particular attention to that work. St. Martin de Porres was born in Lima, Peru, son of a Spanish noble and a free woman of color. His canonization coincided with the rise of the civil rights movement in the United States and the burgeoning independence movements in Africa after a century of colonial rule. (Well ahead of Toussaint, if he is canonized, St. Martin de Porres was named the patron saint of hairdressers.) The dual religiopolitical element historian Davis notes in these three canonizations can be seen at work also in the motives of the succession of New York cardinals who honored Toussaint or pressed for his canonization.

In fairness to Toussaint, it might be said that not all the subsequent decisions taken since All Saints' Day 1990 resonate with what is best known about him. On that day, his disintegrating casket was eased from the earth of the nineteenth-century cathedral churchyard on New York's Mulberry Street. The cemetery had originally served Old St. Peter's Church.

For more than a century, Toussaint's decaying body had lain with the remains of his wife, Juliette, and adopted daughter, Euphémie, under earth and grass that was home to scores of graves shaded by aged trees. All this was behind an old redbrick wall of the city's oldest Catholic burial ground. The ground, on that brisk November day, revealed three caskets in the one space. The Toussaints, close together in life, were close together in death. Later, in clinical surroundings, under the watchful gaze of pathologists and priests, Toussaint's skeleton was removed and examined to confirm that this was, indeed, Pierre Toussaint.

Amazingly, given Toussaint's sense that his family was his most precious possession after his faith, after the exhumation the extraordinary decision was made not to reinter him with Juliette and Euphémie.

The little Toussaint family that always worshiped together at Old St. Peter's Church on Barclay Street was split apart. Rather than create a Toussaint family burial shrine at Old Saint Peter's (where Toussaint was a daily communicant for fifty-six years), Toussaint is now a holy spectacle in midtown. His wife and daughter, essentially forgotten and in earthly separation from him, languish downtown.

Sacrificed to church politics and grandiosity, Toussaint, the model husband and father, was placed in a crypt under the altar of St. Patrick's Cathedral, a lone and lonely layman. The household kneeler at which Pierre and Juliette prayed was placed behind the cathedral altar.

The further irony is that Toussaint's unhappiest experience as a black Catholic occurred in New York's Catholic cathedral.

Pierre Toussaint was well aware that the Catholic Church that had nurtured him as a soul in most places would eject him as a black. On one infamous occasion it did. The incident occurred in August 1842, apparently at a gathering of some importance. In the style of the times, it could have been a concert rather than a liturgical ritual. There were several "masters of ceremony" controlling access and other arrangements. When Pierre and Juliette Toussaint, likely accompanied by Old Cabresse, entered Old St. Patrick's and headed for their seats, they were summarily thrown out.

Louis Binsse, a former white planter from Saint Domingue and Toussaint's friend of many decades, was president of St. Patrick's board of trustees. He wrote a profuse apology on behalf of fellow trustees: "It would be difficult for me to express to you the grief which has been caused me by the insult you have received in the Lord's house. It has given me all the more pain because, wishing to have order in the church, it was I who begged this gentleman to be one of the masters of ceremony. This young man is truly very repentant. . . ."

Toussaint, however, would not have been misled. He knew he was being apologized to because he was Binsse's friend, a man welcomed in high society. The apology had not come to any black man who, somehow inadvertently, with his wife and a friend had been removed from the church. There was no apology from the cathedral rector or New York's bishop. Whatever the sixty-two-year-old Toussaint felt, he kept it to himself in white company, as well as from history's knowledge.

What Toussaint faced in 1842 was unchanged from half a century earlier. In 1790 (when Toussaint, still in Saint Domingue, was eight), Father John Carroll, superior over all the priests working in the United States, traveled to England to be consecrated the Republic of the United States' first Catholic bishop. He became Bishop of Baltimore in the chapel of Lulworth Castle, Dorset, on August 15, 1790. Carroll, uneasy over slaveholding, nonetheless had a slave himself.

Historian Davis reports that Carroll pretended the slave was his sister's property. And for all his sincere work on behalf of slaves—he petitioned Rome to allow the mass to be said in English, so the poor and the slaves could follow it and be drawn deeper into the faith—Carroll wasn't above selling off slaves owned by the former Jesuits to raise money when it was needed. Those Maryland slaves were Catholic slaves, and they represented twenty percent of Maryland's fifteen thousand Catholics. Despite a pious concern for the slaves' souls, in many Catholic eyes—as in the eyes of most other Americans—the slave remained primarily an economic commodity.

This existing black Catholic population in Maryland was augmented on July 10, 1793, when the fourteen vessels fleeing "the Firing of Le Cap" rounded Fells Point, Maryland, and made safe harbor. One ship, according to the Maryland *Gazette* of July 11, 1793, "was a Guineaman, with negroes." "Guineaman" was current usage for a slave ship. As none of the slaves fleeing Saint Domingue were likely to be sold by their owners, who had brought them as personal servants, the writer somewhat overstated the case and likely used "Guineaman" more to indicate that this ship had many blacks whereas the others mainly carried whites. Davis notes that this little armada carried "the nucleus of the black worshipping community that was established in the chapelle basse [lower chapel] of St. Mary's Seminary on Paca Street [Baltimore]."

One intriguing characteristic of the arriving refugees—black and white Catholics—is that they shared a lack of documentation. Like Toussaint, when it came to presenting their bona fides as Catholics to the Catholic institution, those who fled the colony had to be taken at their word, and at the word of their relatives and friends, that they were indeed Catholics. But their word was good enough, for there certainly was no social advantage to declaring oneself Catholic in the United States of the 1790s. (The Catholic priesthood was increasingly refugee, too, but from France, mainly French Sulpicians forced out by the Revolution.)

The white Catholic community in this new United States was eager to be identified as American and republican. Bishop Carroll was chief among them. He had a close friendship with Benjamin Franklin and during the Revolutionary War had somewhat unwillingly accompanied Franklin to Canada. The idea was that the young priest might help persuade the Catholic French Canadians to aid the Revolution. Historian Davis relates that the trip certainly gave those fighting for the Revolution a most favorable impression of the colonial Catholics, an impression bolstered by the Catholic French troops under Lafayette and other French volunteers. Bishop Carroll and President George Washington knew each other; they shared the platform at Washington College, Chestertown, Maryland, in 1785, when each received honorary degrees.

That early cordiality does not disguise the later bigger problem, overt anti-Catholicism. At this moment Elizabeth Ann Seton reappears briefly in the Toussaint narrative, for her journey into Catholicism offers insights into the ever-present social-circle anti-Catholicism—as distinct from the mob anti-Catholicism that caused Euphémie to ask, "Uncle, why do they hate the church so?"

Seton entered St. Peter's Church for the first time on Ash Wednesday, February 27, 1805. She dropped to her knees and exclaimed, "Ah! My God, here let me rest." Seton deserved some rest, but with five children she would get none at home. More than that, she was destitute. She was received into the Church two weeks later, vouched for by her husband's Catholic friend Filicchi. (Was Toussaint present in the congregation? Was Toussaint in St. Peter's Church when, on the Feast of the Annunciation, 1805, Seton made her first communion? She wrote to Filicchi, "At last, God is mine, and I am His. Now let all earthly things go as they will.")

More germane, Seton's correspondence mentions the socially cutting and deeply antipathetic anti-Catholicism of the day, as exemplified by the attitudes of her late husband's family. The interesting contrast is that Toussaint's closest upper-class Protestant friends were not anti-Catholic; just the opposite, they were extremely supportive of his faith and the endeavors allied to it. When he raised money for the Catholic orphanage that Mother Seton had sent her sisters to New York City to open, much of it came from his white Protestant friends. There is strong evidence of their respect for the thoroughness and sincerity of his beliefs. And he was quite outspoken about those beliefs—again, with a suggestion that in his own way he evangelized.

Writes Hannah Lee: "His illustrations were often striking. In speaking to a Protestant friend of the worship of the Virgin, he said, turning to the portrait of a near relation of hers in the room, 'You like to look at this; it makes you think of her, love her more; try to do what she likes you to do.' In this interesting manner he described his own feelings toward the pictures and images of the Virgin Mary."

How unassailable Toussaint seems in such moments. It was a reflection of the same certainty that, before the decade was out, enabled the equally enduring Mother Seton to found in 1809 the first order of U.S. women religious, the Sisters of

Charity, in Emmittsburg, Maryland. (Though in time, that community, too, had slaves to work their land.)

Obviously, the white Catholic conscience was a long way from finding clarity in the matter of slavery. In 1790, Carmelites from Flanders came to the United States to open the first convent (*carmel*) in Port Tobacco, Maryland. Young Maryland women who entered the order brought slaves as part of their dowry. In the second decade of the 1800s, new orders of American women religious, courageously springing up from American soil, similarly were slaveholders. (Two centuries later, many have formally apologized and sought the forgiveness of the surrounding African-American community.)

Religious congregations of men were also slaveholders. When Louis William Dubourg of St. Louis was named the bishop of New Orleans, he donated some of his slaves to male religious. Some Catholic communities sold off their slaves to Catholic slaveholders relatively early; others held on to them until the start of the Civil War. In Maryland, the Jesuits from the earliest days had relied extensively on slaves to work their estates. During the period the Jesuits were suppressed (1773–1814), the slaves continued to work the land under the authority of Father, later Bishop, Carroll. With the restoration of the Jesuits in 1814 by Pius VII, there occurred a haunting chapter in U.S. Jesuit history.

By 1819, with the Maryland Jesuits in financial difficulties, there was strong sentiment to free the slaves. A major problem was that the Baltimore archdiocese was claiming it now owned the former Jesuit property—land *and* slaves—in Maryland. The older Maryland Jesuits, no matter what the cost, wanted the society to assume responsibility for the slaves now too old to work while younger slaves worked the estates. The younger Jesuits argued the society should abandon agriculture altogether and sell the slaves. Some were sold in 1835, and in 1836 the decision was made to sell off the rest.

There was an understanding among Catholic slaveholders that slave families should never be separated, and that slaves should be sold only to other Catholic slaveholders to ensure the slaves could continue in their faith. The Maryland Jesuits did neither. They sold their slaves to Louisiana plantation owners— a terrible fate.

When the new slaveholders' agents came to collect their new property, a few Jesuits took to the woods alongside slaves who fled to avoid being shipped south. As historian Cyprian Davis notes, the transaction was a scandal to southern Maryland Catholics, and it "spelled the end of Catholic practice by Catholic slaves."

Throughout the antebellum period, the attitude of the American Catholic Church toward Catholic slaves, as expressed by such bishops as New Orleans's Dubourg or Baltimore's Arch-bishop Kenrick, was more preoccupied with getting the slaves married or finding ways to "make them fully Christian" than with ending the dreadful institution itself. Some American Catholic bishops actually defended slavery.

It was so controverted a topic that in 1839, when Pope Gregory XVI condemned the slave trade (though not slavery itself except, perhaps, by inference), President Andrew Jackson's secretary of state, a southerner named John Forsyth, publicly criticized the pope.

The earliest Catholic response to the needs of black Catholics came from the black people themselves, encouraged by rare priests, the Oblate Sisters of Providence in Baltimore and the Congregation of the Holy Family in New Orleans. Toussaint was long dead before any elements of the white Catholic institution energetically supported action to focus on the needs of African-American Catholics. Toussaint nonetheless lived through the period when the black Catholic foundation was laid—a foundation, in the case of the Oblate Sisters, dear to the heart of his wife, Juliette—and he financially supported it.

As the United States moved into the 1820s and 1830s, white Catholics, like the general white population, were becoming more anti-black. When, in 1835, Charleston's Bishop John England opened a school for the children of free black families, the whites raised such opposition that he had to close it.

A black Catholic could not be ordained a priest, though one wriggled through the net. Charleston's Bishop England, in Haiti, ordained Toussaint's friend George I. Paddington. Paddington is unusual to the point of uniqueness: a black man born, raised, and educated in Ireland, headed for the priesthood. He becomes somewhat less unusual when one realizes that Ireland at this juncture was closely tied to England, which had a population of at least fifteen thousand Africans, more than a third of them free. (How did the slaves get to England? Like the French, the English were Caribbean planters, and they brought their slaves and black servants with them when they returned to the home country. In the mid-eighteenth century, the famed Pennsylvania agent Benjamin Franklin was in England with two of his slaves, Peter and Tom. When Tom ran away, Franklin didn't pursue him but let him go free.)

Paddington apparently entered the Toussaints' world sometime in the early 1830s. He had received preliminary seminary training in Ireland and had been advised to try for ordination in Haiti—no one in Europe or the United States would be eager in those years to ordain a black priest for domestic duties (the first U.S. black priests were not ordained until long after Toussaint's 1853 death). The priest-to-be undoubtedly stayed with Toussaint, who, well known to the handful of U.S. bishops as a prominent black Catholic, may have assisted with the cost of Paddington's final seminary education. From New York, Paddington sailed to Haiti. In subsequent letters, it's apparent that Paddington expects Pierre's support, and is somewhat truculent when it isn't immediately forthcoming.

Once settled in Port-au-Prince, Paddington became close to

Pierre and Juliette's Haitian friends Diego (sometimes "John") Moya and his wife, Madame T. Moya. The Moyas maintained a strong friendship, too, with Jean Sorbieu in France. In Haiti, Paddington probably also knew Toussaint's cousin Auguste, who had returned to the former colony in the 1820s and gone into business.

The black priest Paddington could neither speak nor write French until he settled in Haiti, from where, in 1836, he wrote to Pierre, in English, that it would have given him "great pleasure to see you again in New York," but Bishop John England of Charleston did not wish him to leave the country to finish his studies in Rome or France. After Paddington was ordained a subdeacon he was made "professor in the new college of La Coupe, eight miles from the city. I remain here probably for the rest of my life. The country and the people are I think the finest and kindest I have ever met."

Bishop England returned several months later to Haiti to ordain Paddington to the priesthood, but Father Paddington did not remain in the country as long as he anticipated. The following year he wrote to Toussaint, "I am by no means satisfied with the state of the church here." He was "anxiously waiting Dr. [Bishop] England's actions" on Paddington's behalf. Four years later Paddington quit Haiti for Rome.

In later letters, when he was living at the Irish College in Rome, Paddington writes that he has been welcomed by the Cardinal of Propaganda Fide, but has declined to be sent to either of two mission countries because he wanted to complete his studies. Nonetheless, he was given permission to celebrate mass in all of Rome's four hundred churches. Plus, he asked Toussaint—it's a recurring theme—that as he no longer has a parish, could Toussaint make him a regular allowance, a *bourse*.

Back in the United States, with anti-Catholicism rampant, America's black Catholics, like their confreres in Haiti, were generally required to shift for themselves. In some key cities,

African-American Catholics might find a sympathetic priest. Pittsburgh, for example, by the 1840s had three thousand black Catholics with their own Chapel of the Nativity under the care of diocesan priest Father Robert Wilson. In Washington, D.C., with a sizable population of black Catholics, Maria Becroft, daughter of a slave, at twenty-two opened a Catholic girls' school for free blacks under the auspices of the enlightened pastor of Holy Trinity Church. Baltimore, now with black nuns, also had a flourishing, dues-paying, black Catholic lay organization, the Society of Colored People, and its documents are historical treasure.

But New York was deadlocked. After a popular French bishop preached at St. Peter's and asked the French population in attendance why they had no French church, the city's French Catholic population pressed for a French-speaking parish. It was built as St. Vincent de Paul's on Canal Street. In 1841, Toussaint gave the first $100 toward its construction. Yet when the new St. Vincent's wanted to open a parish school for black children, Archbishop John Hughes of New York refused to approve it.

Toussaint understood well the American duality. Despite the constant hostile reactions to black Americans by white society in general, there was a parallel lively black world. It included a burgeoning black Catholic community of erudite and insightful African Americans and African Caribbeans. In this black Catholic community's widespread network of correspondents, the discussions went far deeper and were more telling than contemporary whites even remotely suspected. That this is so is captured in one of the letters to Toussaint. It was from a longtime black friend who then had moved to Chicago.

He addressed Toussaint as "My dear old companion." This educated and witty correspondent began, "I am glad to hear that your horrible winter has neither killed you nor given you any serious illness. Thanks to your regular habits and your fervent prayers, you are still in good health and, I hear, prosperous. But you are still a negro. You may indeed change your condition, but you cannot change your complexion—you will always remain black." The Chicago friend then speculates on what this means. He speaks about being black in a white American world. "Many think that a black skin prevents us from seeing and understanding good from evil. What fools! I have conversed with you at night when it was dark, and I have forgot that you were not white. The next morning, when I saw you, I said to myself—is this the black man I heard talk last night? Do they [whites] mistake you for a white man, that you have a passport everywhere? No," continues his friend. His Chicago correspondent then identifies in Toussaint the key element in Pierre's character: "it is because you perceive and follow the naked truth."

His friend advises Toussaint to "continue to learn, since one may learn always. And communicate your wisdom and experience to those who need it. Courage! Let them [the whites] think as they please."

SIXTEEN

THE CIRCLE OF FRIENDS,

THE 1830S

FOR TOUSSAINT AND MOST OF HIS FRIENDS, the 1830s was an unnerving decade. This was so whether the friends were French whites or Saint Domingan whites.

If Saint Domingan whites, the friends realized that despite the French monarchy's overtures to the Haitian government, any reparation payouts for the seized plantations were likely to be minuscule, if they ever materialized.

If the friends were African or mulatto—mainly French-speakers from Saint Domingue—the decade meant coping with increased American bigotry toward blacks. (Racism had reached such a peak that Toussaint himself had apparently determined it was time, after all, to move to Paris.)

If the friends were whites who'd fled Paris because of the Revolution or Napoleon Bonaparte, they were back in the

French capital desperately seeking jobs and a semblance of their earlier lives, neither of which was easy. As Deschamp Lagnel had written to Pierre: "Altogether, we none of us have reason to congratulate ourselves upon coming to France." Another friend wrote Toussaint, "I'm hoping for an appointment in the cabinet [administration] of the Duc d'Orléans." But there were no guarantees. Numa Lagnel, who attended West Point, was one of those who, in the 1820s, warned Toussaint against moving to Paris. ("If you persist in coming make sure you do not in future regret it," he wrote in 1828. "Remain in New York whose charm I miss every day.") Now Numa and his brother were serving officers in the French military for want of some better occupation.

Toussaint's most frequent Lagnel correspondent, Alfred, signed himself "Chevalier des Ordres Royaux du Christ et de Charles III." He was doing better than his brother—he worked for the minister of marine, their mutual friend, Baron Hyde de Neuville. Yet Alfred's letters were always about modest topics and ended with salutations such as, "I pray God to accord you here below, from on high his many precious benedictions."

If the friends were geographically close, and suffering family woes as well as joys, Toussaint was there as a rock. For Mary Anna the decade opened with her son William's death. In 1834, Pierre learned his godmother, Aurore, was dead. Another thread to the past was broken. Catherine Cruger similarly suffered a loss. Then Mary Anna's father died and, in 1835, her husband, Philip. In sickness and grief, people needed Pierre.

The 1830s opened with Toussaint sorrowing but gradually accepting the fact of Euphémie's death. This grieving was prolonged—he lost weight and would see no one. A stern letter from Catherine Cruger helped him pull himself together, yet in 1830, as he began to recover, he was thrown into turmoil by young William Schuyler's demise. There is no record of his words to Mary Anna over this loss of her firstborn. But the mutual grief of children gone must have bound the two ever closer together.

Finally, for the Toussaint friends who were Catholic—and the majority were—this was a decade of ceaseless, slanderous anti-Catholicism. And he showed them how to keep plowing straight ahead despite it. In every tribulation, by mail or in person, Toussaint provided the commiseration, hope, and love that kept him and them on course and eased their passage out of a double pain. And his friends had just done the same for him.

What an extended circle of friends it was. There were hundreds of them in a wide swath from New Orleans through the Caribbean and France back to Baltimore and New York and New Orleans and beyond. And that's without considering the scores of acquaintances from a lifetime of hairdressing customers, without touching on additional friends from the St. Peter's congregation.

What these friends all knew about Toussaint was that he was good fun, as mischievous as he was loving, as constant and reliable as he was entertaining. Hannah Lee has said Pierre was discriminating when it came to assessing his friends: Some he trusted implicitly and totally, with others, though he loved them no less, there was a reserve. He also worried about his friends' souls and was unafraid of calmly keeping his flock in the religious fold.

If he felt they were straying he reached out with his shepherd's crook—a letter—to guide them back in, or said something in person. One senses he even risked offending or alienating them in his concern for their eternal salvation. That he was able to guide and warn them while still keeping his friends reflects the deep and total trust they had in him as a spiritual adviser rather than as merely a wise secular counselor.

Though a few of Toussaint's correspondents did move in the highest realms of American and/or French society, Toussaint was unimpressed by status alone. The Schuylers and Churches were American aristocracy. In France, Catherine Cruger's daughter Angelica was now Comtesse de Bastard (a word signifying the

nature of the royal connection of her husband's family). Instead, like the learned Bishop Bossuet whose work he knew by
heart, Toussaint was quick to tell them not to let these things
take them away from their shared gospel values.

One revealing exchange is the correspondence Toussaint
had with two friends in Paris. Toussaint asked Ninon Bailly if he
ever saw their mutual friend Césarine Meetz Moulton. Bailly
replied: *"Non, non, nous ne voyageons pas dans le même monde"*—
"No, no, we do not travel in the same world. Our life to us is
simple and ignorant of the glitter. That is not where one finds
true happiness." Bailly continues, "Ours is to see our children
grow up. To learn their way, to see our daughters married.
Amélie is seventeen and looking for a husband. In this country,
marriage is a commercial affair—which is not appreciated by
the ladies."

Parallel to this, from the letters of Césarine and her father,
Raymond Meetz, Toussaint knows that Césarine is a major part
of the Parisian *bon ton*. The Moultons have a fine chateau and
will soon have one finer. The balls she gives are widely remarked on, and attract princes and princesses "of the blood,"
ambassadors, and nobility. Her children have a fine carriage
"drawn by two beautiful horses, as they go out with the young
Rothschilds to the Bois de Boulogne." The Moultons travel extensively and "take the waters" at Baden-Baden with their four,
soon to be five, children.

Her husband, Charles, who sounds very much like a modern executive, was "a slave to business," Meetz reports. Nonetheless he was doing extremely well at it, hence their new
chateau. Apparently reinforced by Ninon Bailly's comments,
Toussaint reminded Césarine that God was not impressed by
the high life and she must not endanger her soul. Slightly
alarmed, yet in a letter explanatory rather than defensive, Césarine explained that her social life was a necessity (probably for

her husband's business purposes). She does not deny that she enjoys attending society functions, but says she is not taken in.

"Do not think, I beg you," she implores Toussaint, "that because I go in all the first houses of Paris to the little balls for the Queen, and each evening I have two or three balls to attend and each day a half dozen soirees, do not think," Césarine again stresses, "that these worldly pleasures touch me. No, I tell you sincerely, I am pleased to be invited, but on my word of honor I find them amusing but see them for what they are."

Toussaint knows Césarine very well and apparently takes her at her word, for the topic is not raised again.

To all his friends, Toussaint lived as he spoke, lived what he preached. As Marie Navarre, writing in the third-person style of nineteenth-century correspondents had told him, "the Toussaint who risks his life in the yellow fever epidemics to nurse the sick is a good man who functions in the role of a priest."

Health is a constant in the letters, as when Toussaint writes to Mary Anna Schuyler a "few words just to let you know I'm carrying myself well [in good health] and . . . hope that Monsieur Robert [Schuyler, Mary Anna's stepson who lives with her] is returning to the good health. I have been asking God for him. For health is the most precious of all gifts. We hope to see him [Robert] return to being fine and strong. Alas, dear and good lady, who knows if Heaven listens to the feeble prayers of your Pierre Toussaint."

Toussaint reports he has no additional news for her beyond what she regularly receives from Madame George (wife of George Lee Schuyler, Mary Anna's son). This letter is nine years after William Schuyler's death. George's son, "Little Philip," has become the William substitute in Toussaint's affections. "I can tell you many things of my Little Philip," he writes to Philip's grandmother. "He is always charming and I love him with all my heart. I see him every day and I talk to him about his grandmother, and his uncle [Robert]." Pierre reports that their mutual dear friend Catherine Cruger is well, "thank God, each evening I go to see her"—undoubtedly to dress her hair—"and we talk about you both."

Toussaint signs off, "Adieu my dears."

❖   ❖   ❖

Various Schuylers are regular correspondents, sometimes at Mary Anna's urging. She prods son George on occasion to write to Toussaint: "You know how he loves to hear from you." There's plenty of activity in the extended Schuyler family to write about. Their business interests, for example, connect them to the development of steamships for the new canal and river systems.

Children wed. Mrs. Larue announces her son Louis's marriage, and also, sharply, the wedding of "one of the Garnet girls—better late than never." Children and spouses die. Deschamp Lagnel's daughter "died like a little saint." Children move away. From Paris, Juliette's friend Madame Dumortier writes to say that she is sending her daughter, Zabet, to New York to apprentice her to a fashion house because openings "in the fashion business are so rare in Paris." Juliette's friends are deeply loyal. When Juliette was taken ill, which happened in the mid-1830s, and with even greater severity in the late 1840s, the correspondence is filled with concern.

With some friends, the good-natured ribbing continues. Raymond Meetz asks if Juliette still goes daily to market in "order to cook you her special beef steak?" There's plenty of wry good humor. And there's ironic family wisdom in a letter Toussaint receives around this time from his sister, Marie-Louise. One hears, reading Marie-Louise's lines, the voice of their wise and sardonically humorous old grandmother Zénobie echo down the years as Marie-Louise remarks to her brother, "when people need us we're there to ask. But once we've done it they disappear!" That's a counterpart to Toussaint's ironic rejoinder about two young Frenchmen he helped who then spurned him: "I'm glad they no longer need me."

Toussaint was a handsome man, and one of his admirers, at least, recognized it. Amelia Cruger writes very cleverly, flirtatiously—and possibly daringly for a young white woman: "Lincolntown is a place absolutely without news of interest . . . if you fall asleep over [my letter] I will not complain, particularly if you give me a small corner of your dreams." The Lincolntown mentioned could have been the one in either Massachusetts (where there was a large plantation of that name) or in North Carolina. Whichever it was, there's a sense that the family had sent Amelia out of town, for another correspondent, A. T. Farynus, asks Toussaint about "poor Amelia Cruger, I truly pity her." The writer prays that "God in his mercy will bless her" and dispense her from her afflictions. The afflictions are not identified.

Many people took from Toussaint. Others gave—little gifts and mementoes. His friend Mrs. Miller on Fifth Avenue, wrote, "My dear Toussaint, accept from your friend a souvenir for to-day." It was Thanksgiving Day. Toussaint had regularly called on Mr. Miller, who was ill. Affixed to the back of a crucifix above Toussaint's writing desk at home was the handwritten label: "From a grateful priest." Sarah Ann Moore wrote: "Dear Toussaint, when I first received these rosaries I destined one of them to you, for I recollected the value you set upon a sprig of olives which I brought you from Rome. The rosary I now send is made of fruitwood from Mount Tabor and has been consecrated by being laid on the Holy Sepulchre in Jerusalem." The rosary was certainly destined for the wall shrine above Pierre and Juliette's prie-dieu.

In forty years of letters Toussaint's friends tell him things about himself that he was embarrassed to hear, even in his earliest days in New York. In 1815, for example, when his aunt Marie Bouquement died, Catherine Cruger, at that time in Wilmington, wrote, "I have need to tell you that I have learned of your pain. The grand age of your good aunt [she was about sixty] is a reason for resignation, for this is the natural order and you have consolation in the certainty you acquitted your duties toward her."

Catherine then switches course in her conversation: "The best that a good soul has the power to have," she told Toussaint, "you have it." She then carefully reveals Toussaint to himself, and to the world. "Truly Toussaint, it is difficult to find anyone better than you. I would tell you it is impossible if I did not know it would wound your modesty."

Behind the often flowery sentiments of early nineteenth-century letter writing, one repeatedly detects in Toussaint's correspondents these same feelings of genuine admiration for his spiritual qualities. These hints and allusions matter, for they are what exists as an independent source regarding his character. Most mature adults do not like to have their "goodness" remarked on, and most mature correspondents hesitate to write as boldly as his very close friend Catherine could. One friend said of Toussaint, "he has the best *instincts,* he was *born* good." That is unfair to Toussaint. As any person knows, being good is a daily task, not a permanent state. Toussaint worked at being good.

Twenty years after Catherine Cruger's letter, Pierre's friend Loïsa, Comtesse de Boesteind, wrote from Paris: "I see you always opening your heart, always content with your little songs." (Toussaint had a good voice. Does this mean he sometimes quietly sang as he dressed his customers' hair? Did he quietly sing to himself as he walked along New York's streets, going from one appointment to the next? He was merry enough to do either or both.) Loïsa continues that every Sunday in church "I thank God always for the merits of Toussaint."

Expressions of his generosity of time, effort, and money expended on others mark much of the correspondence. And it is the sheer quantity of them that suggests how remarkable a man Toussaint was.

In 1835, Madame Larue boldly presents Toussaint the Christian to Pierre himself—not as a good servant of Jesus but as far more: as a "disciple." Madame Larue at first writes in general terms. Note how she suddenly switches tempo to set the Christian Toussaint before us, starkly and simply, as a man of faith. "We are dependent on God's holy wishes to remedy things," she writes. God gives "resignation—calm to sweeten and mitigate [misery] and gives us hope in divine grace. Sometimes we're punished, sometimes rewarded," she says, and adds, "and what reward my good Toussaint! A place of royalty [in Heaven]."

Now she places Toussaint in context: "*You* know the life of a Christian, a life of the Cross of Combat and Suffering. Our divine Saviour—who traces the road during his mortal life and said, 'who will follow me is my disciple'—He knows *your* grand piety my dear Toussaint." And Madame Larue is telling Pierre: So do I, and so do your friends.

Another white person, a lodger in the Toussaints' home, drew this comparison: "Juliette was a good woman, but unlike Toussaint. She was flesh and blood, while he was possessed of the spirit of one man out of many thousands." Again, Toussaint is singular. And it is as Christian that they see this singularity. Juliette's friend visiting from Baltimore writes in her thank-you to Juliette and Pierre of the prevailing Christian goodness of the household. Father Lombart, the parish priest of La Raie in Saint Lucia in the English Antilles, stayed with the Toussaints. He departs impressed, "at your home I received much expression of goodness and a charity solidly Christian." From Paris, Jane Sully Morin adds, "Toussaint, you give us all an example of the piety of God."

Toussaint's friend Diego Moya, writing from Port-au-Prince

after the New York fire, speaks of his affection for Toussaint as "loving a good Christian who is a good friend, whether in misery or in opulence."

God's grace and requests for prayers are frequent comments. "Adieu, my good friend Toussaint," writes Comtesse Loïsa, who stresses, "I beg you pray for me." His friends need his prayers, and are always asking for them. Loïsa de Boesteind probably spoke for them all when she wrote: "I count on the affect of your prayers and never think not to have confidence if Toussaint prays for me."

Mary Anna Schuyler remains our best guide: "Adieu, my excellent Toussaint," she writes in closing one letter. "I think always of you and that you pray for me and that this God you serve is so living in your soul that His balm is salutary and for us so necessary." When two families were fighting, Toussaint helped them reach an accommodation with each other. His correspondent remarked, "you helped them find happiness again. You are a very, very good man." The sentiments, almost all expressed in French, are heartwarming. To the writers Toussaint possesses the "good heart."

In 1829, just before the decade under consideration opens, Juliette's close friend, her cousin Fanny Montpensier, the most prolific of letter writers, was pressing both Juliette and Pierre quite hard on behalf of the newly founded Oblate Sisters. The sisters were a wonderment considering that in the United States most blacks were slaves. Women had few freedoms and practically no legal rights. Yet there, in a slave state, Maryland, was a little band of free black women determined to found a religious order to serve the black community.

Elizabeth Lange was born about the same time as Pierre Toussaint, though in Cuba. Like his sister, Marie, and some members of her family, and thousands of other Saint Domingans during the cresting of violence, Elizabeth's parents had quit the French colony for the nearby island of Cuba for safety's sake. Eventually, when Elizabeth was a teenager, the Langes moved from Cuba to join the numerous *gens de couleur* who were Saint Domingan exiles in Baltimore. This was the solid and strong Catholic community that met for worship in the basement chapel (*la chapelle basse*) at the French Sulpician seminary.

As she entered her twenties, Mademoiselle Lange turned her attention to the needs of black children. Three other female *gens de couleur* joined her in teaching the *chapelle basse* community's children. Lange wanted to found a religious congregation and one of the Sulpicians who had lived in Saint Domingue, the aristocratic Father Jacques Joubert de la Muraille, strongly supported her. The Oblates Sisters of Providence were formally founded in 1829, and two years later Pope Gregory XVI formally approved the new congregation.

In October of the Oblates' founding year, Montpensier wrote to Juliette, "I can tell you with satisfaction that our convent prospers." Four hundred gourdes had been raised from the dowries of young women entering. "How happy for us to have such a fine establishment for the people of color." Fanny then makes the pitch she was to keep up for the next two decades. In the New York markets, Juliette was deputed to find lovely goods (frequently kerchiefs for headscarfs) that could be then sold at a nice profit in Baltimore to benefit the convent, which "is very poor. My dear friend, make a little contribution to aid our new institution. God bless you if you will seek contributors." She wanted Juliette to ask Pierre to make the Oblates establishment a goal of his charity, too. And to some extent, through Juliette, he does.

Apart from his hairdressing work, Toussaint has his usual church duties to attend to: the orphans and St. Peter's various organizations. The new church is being built, funds are scarce, the Society of St. Peter is the major fund-raising body, and Father Power reminds Society members whenever a meeting is coming up. He tells Toussaint he hopes to see him at the meeting "immediately after vespers."

In this period, as Toussaint enters his fifties, he is not merely in his prime but in some ways at his peak. He is wise in the ways of the world and wealthy. His income from his house calls and the hairdressing establishment on Church Street probably approached $100,000 a year in today's buying power (there was no income tax). But augmenting that was the income from his investments. He had been carefully buying property and investing in insurance companies and, perhaps, banks. Soaring inflation in the early 1830s had caused rapid rises in property values—beneficial to Toussaint for they were driven by wild speculation on Wall Street and in land in Manhattan.

The same inflation was leading to workers' strikes, short-lived fledgling trade unionism, disturbances demanding affordable food. There was also a cholera epidemic sweeping the city. Juliette, taken ill while visiting Baltimore, received such a "fright" in thinking she'd contracted cholera before leaving Manhattan that she remained in Baltimore a month longer than she'd anticipated, until the epidemic began to fade.

Manhattan was being modernized. One element of which was the founding, in 1823, of the New-York Gas Light Company to serve Manhattan below Grand Street. Its cast-iron gas lines ran under the city streets to provide lighting, though not heating, to the cavernous warehouses and office buildings that dominated the Lower East Side. How this all affects Toussaint will be seen momentarily.

The Lower East Side was the enormously prosperous and booming commercial district that sustained and drew its energies and income from the nation's busiest seaport. Cast iron is a notoriously brittle metal, subject to rust. Surrounded by water or damp, in subzero weather, the rust-weakened piping is vulnerable as the earth around it freezes and expands—and crushes the piping. If the stories from almost two centuries ago are to be believed, sometime around nine on the evening of December 16, 1835, such a gas pipe broke in a building near Exchange and Pearl Streets.

For New Yorkers, the "Great Fire of 1835" evenly split the decade of the 1830s in two. For Pierre Toussaint it meant a major decision reversed. December 16 was a bitterly cold day. Once darkness came, the freezing daytime temperatures plummeted. By midnight it was twenty below zero. Furious gales created a windchill factor that descended to thirty-five below freezing. Or worse.

Around 9:30 on that December evening, a night watchman named Hayes, patrolling Exchange and Pearl Streets, smelled smoke.

Hayes called two more watchman and the three broke open the door of a five-story warehouse. They faced a wall of flames. Subsequent investigation said stove coals had ignited gas escaping from a leaking pipe. The watchmen sensibly turned tail and fled for help. Within fifteen minutes two entire city blocks were engulfed as dozens of buildings crackled like kindling in the desperately cold night air. The winds quickly fanned the fire to an inferno that would burn for two days. Brooklynites flooded out of their houses to gaze across the East River at the horrific spectacle of the city burning. The fire was so intense and the flames rose so furiously into the sky that the glow could be seen as far as Philadelphia to the south and New Haven to the north.

All sources of water, including the wharfside reaches of the East River, were frozen solid. Firemen "poured brandy into their boots to keep their feet from freezing." Buildings were blown up to keep the fire from crossing Wall Street and moving south. More gunpowder was rushed from the armories and detonated to raze additional buildings and prevent the flames crossing Coenties Slip and heading north.

Onlookers thought it was a glimpse of hell. When flaming

liquids flowed from the warehouses onto the ice they continued to burn and gave the impression that the ice was on fire. An enterprising young engraver, the twenty-two-year-old Nathaniel Currier, quickly made a name—and quite a considerable profit—for himself selling depictions of the scenes.

Even as the flames roared the looters moved in. And right behind them were the hastily summoned troops to drive them back out. Which they quickly did.

Fifty hours later, with smoke still rising from the acres and acres of charred city, the reckoning began. Where almost seven hundred buildings had once stood, most filled to the brim with commercial goods, there were now only ashes. Amazingly, only two lives were lost. But the devastation in dollars was enormous—at least half a billion dollars by twenty-first-century reckoning. The devastation triggered a severe recession that affected U.S.-European trade and plunged the region into bankruptcies and unemployment.

Practically all two dozen city fire insurance companies immediately ran out of funds and failed. Included among them were the companies in which Pierre Toussaint was most heavily invested. Now came his decision reversed: Toussaint at this point was finally about to leave for France. The anti-Catholicism fanned by Protestant evangelicals and the antiblack bigotry led by Irish Catholic racists produced riots and an inferno of hate as searing as anything whipped up by the gale-force winds that burned half of New York's commercial district to the ground.

In the late 1820s and immediately thereafter Toussaint had held off considering France for two reasons. The first was the period up to and immediately following Euphémie's death. The second was because his French friends said he could not survive in Paris at the same financial level he was achieving in New York.

Midway into the 1830s, however, the industrious Toussaint, through eighty-hour workweeks, personal industry, and judicious investments, had brought himself to the moment when he could move to Paris and never work again.

Overnight, the fire financially all but wiped him out.

Conservatively, he lost an estimated ninety-five percent of his net worth in those two days, possibly as much as $900,000 in today's money. Paradoxically—but then, what does one expect of Pierre Toussaint?—the manner in which he handled the loss added to his stature: "Some of his friends, who knew of his slow, industrious earnings, and his unceasing charities, thought to get up a subscription to repair his losses. As soon as it was mentioned to him he stopped it, saying he was not in need of it, and he would not take what many others required much more than he did."

What no one except Toussaint and Juliette truly understood was that the fire had consumed their only chance of true freedom.

SEVENTEEN

PILLAR OF STRENGTH,

1835–1839

TOUSSAINT'S IMMEDIATE RESPONSE to the great conflagration was to offer help and commiseration to those badly hurt by it. "The Great Fire of 1835 changed our fortunes," said one friend. "The first person who came to us early the next morning to proffer assistance was Toussaint."

For Toussaint the consequences were crushing. In time, Marie Navarre in Paris understood perfectly. In her first letter following the fire she wrote how concerned she was for all their friends whose lives and fortunes had been devastated. In complete candor, Toussaint replied that he was one, and revealed the extent of his losses. She then wrote of her grief on his behalf, and not just over the significant loss of fortune. Knowingly she said, "I am doubly grieved and anxious, for your loss is an obstacle to your coming to France."

The fire was more than a mere obstacle: it had ended forever Pierre and Juliette's opportunity to live truly free as a black couple in a white world. Toussaint had to permanently put aside his dream. (Almost exactly a century later an entire legion of American blacks, artists like singer Josephine Baker, in 1925, and writer James Baldwin, in 1948, moved to France to live the life that now evaded Toussaint.)

Putting aside the misfortune that befell him, Toussaint and Juliette simply carried on with their lives as industriously as before. And indeed, far more interesting than these financial issues is the way in which the Toussaints' home was now the central pillar connecting, almost morally supporting, an impressive transatlantic, Caribbean, and nation-girdling array of mainly anxious and unsettled friends.

Toussaint became their center.

This comment should not be taken lightly. Toussaint is key. Nearly two centuries later one can too easily dismiss the turmoil of the times—and miss the centrality of Toussaint's presence and persona to his circle of friends.

Look what most of them had to face. If it was dislocation and uncertainty, Toussaint kept them all in touch with one another so they didn't feel alone. If they were Americans, they felt the anxiety of financial collapse as a result of the Great Fire and the recessionary aftermath. Toussaint was there, solid, stolid, a visible sign there was no need to panic. He had not done so himself, even though they knew his losses were enormous.

If it was his Catholic friends, deeply alarmed by the rising tide of religious bigotry and inflammatory falsehoods, Toussaint was unshakable, impervious, trusting in God—their example of fortitude and determination. To his African-American and mulatto friends, he was a solid refuge—and despite his losses the financial key to helping them escape to better situations. Which brings the conversation back to Toussaint's white female Protestant friends, many of whom were members of—or sympathizers with—the aims of the increasingly hated American anti-slavery society. If Toussaint no longer had the money himself to assist in emergencies, they would do it—and did.

They had reason to. In 1834, New York's racial hatreds erupted into a race riot. Proscriptions against blacks and the incredible viciousness now evident in the streets was fearsome. Still, Toussaint continued to walk from one house to the next, working and visiting.

The anti-Catholicism was blatantly evident in the scurrilous pamphlets and books gleefully produced by Protestants with absolutely no interest in truth. The fundamentalists spread malicious rumors; the publishers Harper Brothers put out the scandalous *Maria Monk* and made a name and fortune for themselves; and in general a fine old religious bigotry whipped up passions against the Catholics. Toussaint simply continued as before, attending daily the six A.M. mass at St. Peter's.

In 1836, the old church, as if to signal that it needed stronger foundations to continue the fight, actually collapsed. The roof fell in—thankfully no one was injured—and the decision was made to raze and rebuild. (There was St. Patrick's Cathedral to worship in during the reconstruction.)

Faced with such racial and religious virulence, some of Toussaint's black friends migrated south to New Orleans, where their numbers as free blacks might give them a modicum of protection. The attraction of New Orleans was understandable. Until the 1803 Louisiana Purchase, the people of New Orleans had been French (or, briefly, Spanish) citizens. When Toussaint's sister, Marie-Louise, had her freedom, she headed there in part because *gens de couleur* had the same rights (in principle, at least) as all other French citizens. Further, at the time Marie-Louise arrived, sometime before 1810, more than half of New Orleans's eight thousand population was black.

These blacks at many levels felt they had a special claim on the city. As Catholics they were well served by the twin-towered

St. Louis Cathedral and, until 1829, by Father Antonio de Sedella—Père Antoine. He was a fiery fellow who spoke his mind, was loved by the people, and died at eighty-one. The city had enjoyed for decades the work of the Ursuline Sisters. Even a decade after the Louisiana Purchase, the people of New Orleans, as new U.S. residents, were largely French-speakers. Most of them didn't mind that their mayor, Nicholas Girod, neither spoke nor read English.

New Orleans, in so many ways a disreputable city, was thoroughly Catholic and human. It was a Latin Catholic city where good and evil were seen as companion elements in the human condition in all its variety. Essentially, though, the city had become a haven for blacks. When Collinette, Fanny Montpensier's sister in New York, announces that she, too, is leaving for New Orleans, the migration makes sense to other black Catholics. The biggest risk relocatees had to face was from yellow fever. As prevalent as it was in New York, in New Orleans it was practically pandemic: almost thirty thousand people died in New Orleans during the twenty-three epidemics between 1817 and 1860.

It comes as no surprise, given the preponderance of Africans and *gens de couleur* and their needs, that the city nurtured the second Catholic community of black women religious.

In 1842, after many attempts and trials, the Congregation of the Holy Family was established by a remarkable young woman, free person of color Henriette de Lisle. She had to create her congregation surreptitiously, a legal ruse was necessary, but those African women of Saint Domingue heritage, like Delille and Lange and Zénobie Julien, were not easily dissuaded once their minds were made up.

The letters from New Orleans to Toussaint poured in. By June 1838, Charles and Euphrasie Floremans wrote to Toussaint to report that they had arrived safely and in good health after a three-week voyage. Auguste Collon was being "persecuted" in New York. He needed money to flee to New Orleans.

It seems that the Schuylers, Crugers, and others, along with Toussaint, helped find the money that made the Collon family's flight possible. At a time when enslaved blacks rode the Underground Railway north, many free blacks traveled the coastal steamers south—to New Orleans.

Other Toussaint friends, those with connections to Saint Domingue, as they still called it, fled New York for safety in Haiti. Not with happy results as a rule. Juliette's friend Joséphine Walmie wrote, "this is a poor, miserable place to live in and I am sick and tired of the place. My boy also. We are getting better. The climate don't appear to agree with us and my greatest desire is to get home once more."

Johardinette Chardin returned to Haiti with her family. From Cap Haïtien she told Toussaint that she had passed his letter quickly to St. Marc and urged the man to whom she entrusted it to ask around widely about Pierre's family, and then to do the same in Port-au-Prince. She said she had not yet received any news but would inform him immediately when she did. In the meantime, she said, she found "the country in a sad situation, there is sadness throughout the country, and commerce is dead."

Sadly, there is no evidence that Chardin's "monsieur" discovered the whereabouts of Zénobie, Ursule, or other family members, and none to suggest Toussaint ever learned any more about his family.

In New York, riots, recession, and inflamed bigotries were now the frightening backdrop to Toussaint's activities—and to his continued calm and cheerful, hardworking presence. And as if he weren't already busy enough, his friends' demands by letters kept him busier yet. They wrote to borrow money, or for a package of hair to make a wig, or for the name of a good French baker in New York City. Someone had returned to Paris and left old clothes behind—"camisoles and ladies flowers"—that they wanted him to sell. Another wrote: "Here's the key to the house, please tell the servant to wash the drapes and prepare the rooms." Toussaint himself replied to a similar request from Mary Anna Schuyler as the family prepared to return to the city from Rhinebeck, New York: "Madame, I have the honor to let you know that your house is ready but the paint still smells a lot." He had presented her compliments to their friend Baron de Neuville (the French ambassador) who was back in the city "last week, his wife is well. He left again on Sunday."

Friends and acquaintances felt free to request almost anything. One wrote that her friend's husband was coming to New York, and would Toussaint please send back with the man "a small sack of manioc." Another asked him to "please hurry" to the French consul to trace missing papers. One of the McDowells was "very sick, I've lost everything," and sent lengthy begging letters. When J. Ionesco was inquiring about a room to rent in Toussaint's home for himself and his wife, he assured Toussaint that they were "decent and honest—and will stay a long time if the price is reasonable."

Pierre was the accommodation-finder for visitors. He was the employment agency. If people wanted servants, or wanted work themselves, Toussaint was the first person they turned to. "I'm looking for a French girl to live in." Another wanted "a French cook and a French servant." Wrote another, "If the mattress man had not been paid, please pay him for me."

Some wrote with considerable precision—and of course, Toussaint did know people in service: "Mrs. Harvey will be very much obliged if Mr. Toussaint in his visits to his friends could find a substitute to take Marie's place. She wishes to go to France as soon as she can find an opportunity. And if Mr. Toussaint should hear of any lady who needed a companion to accompany her to England or France, they could not find a better attendant than Marie. Mrs. Harvey is also anxious to find a companion for a friend of hers in Philadelphia. If Mr. Toussaint hears of one, would he mention it to her brothers as she leaves the city tomorrow for Hyde Park and will not be in town until the first of October."

Biographer Lee wrote that Toussaint's "ingenuity in contriving means of assistance to others was remarkable. A French lady who was much embarrassed in her circumstances by the depreciation of her small property and the failure of her rents, consulted Toussaint on the possibility of doing something for her [own] support. He suggested she teach French. She said very frankly she was inadequate to it, that she had no grammatical knowledge. 'Madame,' said he, 'I am no judge but I have frequently heard it said that you speak remarkably pure and correct French.' This was really the case, for she had been educated in the best society. 'That is a very different thing,' she said, 'from teaching a language.'

"Toussaint, after some moments of reflection, said, 'Should you be willing to give lessons for conversing in French?' She replied she'd be quite willing. He at once set about procuring scholars among his English friends, many of whom appreciated the advantage of familiar and correct conversation for their children. Thus, pupils were not wanting for the lady, and she was able to support her family by these simple means until the sudden rise of her rents relieved her of some embarrassment."

What Toussaint had proposed "was quite an original idea . . . at that time," Lee said, "though it has since been adopted even in our own language." (New York's English-speakers of the period who wanted French language skills relied on local tutors and an abundance of French grammar books. Around the turn of the nineteenth century, those books were usually published in England, though later in Philadelphia and Boston. The American market for French primers was a sure source of income to people like the French master Mr. Porny at England's prestigious Eton College. By 1803, his *Practical French Grammar* was already into its eleventh edition.)

In their letters, Pierre's French friends urge him to look for their lost relatives—often sons wandering around America. Marie Navarre just before Christmas, 1838, pleaded, "give me the gift of writing news of my son. Our good Auguste has been charmed to return to the city [New York] in which he was born," but apparently Auguste wasn't much of a correspondent. Similarly, in Paris, Madame Lagnel was worried about her son Jules and asked Toussaint to make inquiries. Others, like Fanny Cottenet, gently chided Pierre for not writing often enough. This was a frequent complaint from correspondents who usually were ladies and gentlemen of leisure with little demand on their time—unlike Toussaint, who was putting in a regular twelve-hour workday or more.

The Toussaints always supplied New York accommodations for their French friends' wandering children. Edward McDowell, young son of Pierre's friends Ninon and L. McDowell in Paris, wrote from Charleston, South Carolina, to introduce himself, announcing that he was in the United States and undoubtedly paving the way for an invitation to stay with the Toussaints in Manhattan. "I await your response," said the young McDowell, "with lively impatience." His father, Ninon, told Toussaint: "I hope you give him those good counsels a young man of his age always needs."

Sometime later it is the parents of these young men who are writing—to thank Toussaint for his timely advice to their sons. Somehow Toussaint had a way of getting through to young men to reinforce the codes of conduct they already understood—and may have been testing in the freedom of being away from home. And it wasn't just young men he could relate to. Another friend of Pierre's, referring to his daughter working in New York, whose care was supervised by Toussaint when she was taken ill, thanks Toussaint for his ministerings and "good heart." The friend adds, knowing Toussaint will see to it, "I hope she goes often to church and makes her Christian devotions."

Otherwise, in Manhattan, nearby friends and acquaintances seek "a loan of two dollars until I get my money the first of the month"; another requests $100; a third addresses him as "bene-factor" and tells Toussaint, "you say with truth that the unfortu-nate always have recourse to you." That writer wanted to stop by in person for an immediate loan. Eugene McCarty, possibly writing from Haiti, says "in the name of Christ I need to leave here" and seeks $25 for his passage. Miss Gillingham needs pupils; Cotonie Sorbieu's cousin Emilie Goudain in Long Island needs advice about hair loss. A seminarian in Paris needs $100, which Toussaint supplies by return *paquebot*.

There was other, more detailed, deeper correspondence of the type he enjoyed with Madame Larue and Sorbieu. Fanny Cottenet is in that league. She sends an intense yet perceptive note thanking him for his letter, which obviously dealt with mat-ters of faith, for she writes that she will read and reread it. Ob-viously referring to his own conduct, she tells Toussaint: "What a need there is to be good and religious [on behalf of] those who are afflicted in this sad world," and adds that she is enlivened by what he says and with all her heart "wants to resemble Christian perfection."

Was Toussaint a proto-feminist? At the very least he saw women as equals. Cottenet provides that insight. Traveling in France and Italy (he has sent her a language dictionary), she re-galed Toussaint with a lengthy, wry, and at times hilarious account of her visits, including one to the monastery at Char-treuse. There were twenty-six friars, she wrote, and their life was severe. They were not permitted to eat meat, and rarely spoke. "They have reveille many times during the night to go to the church to say their prayers! It is a life of deprivation. Women are not allowed in the chapels! One is obliged to look at the magnificent mosaics through a grille like a criminal. I am to tell this immediately to Toussaint, this affront to our sex!"

The Toussaints were a regular lodging for priests and seminarians who needed a place to stay overnight on their travels. At journey's end, they wrote their thanks. From Le Havre, Father Matthew Herard recounted his "wonderment. Finally my dear Toussaint here I am newly on French territory, oh what a joyous spectacle." Herard, Toussaint's New Jersey friend, had stayed with the Toussaints before embarking in New York. When Herard arrived in Le Havre he spent an evening with the Larues "at their new and superb house," and was invited by the Larues to dine, but he had accepted an invitation from the pastor of Le Havre's "Grand Eglise," who also invited Herard to say mass. Toussaint probably helped make the trip possible. Writes Herard, along with his thanks, "Pray to God for me Toussaint."

Wives and husbands reveal intimate details of their lives to Pierre, simply for the joy of sharing with someone. His friend and regular correspondent Madame Naomie Bailly asks him how could she be ungrateful toward a God who has given her "a good mother, an excellent husband, two good children. And friends I love. Why do I merit such happiness? I ask God to keep my husband safe and sound, and that my son conduct himself honestly in New York."

Not everyone is lovingly good-natured all the time. Toussaint, through the mails, becomes an arbiter of disputes. Raymond Meetz asks Pierre for his counsel in reuniting friends in a dispute. The central problem, Meetz confides to Toussaint, "is that on the part of some, Vanity, Pretentions and Ignorance create barriers to listening." E.J. writes snippily to Pierre about an acquaintance, "I really can't forgive her for being so rude. I could never do what she does—if you're a friend you're a friend for life. I'm not going to run after a woman just because she's rich."

When one Toussaint correspondent actually turns rude, that

is quite out of character among his friends, but there's an explanation. Mademoiselle Françoise Souty complains she has not received the money Pierre had said he would send. She writes: "You have written to me three times. The first to say you are going to send it. The second to say you have sent it, and a third one—I'm not going to mention." He had sent the money. Poor Souty was actually deteriorating mentally, as his correspondents Marie Navarre and Deschamp Lagnel wrote to inform him. In her illness, said Lagnel, she had "become entirely an imbecile," and indeed she was soon dead.

Toussaint was the international banker shifting other people's money around. When Jean Sorbieu wanted to help two people with monetary gifts, he sent the money to Toussaint with instructions not to let the recipients know the source of the money, "because of the jealousy." Certainly Pierre could move money around the eastern seaboard and Caribbean with effect. Juliette's cousin Fanny constantly has Juliette sending sizable orders of food and other wares south to Baltimore. The financial network part of it was informal but effective and Juliette (actually Toussaint) was paid quickly. At Fanny's instruction, Father Joubert in Baltimore gave money to the Sisters of Charity in Emmitsburg, Maryland. Then, in New York, the Sisters running the orphanage on Prince Street gave Toussaint the required amount.

Equally so in the Caribbean. Using goods instead of cash, Toussaint could quickly ship tobacco or other quality wares from New York to almost any Caribbean destination. And he frequently did.

Yet the crux of most of the correspondence throughout fifty years of letters was always family matters, health, and the wish to be remembered to relatives and friends. Even when business pressed, it was usually a family matter.

Occasionally there is overt discussion of the economic or political situation. Diego Moya wrote in 1838 from Port-au-Prince:

"Let us now speak of politics. I have the honor to send you the treaty between France and Hayti, that you may see the conditions of agreement between the two powers. If I were to give you all the details, I should have to write a journal. But you will have them before your eyes. I can tell you, however, that since the arrival of Baron de Lascase there has been nothing but fetes, dinners, breakfasts, and balls, in the city and the environs. Le Baron de Lascase gave a ball to the Haytian ladies; never has any thing like it been seen in Port-au-Prince. The company was the captains of frigates and brigs, as well as their officers. Ah! it was a splendid ball. They left, the 23rd of March, with two Haytian missionaries, who have gone to France to get a receipt for the money which has been given, and to see to the ratification of the treaty."

Reparations at last for the ousted planters? Very little, and very late.

In the late 1830s—when Meetz asked of Gabriel Nicolas's whereabouts and if Diego Moya's brother is happily married, and "have they [the brothers presumably] made their peace"— he noted that "people are once again attending soirees and balls." Manufacturing (crippled by lack of demand in New York following the 1835 fire) had started to revive in France and England: "our manufacturers are beginning to receive orders from your city."

The final year of the decade opened with the happy January announcement from Césarine that she is thirty—and pregnant again, with her fifth child. She described herself as "very fat, fatter than before and very red." She's looking forward to seeing Toussaint, for once the baby is born she intends to travel to New York. (The child arrived and was christened Henry. Plans were made for an 1840 voyage to America.)

Even more jolly were the letters from the Phoenix daughters on their farm in Sodus, New York. "We are keeping a pair of oxen and a pair of horses to till the ground. And Papa has given us a beautiful pair of carriage horses for our own use." They are not suffering financially, for Papa is also building them "a little English cottage."

The Phoenixes' happy situation is in marked contrast to the woes faced by Jerome Villagrand's daughter, whose husband runs a school in Botecourt County, Virginia. The school is in financial trouble due to the fiscal irresponsibility of her brother-in-law. But Villagrand himself is uncomplaining and wishes Pierre and Juliette good cheer and "a happy and prosperous New Year."

Andrew Morning takes care of his own cheer—Morning wants to make some beer. He drops a note to Juliette asking if he might borrow "until tomorrow" a medium-sized mash tub. We can be sure the obliging Juliette obliged.

The decade that wiped out Toussaint's fortune had little impact on Juliette and Pierre's lives and none at all on their friendships.

EIGHTEEN

"Saint Pierre," THE 1840S

TIME QUICKENS. Advancing age does that. Toussaint could measure the speed of change in his life in Atlantic crossing times.

When he was born in 1781, the voyage from Saint Domingue to Le Havre took eight to twelve weeks. By the time he left the island in 1797, it was closer to five weeks. Two decades later, in 1818, his friends are commenting on their twenty-five-day New York–Le Havre crossings. By the 1840s, his Paris friends the Moultons and Lagnels urge him to at least visit—for the steamships make the journey in twelve to fourteen days. If Toussaint was tempted he didn't mention it, for Juliette's health was worsening.

Another measure of time for Toussaint was the succession of U.S. presidencies—he would live under fourteen. Born before the United States had a president, President George Washington had just completed his eight years (1789–1797) and left office to make way for President John Adams (1797–1801) as Toussaint landed in New York. Thomas Jefferson (1801–1809) was president when Toussaint was freed in 1807. (Toussaint would have known something of American politics as he dressed hair and listened to conversations in the households of the Schuylers, Churches, and Hamiltons. He may have known the stories of the times when, in Jefferson's words, Jefferson and Alexander Hamilton were "pitted against each other in the Cabinet like two cocks." And after Hamilton died in 1804 from the duel with Aaron Burr, Toussaint would have heard much of the grim background to that disagreement. Toussaint, said his friend Raymond Meetz, "always knows what is going on in New York.")

In the years when Toussaint was wed (1811), Euphémie adopted (1815), and Pierre was reconnected with his godmother, Aurore Bérard, James Madison (1809–1817) was president. James Monroe followed (1817–1825) as Toussaint first considers a move to France. President John Quincy Adams was in the last year of a four-year term (1825–1829) when Euphémie died. By the time of the Great Fire, Pierre was into his seventh U.S. president, Andrew Jackson (1829–1837). Now, as the 1840s open under Martin Van Buren (1837–1841), Toussaint still has six more presidents to go (William Henry Harrison, 1841; John Tyler, 1841–1845; James Knox Polk, 1845–1849; Zachary Taylor, 1849–1850; Millard Fillmore, 1850–1853; and Franklin Pierce, 1853–1857).

And yet, for Toussaint, perhaps the most fitting measure of time is to chronicle his life alongside that of the church in which he always worshiped: St. Peter's. When the 80-foot wide, 120-foot-long St. Peter's Church was dedicated on November 4, 1786. Toussaint was a slave boy of five in Saint Domingue. When he arrived in New York, the pastor was a member of the Order of Preachers, Dominican Father William V. O'Brien. The Irish-born pastor arrived in 1786 and served the church for twenty years, "a period of peace and remarkable growth," wrote the indefatigable chronicler of St. Peter's Church, Leo Raymond Ryan.

From its own opening in 1876, St. Peter's, by the start of the 1840s, had fostered in the city nine more churches and a cathedral, yet the parish was forever broke. At various times St. Peter's owed Trinity Episcopal Church for the land it stood on, and on occasion attempted to borrow money from Trinity's trustees.

Even at the start St. Peter's trustees loaned their personal funds to see the church completed, and despite a thousand-dollar gift and altar vessels from King Charles of Spain, Father O'Brien had to go on a fund-raising tour to Cuba and Mexico. Travel was slow, O'Brien was gone for three years. A fellow Dominican, Father Michael Burke, served the parish in his absence.

During his lengthy tour, the hardworking Father O'Brien, a noted orator and scholar, raised a further $4,920 through which, wrote the trustees, the church "has been extricated from the danger." It was one of many temporary fixes. Despite a congregation, at its peak, of sixteen thousand Catholic New Yorkers, St. Peter's had to acknowledge that practically all of them were fearsomely poverty-stricken. (When St. Peter's had to be rebuilt, it limped along financially until, in 1844, it lapsed into bankruptcy.)

Toussaint could not have been more fortunate in the example of his pastors. In 1798, the year after Toussaint arrived in New York, a prolonged yellow fever epidemic saw "Father O'Brien weighted down with the cares of tending the sick and burying the dead." From his earliest days in the country, Pierre had a model for Christian service. Nor was he the only one with such a model.

St. Peter's, the small church on Barclay Street, has a major claim in the Catholic annals—how many churches can show that three of their parishioners have had their cause pressed for can-

onization? From her reception into the Catholic Church at St.
Peter's parish, Elizabeth Seton went on to a life of service and
was canonized in 1975. The second cause is that of Mother
Juana Adelaida de Santa Teresa, O.C.D.—born Theresa
O'Sullivan in New York in 1817. Theresa joined the Carmelites
in Cuba, served in Guatemala, and died in Spain in 1893. Her
cause was begun a few years later. Toussaint's cause was begun
in 1989 and the Propio presented to Rome in 1993. He was declared "Venerable" by Pope John Paul II in 1996. Like Mother
Juana Adelaida, he is waiting for a miracle or two.

In 1807, Pastor O'Brien, exhausted from battling three annual yellow fever epidemics, resigned from the church. Three
years after that the parish voted him a $500 annual pension, the
same stipend as the pastor received. (O'Brien died in 1816.
When the new church was built, his remains were placed in the
basement wall with a commemorative plaque. The wording included Matthew 25:36: "I was sick and you visited me.")

The faltering parish finances, though a tremendous worry
for the succession of St. Peter's pastors and priests, did little to
actually impede the daily work of the church. And in fact, despite the shortage of money, St. Peter's next pastor, Jesuit Father
Anthony Kohlmann (1805–1815), who officiated at Pierre and
Juliette's wedding, took on a greater debt. In 1808, Pope Pius
VII divided the only existing American diocese, Baltimore, into
five. The additional dioceses, with Baltimore now an archdiocese, were Philadelphia; Bardstown, Kentucky; Boston; and
New York. Kohlmann decided that if New York was going to get
a bishop, he'd better have a cathedral. A remarkable priest and
pastor, Kohlmann was another linguist priest who spoke English
and French fluently in addition to his native German.

The Episcopal appointee to New York, Father Richard Luke
Concanen, was an Irish priest who had refused a bishopric in
Ireland, and didn't want New York either. Kohlmann, who ar-
rived in the United States in 1804 from Germany, was named

vicar general—the diocese's administrator. It was not a propitious moment for cathedral building—there was a prolonged business depression. Scores of major firms failed, and "500 ships sat rotting at anchor, sailors were destitute, merchants shut up their premises." Yet Kohlmann proceeded to build what is now Old St. Patrick's with a maximum of energy and, to save money, a minimum of unnecessary furnishing and detail.

For political reasons, Concanen was detained in Naples, where, in 1810, he died. Meanwhile Kohlmann had established a Latin school that would have been the Jesuits' future college in New York had not Georgetown taken preference, and Kohlmann was recalled in 1815 to serve there. But not before a famous law case he successfully fought over the sanctity of the confessional. As a result of Kohlmann's stand, the protected nature of the Catholic confessional gradually became the legal norm for the entire country. What Kohlmann represented to Toussaint was, of course, a man who knew when to stand fast. (Another Jesuit, Father Benedict Fenwick, pastor from 1815–1817, welcomed the first New York bishop to actually arrive in the city, Bishop John Connolly, in 1815. There were sixty thousand inhabitants, fifteen thousand Catholics, and three priests, all Jesuits.)

There were several other admirable St. Peter's pastors, but the third one of towering stature during Toussaint's years was Dr. John Power (1822–1849). Father Power was not simply Toussaint's pastor, he was also a friend and admirer, and a major figure in Toussaint's circle. (He preached the first sermon in the rebuilt church and worked tirelessly to pay off its debt. He died the year after it went bankrupt.)

Power is regularly mentioned in the Toussaint correspondence, and was held in the highest esteem. With a financially strapped parish, Power kept up the pressure on others, but on no one more than himself. Toussaint is one of many to receive regular notices from Power that stressed, "I renew my request that you will not fail to attend [a scheduled St. Peter's Society meeting] with your friends, and thus confer an obligation on a pastor ever anxious for your happiness here and here after." Power had established the Society to work specifically toward the reduction of the parish's rebuilding debt. Dues were $3 a year.

What brought about the bankruptcy and the ignomy that killed Power was something that had bedeviled St. Peter's from its start: the rivalries between the laboring Irish Catholic majority and the better-educated French minority. Long before Toussaint's (or Power's) advent on the scene, differing views had created the first schism in the American Catholic Church even before the city's first Catholic church was opened. It was a complex battleground—outside the scope of this book—known as "trusteeism." (Essentially its basis was an anguished and prolonged disagreement about who actually controlled the parish properties and income. It was also a question of U.S. law and American practice confronting a European church's expectations. In Manhattan, the French sided with one priest, the Irish sided with another. As the nineteenth century opened, these disagreements were not limited to New York.)

That the French-Irish rivalries cut across history is evident in the fact that for the past two centuries, New York has had only one French-born bishop. Without exception, all others have been Irish or Irish-American.

French-speaking Catholics like Toussaint reveled in the presence of Dubois and the visits of Boston's Bishop Chevereux, a priest and bishop of singular quality. Chevereux was friend to many in Toussaint's circle, including Madame Larue and Catherine Cruger. When Catherine died, Chevereux praised her life and work even though she was not a Catholic.

Father Power spoke not only French, but also Latin, Greek, Spanish, Italian, and Gaelic. He was instrumental in the founding of New York's first Catholic newspaper, *The Truth Teller,* and in inviting, on Easter Sunday 1841, the visiting French bishop, Charles-Auguste de Frobin-Janson, bishop of Nancy, to preach. In that gesture, Power sealed St. Peter's financial fate. The French bishop appealed to the French congregation for funds to build a French church in New York. Toussaint came forward with the first donation: $100 (about $2,000 today), for what became the St. Vincent de Paul church.

Without the French parishioners' contributions, for most had left and registered as St. Vincent parishioners, St. Peter's could not pay off even the mounting interest on its debts. In 1844 it fell into bankruptcy. Eventually the New York bishop stepped in to redeem its fate. One oddity, however, is noted. Despite his loyal support of St. Peter's for more than forty years, there is no record that Toussaint made any financial contribution toward the new building or to prevent the bankruptcy. It is quite possible that he was instead funneling what money he could spare to his two main charities, both Catholic orphanages. Possibly in Euphémie's memory, he was as generous as circumstances permitted to the Sisters of Charity's orphan asylum in New York and the Oblate Sisters' "school for children or orphans of color" in Baltimore.

For the first eight years of the 1840s, Pierre and Juliette are energetic and generally in good health (though Juliette had a very serious illness in 1836 and was plagued by rheumatism). In the 1840s, when Toussaint was still as hard at work as ever, the worsening arthritis in his right knee made his long-distance walking to appointments a further challenge.

But he was consistent. Before his losses in the Great Fire, a friend asked him: "Toussaint, you are richer than any one I know; you have more than you want, why not stop working now?" He answered, "Madam, I have enough for myself, but if I stop work, I have not enough for others." The same was true after the fire and through the 1840s. The early New York priests and bishops were notoriously overworked. Toussaint could commiserate and, seeing their lives, could scarcely complain about his own twelve- to sixteen-hour days.

Juliette goes periodically to Baltimore to stay with Fanny and visit Noël family members and the Oblate Sisters. At least one member of the Noël family enters the convent during this decade. Pierre, too, traveled; to Baltimore on more than one occasion; to Philadelphia to see the new chapel to Blessed John Neumann (C.SS.R); and to Boston, perhaps. There is reference to him visiting Nevis, not the Caribbean island but one of the Schuyler family estates, to see young Philip Schuyler.

Much is missing from the historical account. No Bérards wrote after the 1834 letter from her sister that announced Aurore was dead. There is no date for Jean Sorbieu's death, and no further mention of Gabriel Nicolas. The fate of Pierre's sister Marie-Louise is not known, nor that of his brother. Mary Anna sees Toussaint regularly, and writes only from abroad or on other travels.

> I have returned from church. The service was performed in a Catholic chapel, with all the insignia. I thought of my dear Toussaint, and send my love to him. Tell him I think of him very often, and never go to one of the churches of his faith without remembering my own St. Pierre, *and nobody has a better saint.*

Judged solely on the number of letters that have survived, Toussaint's major correspondents into this decade were Césarine Moulton and her father, Raymond Meetz; Madame Larue in Le Havre; the Lagnels in Paris; and in America the children of early friends such as Charles Phoenix in Sodus, New York, and B. D. Villagrand (daughter of his co–best man, Jerome Villagrand) in Virginia. Only the letters of Juliette's friend Fanny cover a longer period than Larue's—from the 1820s to the

1850s. A letter from Fanny is the last letter received by Toussaint before his death in 1853.

There's happy news to kick off the decade. In March 1840, Raymond Meetz wrote: "soon you are going to have the advantage of seeing our Césarine and we regret her departure and her absence . . . you know my disquietude over the sickness and perils of the crossing . . . in the end, my dear, we must have confidence in God, and count on providence as our protection. Your response will tell me of their happy arrival—on the Batterie [the New York Battery] the first or 2nd of May." Soon Villagrand's daughter is writing from Botecourt Springs, "in your last letter you told me of Mrs. Moulton's arrival. She has without doubt eclipsed all the fine ladies of your city with her beauty and splendour—give me all the details."

Father Paddington, probably the Western Hemisphere's only black priest, is in Ireland, en route to Rome. His letter positively explodes with happiness. "I have found all my family and was with my old friends who are in good health and so pleased to see me, again and again as affectionate as possible." From "morning til night" he is visiting, and being entertained at lunches and dinners galore. "All the priests have received me with the greatest respect possible; lunch with the vicar general and dinners at all the churches after saying mass. Finally, in spite of the urgings of all my friends" off he goes again: Bristol, London, Southampton, Le Havre, Rouen, Paris, Lyon, Avignon, Marseille, Geneva, Sivourne, Civitavecchia, and Rome.

While Paddington has somewhere fresh to stay each day, the busy work for Toussaint continues. A Paris friend writes: "I am advising you Toussaint of the unhappiness that I have lost my wife. Would you please obtain for me my marriage certificate from the French consul." (He enclosed $29 "to my account"— Toussaint had apparently loaned him money.) "I beg of you haste," he wrote. Another writes from France that his uncle has died. The uncle, mentally ill, did not leave the address of the man handling his affairs in New York. Can Toussaint locate this man? From the Montreal seminary Collège de St.-Hyacinthe, Michel McDonell asks for help—he is living off 25 piastres a month whereas the other seminarians have 50. "Thank you for the service you have rendered me and the friendship you have always shown me, particularly in the critical circumstances of my last visit to NY." There are many pleas for money. And Toussaint is still the confidant: "I value your discretion and I beg you that you not make known to my sister the extremely great secret in this letter." (The information concerned the writer's father.)

The Toussaints are an understanding pair. Adèle d'Armagnac in Baltimore knows in advance she'll be forgiven when she apologizes to Juliette, "sorry if my letter caused you despair—do not keep the bad part, consider that I was sick when I wrote it." Loïsa de Boesteind, by contrast, can be relied on for good humor, or reassurance. "The long sojourn I have made in Italy gives me a little chance to correspond with New York, my good Toussaint, and to give you some tokens of the trip as a souvenir. You are always in my prayers and I love to think you do not forget me in yours. The little dictionary you have given me goes with me always, even when there is no need for it. It reminds Loïsa of you every day. I never participate in our church at a religious ceremony without thinking of you, without missing you."

As the decade begins to check off the years, the Villagrands' little school is not prospering in Botecourt Spring, Virginia. One of Villagrand's daughters, Estelle Johnson, writes that her brother-in-law, a wandering artist, committed the school without their knowledge to a $1,000 debt. "This is the cause of our ruin." Friends of her husband, Mr. Johnson, are hoping to obtain for him a place as a professor at the university at Charlottesville. Pray for us my friend, for there is nothing more efficacious than the prayers of the good."

The trek to New Orleans continues for the Toussaints' black friends. And he is still assisting in their exodus. One friend wrote: "After 20 days [aboard ship] we have arrived in New Orleans tired but in good health. We've been here 3½ months. We are all installed in the same house with my brother who is aided in his commerce by his wife who runs a grocery store that makes a small profit. I think New Orleans offers many resources and in July next the railroad will reach here. A great many strangers abound in New Orleans, the majority émigrés like us. Present our respects to Madame Schuyler, embrace Madame Toussaint for us, and pray think of our friendship and our eternal thankfulness to you."

Gumbo remains a culinary glue in the long-distance relationships. N. Bailly's son has died. He knows Toussaint will understand his grief. Referring to Toussaint's losses in the Great Fire, Bailly adds, "We admire your philosophy and courage in that you lost so much money but continue to give it. Thank Juliette for the gumbo."

If the gumbo has never stopped it is because Toussaint is an assiduous seeker of supplies. Clair Gautier in Philadelphia tells Toussaint, "My dear countryman, regarding your desire to buy a quantity of gumbo seasoning, we have to be in season for gumbo, my dear countryman, and that moment has nearly passed. I have found five half packs at two shillings the half pack. I will send it with Mr. Alexander." In Paris, Marie Navarre's sons have eaten all the gumbo he sent "and we are obliged to Madame Toussaint for it. Saved for special occasions, and delicious meal." Her husband is retiring from his business, the years are flying by. The Baillys, too, have gumbo: "We have received with pleasure the gumbo you sent. We are persuaded this is homemade. Thank Madame Toussaint for us. When we eat it we shall drink a toast to you both. I wish I was a bird so I could fly to New York for a visit."

The events that fill daily life continued: a meeting of the

fabriciens of the new French Church on Canal Street; requiem masses and memorials for deceased friends. The Toussaints moved from Reade Street to Franklin Street in 1845. Toussaint would have bought the Reade Street premises but the asking price was $6,000 and Pierre had decided $5,000 was his maximum. He still maintained his hairdressing shop, now at 141 Canal Street.

Friends gathered afresh—now in the front parlor of Franklin Street, the first home the Toussaints owned. The welcome, jollity, and reassurance these friends had always experienced in the Toussaint home they carried with them for the rest of their lives. Nothing changed in the move of a dozen blocks.

The Moultons, too, are moving—into their Le Château de Petit Val. Césarine writes in these years with a mixture of joy and sadness, and that mixture begins to set the tone for the balance of the decade. In 1843, Césarine has told Toussaint she is preoccupied with "the health of our son Fred who you saw on our last voyage [three years earlier]. One sees the huge veins stand out in a huge forehead white as snow. He thinks all the time and I think he is too advanced for his age. He is very nervous with heart palpitations and little [movements]." She describes the attributes of her other children with some amusement. A year later, sadly, she notes Frederic has died. The child struggled for "six long months. Each day," wrote Césarine, "we thought it would be the last. His resignation, his patience, his piety were an example even for those with white hair. He said to me one time: 'Dear little mother, why must I suffer? Is it because our Saviour suffered?' "

What a loss for the Moultons. What a loss, too, that Toussaint's letters to his friends—Césarine, Mary Anna, Catherine, Jean Sorbieu, and the many others—written at the moments of their greatest sorrow, have not survived. What consolation did he bring in the written word to those gripped by grief when he could not be present in person? What did he say?

Toussaint knew the Moulton children. The elder sons were in college. Charly, the firstborn, of all Toussaint's correspondents, is the only nonfamily member to address him in the familiar *tu*. Charles said he writes on July 4 and wonders what it is like in New York that day. "Write to me and tell me if the day was good or bad," he asks Toussaint, and adds, "Why don't you come to France for a visit. It is not a long trip traversing the ocean in a steamship. We would be so happy to receive you."

Alas, it could not be. By 1849, Juliette was totally bedridden.

One friend who wrote that year tied together a lifetime. Their acquaintanceship may have begun in their mutual Saint Domingue childhoods. The writer referred to Toussaint as "venerable" (a foretaste of the title the church conferred on Toussaint one hundred and fifty years later): "My Dear and Venerable Compatriot, so far off as I am from you, I think of you always. I wend my way to Franklin Street at least once a day, in imagination."

Juliette was failing. The letters from her lifelong friend Fanny were constant, filled with concern and anguish. And prayer. Fanny was trying to reassure Toussaint as well as herself. Juliette dearly wanted her to come to New York for a final visit. By 1851, Fanny was filling her letters with news of the Noël family and the Oblate Sisters, and she counseled patience to Toussaint. She also told Pierre that new laws were going to be enacted that were "very unfavorable to people of color."

Toussaint was hopeful. "As in Euphémie's case, Toussaint was sanguine that Juliette would recover. He said, 'She is much younger than myself—she is strong, very strong. She is nervous—she will soon be better.' But it became evident that she grew more ill, and he could no longer shut his eyes upon her danger.

"I often went to see Juliette," a friend told Hannah Lee. "She indicated the prie-dieu in the hallway between their bedrooms. 'Ah,' said Juliette, 'he prays for me there—it is all the comfort he has; he will soon be alone. Poor Toussaint!' "

Juliette died on May 14, 1851.

Lee wrote: "He never recovered from the shock. It seemed to him most strange that she should go first, and he be left alone; yet he constantly said, 'It is the will of God.' " Fanny was mortified with grief. "Had I known that Juliette was so sick I would have made the sacrifice to come to New York to see her."

Said Lee, "Every man must value the respect of his wife, and Toussaint could not but be gratified with the evident delight Juliette received from the attentions paid him. When her friends congratulated her on having such a good husband, her frank, happy smile gave a full assent to their commendations. One of the methods in which Toussaint did essential good works [was] by bringing up colored boys one after another, sending them to school, and, after they were old enough, teaching them some useful business. In all these plans of charity Juliette united."

"Juliette," said a white lodger, "was a good woman."

The good wife of a good husband.

The requiem mass for Juliette was celebrated in St. Peter's Church. Toussaint asked, and this was respected, that only black friends accompany the cortege on foot through the street to the cemetery. The white friends were in attendance at the St. Patrick's graveyard when the funeral party arrived.

Madame Marie Rose Juliette Toussaint was laid to rest in the same plot as Euphémie.

$\mathscr{R}$EST IN $\mathscr{P}$EACE

JULIETTE WAS GONE. Toussaint's circle was closing in. One friend whom he continued to visit daily was Mary Anna Schuyler. He was now seventy, she sixty-five, neither of them in particularly good health. He continued to attend to the details of his life. He had early drawn up a will; now he amended it. But it was as much a statement of faith as a disposition of his estate:

> It was the holy will of God to take from me my beloved adopted daughter, Euphémie and I submitted to the blow with faith in the wisdom of my Heavenly Father but then especially did I appreciate the friendship and sympathy of my two friends Catherine Cruger (who has finished her life of constant benevolence and disinterestedness) and Mary Anne Schuyler, now of the City of New York.

He'd intended his estate would go to their heirs:

Though the pleasure of my Heavenly Father has taken from me my beloved wife, Juliette, and her mother, Claudine Gaston, and thus all the provisions of my said will become inoperative. . . . It was once in my will, before it please Almighty God to remove him from this world to higher duties, that this part of my estate be enjoyed by William Sawyer Schuyler, the eldest son of my friends Philip J. Schuyler and Mary Anne Schuyler, as one upon I had placed my warmest and deepest love. But my Heavenly Father had seen it good to call his pure spirit to His own immediate presence. . . .

I pray that Philip ["Little Philip," son of Mary Anne's son George Lee Schuyler] may live to equal virtue, truth and kindness of heart which won for his departed uncle, William, the love of all on whom his smile of gladness fell.

There were the expected bequests. To Father Quinn, St. Peter's pastor, $100 for his personal use and a further $100 for masses for the repose of Toussaint's soul ("when that should become necessary," added Toussaint, in a mischievous touch). There were gifts to be purchased for those who cared for him, a few surviving friends.

But he was not dead yet.

Indeed, he had another loved one to bury. Mary Anna Schuyler now fell ill. "One bitter pang remained for him; to watch by the death-bed of that being who, from her exalted station, had poured strength and consolation into his wounded heart; who had often left the gay circles of fashion to speak to him words of peace and kindness, and who, when the shadows of death were coming over her, gave orders that Toussaint should always be admitted."

He went daily to sit with her in her room, seated quietly, saying prayers if she was sleeping. She died in the spring of 1852. "The last time I saw Pierre," wrote one friend, "he was seated

among a group of mourners, beside the coffin of a lady vener-
ated for years in the highest social sphere of the city. She was almost the last tie that bound him to the past. He had visited her
daily for thirty years, and brought his offering of flowers; and
there he sat, with his white head bowed in grief, and every line
of his honest sable face wet with tears. It was a beautiful homage
to worth—a beautiful instance of what may be the disinterested
relation between the exalted and the humble—when the genius
of character and the sentiment of religion bring them thus together.

Hannah Lee notes: "His health was now evidently failing,
yet morning after morning, through snow and ice and wintry
frosts, his slow and tottering step was seen on his way to Mass,
which he never once failed to attend for sixty years, until a few
months before his death; and later in the day, his aged frame,
bowed with years, was to be seen painfully working its way to a
distant part of the city, on errands of love and charity. A friend
said to him thoughtlessly, 'Toussaint, do get into an omnibus.'
He replied, with perfect good humor, 'I cannot, they will not let
me.'

"As he grew more feeble he was obliged to give up his attendance on the church. This occasioned him some depression.
One of his Protestant friends who observed it said, 'Shall I ask a
priest to come and see you? Perhaps you wish to confess.' After
a long pause he said, 'A priest is but a man; when I am at confession, I confess to God; when I stand up, I see a man before
me.' "

Hannah Lee traveled down from Boston to visit him.

"When I last saw Toussaint, I perceived that his days were
numbered, that he stood on the borders of the infinite. He was
feeble, but sitting in an arm-chair, clad in his dressing gown,
and supported by pillows. A more perfect representation of a
gentleman I have seldom seen. His head was strewed with the

'blossoms of the grave.' When he saw me he was overcome by affecting remembrances, for we had last met at the funeral obsequies of the friend so dear to him. He trembled with emotion, and floods of tears fell from his eyes. 'It is all so changed! so changed!' said he, 'so lonely!' He was too weak to converse, but his mind was filled with images of the past, of the sweet and noble lady to whose notes we are indebted. The next day I saw him again, and took leave of him to see him no more in this world. It was with deep feeling I quitted his house—that house where I had seen the beings he dearly loved collected. It was a bright summer morning, the last of May; the windows were open, and looked into the little garden, with its few scattered flowers." Hannah knew few of his visitors—the old friends were gone.

After Lee returned home, a friend from earlier days, Eliza Hamilton Schuyler, Mary Anna's daughter-in-law, was his most regular visitor. She sent notes to Hannah Lee regarding Toussaint's condition. In June, just before his death, Eliza wrote:

> Toussaint was in bed to-day; he says it is now the most comfortable place for him, or as he expressed it in French, "Il ne peut pas être mieux." He was drowsy and indistinct, but calm, cheerful, and placid—the expression of his countenance truly religious.
>
> He told me he had received the last communion, for which he had been earnest, and mentioned that two Sisters of Charity had been to see him, and prayed with him. He speaks of the excellent care he receives—of his kind nurse [she is a white woman]—and said, "All is well." He sent me away when he was tired, by thanking me.

A few days later, Hannah Lee received the note she knew was inevitable:

Excellent Toussaint! he has gone to those he loved. His departure took place yesterday at twelve o'clock [June 30, 1853], without pain or suffering, and without any change from extreme feebleness. I saw him on Sunday; he was very low, and neither spoke nor noticed me.

On Monday, when I entered, he had revived a little, and looking up, said "Dieu avec moi"—"God is with me." When I asked him if he wanted any thing, he replied with a smile, "Rien sur la terre"—"Nothing on earth."

I did not think he was so near the gates of heaven; but on Thursday, at twelve o'clock, his spirit was released from its load. How much I shall miss him every day, for I saw him every day—every day!

The New York newspapers reported his passing. Some at length. These are excerpts:

Pierre Toussaint, whose funeral will take place this morning, at ten o'clock, from St. Peter's Church, Barclay Street, was born in the servitude of St. Domingo. All knew his general worth, but few were acquainted with the generous qualities of his heart, and with those principles of disinterested and genuine kindness which governed his daily conduct.

His charity was of the efficient character which did not content itself with a present relief of pecuniary aid, but which required time and thought by day and by night, and long watchfulness and kind attentions at the bedside of the sick and the departing. Thus goodness springing from refined and elevated principle, and from a sense of religious duty, which never permitted him to omit a most scrupulous compliance with all the requirements of his faith, formed the prominent feature of his character, and made his life a constant round of acts of kindness and sympathy.

By such a life, governed by such principles of integrity, charity, and religion, Toussaint secured to himself the respect, esteem, and friendship of many of our first citizens; and though death has made the circle small in which he had moved, there are yet remaining many who remember his excellence and worth with the kindest appreciation.

The New York *Evening Post* stated:

. . . Toussaint is spoken of by all who knew him as a man of the warmest and most active benevolence, the gentlest temper, and the most courteous and graceful, yet wholly unassuming manners. The successive pastors of St. Peter's Church had all the same opinion of him, and it is said, that, when the present pastor came to bury him, he observed that he had not such a man left among his congregation. It is related of a gentleman, formerly of this city, distinguished for the wit and point of his conversation, that he was one day talking with a lady, who instanced Hyde de Neuville as more fully illustrating her idea of a perfect gentleman than any other person she had known. He replied: "The most perfect gentleman I have ever known is Pierre Toussaint."

The *Home Journal* correspondent said:

We cannot allow this brief announcement to form the sole record of one whose example is a higher vindication of his race, or rather a nobler testimony to the beauty and force of character, than all the works of fiction that studious invention ever conceived. Pierre Toussaint for more than sixty years had been the most respected and beloved Negro in New York. . . . A very few of the brides, whose tresses he so daintily arrayed, yet survive; and as long as any of them lived, Pierre paid them regular visits, and was always certain of a kind reception.

He devoted himself to social and benevolent duty. His relations in the former respect were threefold: first, to his cherished lady friends and their families, whom he had attended in youth, and towards whom he exhibited a disinterested and loyal attachment, which seemed to belong to a past age or a different country, so unique and touching was its manifestation; second, to the French population of New York, to which he was attached by early association and native language; and thirdly, to his own race. By these so widely different classes Pierre was both respected and beloved. He moved among them in a way peculiarly his own. He possessed a sense of the appropriate, a self-respect, and a uniformity of demeanor, which amounted to genius.

For sixty years he attended Mass at six in the morning, as punctual as a clock, until prostrated by illness. His days and nights were given to visits, ministrations to the sick, attendance upon the bereaved, and attempts to reform the erring and console the afflicted. Often strangers paused to look with curiosity and surprise upon the singular tableau presented in Broadway of the venerable Negro, with both his hands clasped in greeting by a lady high in the circles of fashion or birth, and to watch the vivid interest of both, as they exchanged inquiries for each other's welfare.

Eliza provided the description of Toussaint's funeral. "I went to town on Saturday, to attend Toussaint's funeral. High Mass, incense, candles, rich robes, sad and solemn music, were there. The Church gave all it could give, to prince or noble. The priest, his friend Mr. Quinn, made a most interesting address. He did not allude to his color, and scarcely to his station; it seemed as if his virtues as a man and a Christian had absorbed all other thoughts. A stranger would not have suspected that a black man, of his humble calling, lay in the midst of us."

Eliza recounted that the eulogy spoke of the aid Toussaint

had given "to the late Bishop Fenwick of Boston [previously St. Peter's pastor], to Father Power of our city, to all the Catholic institutions." This, she said, "was dwelt upon at large. How much I have learnt of his charitable deeds, which I had never known before! Mr. Quinn said, 'There were few left among the clergy superior to him in devotion and zeal for the Church and for the glory of God; among laymen, none.'

"The body of the church was well filled with men, women, children, nuns, and charity sisters; likewise a most respectable collection of people of his own color, all in mourning. Around stood many of the white race, with their eyes glistening with emotion. When Juliette was buried, Toussaint requested that none of his white friends would follow her remains; his request was remembered now, and respected; they stood back as the coffin was borne from the church, but when lowered to its last depository, many were gathered around his grave."

Many other touching remembrances might be added. One French lady said: "He dressed my hair for my First Communion; he dressed it for my wedding, and for christenings, for balls and parties." And then she added why they loved him: "At burials, in sickness and in trouble, he was always here."

"He was always here." For rich and poor, for black and white, for friend or down and out.

One of Catherine Cruger's daughters, likely Henrietta, wrote to Hannah Lee: "If my mother were living, how much she could tell us of Toussaint! But unfortunately," she wrote, "I never kept notes of the many incidents she used to relate of his character; I regret it sincerely now. At the time of Euphemia's death we were in France, but most deeply did we feel for him.

"When we returned I saw him constantly, and began to comprehend him, which I never did fully before. I saw how uncommon, how noble, was his character. It is the *whole* which strikes me when thinking of him; his perfect Christian benevolence, displaying itself not alone in words, but in daily deeds; his entire faith, love, and charity; his remarkable tact, and refinement of feeling; his just appreciation of those around him; his perfect good taste in dress and furniture—he did not like any thing gaudy, and understood the relative fitness of things."

OSTSCRIPT

HE WAS SAINTLY, but was he a saint?

His white friend Mary Anna Schuyler said yes and committed it to writing, "My *Saint* Pierre."

Henrietta Cruger saw holiness in Toussaint's decision to never let the world dictate his conduct: "He entertained an utter aversion to all vain pride and assumption. I recollect how invariably he consulted the dignity of others, as well as his own. His religion was fervent, sincere, and made a part of himself; it was never," she emphasized, "laid aside for worldly purposes."

His black friend in Chicago seemed convinced, and said why: "because you perceive and follow the naked truth." The friend meant, of course, a particular truth. The truth that is the beatitudes. The truth in the Way, the Truth, and the Light.

It is possible today to go to St. Peter's Church in New York City where Toussaint worshiped. One may sit in the pew he sat in, or in the same pews his mourners sat in. One may gaze on the same altarpiece and carvings they saw. Seated, and thinking about Toussaint's life, it is not difficult to understand, as those present one hundred and fifty years ago understood, precisely what Father Quinn meant when he eulogized:

> Though no relative is left to mourn for him, yet many present feel that they have lost one who always had wise counsel for the rich and words of encouragement for the poor.

Father Quinn would then have looked out at the crowded church, on those who had known Toussaint well, and those whose lives he had only lightly touched, as he added,

> And all are grateful for having known him.

$\mathscr{A}$PPENDIX

KEY DATES IN TOUSSAINT'S LIFE

On the cover of the 1993 deposition submitted to Rome proposing the beatification and canonization of Pierre Toussaint (Congregatio de Causis Sanctorum Prot. N. 1647), the dates for Toussaint's life are given as 1766–1853. The first date is undoubtedly incorrect. These are the dates based on the Hannah Lee biography, which also states he arrived in New York in 1787.

Subsequent research and writing (P. H. Gaschnignard and G. Ladevic), acknowledged within the deposition, strongly suggests that Toussaint was not born until at least 1780. There is now documentary evidence that Jean-Jacques Bérard did not arrive in New York until 1797. (This evidence was generally accepted by Archbishop M. N. L. Couve de Murville in his 1995 Catholic Truth Society pamphlet, "Slave from Haiti: Slave from New York?" He suggested 1778 for Toussaint's birth.)

This author has fixed Toussaint as five years junior to his godmother, Aurore Bérard, and five years senior to his sister Rosalie. Rosalie's age is known from the record of her freedom, granted in New York in 1811. Her given age was twenty-five. If Pierre was five years older, and he was no older than that, for they were childhood playmates, he'd be thirty, and again the birth year would be 1781.

French investigation has determined that Aurore, the youngest of the Bérard children, was born in 1776. It was not unusual for children to be godparents in French colonial practice. Allowing that Aurore was five when she became Pierre's godmother, that, too, would have been in 1781. Margaret Silsby, an American historian who studies the women in Toussaint's life, believes Toussaint was born even later than 1781.

Because Lee wrote the memoir after Mary Anna's and Pierre's deaths, she had no one with whom to check her dates and facts. No one remained who'd known Toussaint in earlier life, and if they were still alive, they were unknown or inaccessible to Lee. Besides, Lee could not speak or read French, nor could her sister. Plus Toussaint's English was fractured, not fluent. There was room for misimpression and misunderstanding. In addition, no documentation exists in Haiti, and no documentation survived the trip from Saint Domingue to New York. The most likely explanation for the 1766 date (and it would fit) is that this was the birth year of Toussaint's master, Jean-Jacques Bérard.

The major point, however, is much simpler. While Toussaint's age has a bearing on his experience and wisdom as he made his decisions, in fact his life's acts and deeds and friendships remain as they are regardless of his birth year.

CANONIZATION CAUSE

The Relator of the Cause, Prof. Dr. P. Peter Gumpel, S.J., submitted the two-volume *Positio* on November 14, 1993. Since that time, while miracles have been attributed to Pierre Toussaint by families of persons cured through Toussaint's intercession, at the time of this writing no miracle has been confirmed by the Congregation for the Causes of Saints.

DOLLARS AND SENSE

Throughout the Toussaint correspondence many currencies are used: gourdes; francs; livres; pounds, shillings, and pence; even piastres. In the text, where the actual sum mattered to the context, many amounts were translated into twenty-first-century dollars. Others were retained simply to preserve the eighteenth- or nineteenth-century flavor.

On his death, Toussaint left a recorded appraised estate of $19,430. All of it was listed as "personal" rather than business or investment wealth. According to Georgiana Schuyler Brandt, Mary Anna Schuyler's granddaughter, the actual sum was nearer $30,000. The difference may come from the fact that Georgiana's father, George Lee Schuyler, held real estate on behalf of Toussaint.

"Toussaint left quite a little fortune, some $30,000, a third share to my brother. In his later years when there was a loss of [Schuyler] fortune, part of this sum was spent on my brother's education. My father [George Lee Schuyler, Mary Anna and Philip's second-born son] assisted Toussaint in his investments—he held real estate for him when it was against the law for Negroes to hold real estate."

What that $30,000 is worth in today's money ($750,000) is fairly easily arrived at through U.S. Department of Labor Consumer Price Index tables. There's the added factor that Toussaint lived in a virtually tax-free society: no income tax, sales tax, or inheritance duties.

In one sense, what the $750,000 tells us is that Toussaint bounced back fairly well financially after his enormous losses in the Great Fire of 1835, primarily because of Manhattan real estate prices resuming their inexorable climb. It also says that before the fire, Toussaint was wealthy indeed.

After Toussaint's death, his estate spent little money. There was

$40.15 for his headstone, engraved and erected by stonemason Hart in the Mulberry Street burial ground of Old St. Patrick's, plus $9.13 paid to the sexton for his services.

Pierre's several-thousand-word will, the longest piece of writing attributed to him (though translated for him), is a matter of public record in the Toussaint Papers of the New York Public Library. It is a declaration of his love for his immediate family and friends, a clear statement of his reliance on God, and yet further testimony to his innate generosity of spirit.

> Signed, sealed, published and declared by the above named Pierre Toussaint as and for the First Codicil to his last will and testament dated the fifteenth day of September one thousand eight hundred and forty-two, in the presence of us who at his request, in his presence and in the presence of each other have subscribed our names as witnesses to the execution thereof.
> Washington I. Morton of the City of New York, residing 54 Varick St. Robert S. Bullers of the City of New York, residing at No. 10 Beach St.

RACE VERSUS CLASS ISSUES

There is in Lee an account of an occasion when Juliette and Pierre Toussaint invite four white women to call for afternoon chocolate. Hannah Lee sees the event only in relation to race whereas issues of class and nationality (two visitors were French) could equally be key to what transpired:

> One of the [Toussaints'] social parties was pleasantly described to me by a white American acquaintance who had called on them, and whom Juliette invited with a companion to visit her. [There's little doubt the two American visitors were Lee's sister Mary Anna Schuyler with her sister-in-law Cather-

ine Church Cruger—the latter back in America on a visit home from France.] They belonged to the household of one of his most cherished and respected friends. They found only two Frenchwomen as guests beside themselves. The table was most neatly set out with snowy damask table-cloth and napkins, and exhibiting many of the elegant little memorials pertaining to the tea-table which had been sent to them as presents from their friends in Paris. Juliette sat at the head, and waited on them, treating them with her delicious French chocolate, but of which she did not herself partake. When they had finished the repast, they went into the contiguous room and Toussaint joined the party. It was thus his sense of propriety led him to draw the line. He never mingled the two races. This might have been in some measure the result of early teaching, but there was evidently a self-respect in avoiding what he knew was unwelcome.

Of course, Juliette and Pierre did mingle the two races. Hannah Lee says as much herself, that many pale faces visited them at home.

The four white women had come to the Toussaint home for chocolate. The outside world witnessing this, as indeed it did in gossipy New York, did not know whether Juliette and Pierre actually broke bread at the same table as their white friends. And apparently the Toussaints were not concerned with the impression given to the world. (This particular event would likely have been in the 1830s, after the death of Toussaint's niece, Euphémie, or Lee would have mentioned Euphémie providing the musical entertainment, which she invariably did at Toussaint social gatherings.)

The question is why Juliette and Pierre did not also participate in the chocolate and the light repast. Hannah Lee gives the impression it was more a matter of race than of social class.

Toussaint, of course, had to operate on several levels within the two different communities represented by his visitors: the American white community and the French white community.

In front of visitors, he would never assume a familiarity with Catherine or Mary Anna that might be present in less formal settings. The Toussaints did not take chocolate with Mrs. Schuyler and Mrs. Cruger because, in Toussaint's mind at least, he was in the service trade. Whatever else they were—and Mary Anna and Catherine, as Schuylers, were his friends and visited more than once—they were also his clients, and members of New York's first families.

Even in the twenty-first century, an American servant, a butler, would never dine at table with his American employer. Extremely strong social conventions did not allow it in Toussaint's day, and do not allow it now.

By contrast, Juliette and Pierre might well have taken chocolate with their white French visitors, for under French law, blacks and whites were equal. Toussaint was very aware of that difference in his status.

Consider the same social nuances in the case of Euphémie's piano instruction. Césarine Meetz, the accomplished teenaged musician daughter of Toussaint's French émigré professional musician friend Raymond Meetz, offered to come to Toussaint's home to teach Euphémie the piano. Without payment—just out of friendship for the family she loved and to help an obviously talented little girl.

Toussaint would not hear of it. It would not be proper. Mademoiselle Meetz, possibly eighteen at the time, was a young French lady. Her father was well connected at the French court. Her regular attendance at 105 Reade Street as a volunteer tutor would appear, in Toussaint's judgment, too close to a servant function for Pierre to permit it. (A young lone white woman regularly visiting a black man's home might arouse other forms of gossip, too.)

A compromise was reached. For four years Juliette or another adult escorted Euphémie to the Meetzes' residence for the lessons.

However, when Césarine wed and returned to Paris as Mrs. Charles Moulton, Toussaint promptly hired a male tutor. This was his Saint Domingan acquaintance Monsieur Gentil. He was white and socially superior to Pierre. Yet Gentil taught Euphémie in the Toussaint home. The difference between Gentil and Mademoiselle Meetz was not primarily that the well-born Gentil was male, but that he was earning his living as a piano teacher, just as Toussaint was earning his living as a hairdresser.

TOUSSAINT'S EDUCATIONAL LEVEL

Though it has been suggested, it is unlikely Toussaint was self-educated, though he read widely on his own. His handwriting and French grammar point to some formal training. The options are that he was home-schooled with the younger Bérard family children in their nursery or that Jean-Jacques Bérard took Pierre under his wing when the master was still single and not long removed from being a student himself. An equally plausible third option is that Pierre was taught by a local priest from St. Marc.

At times Lee has Toussaint speaking a quaint American plantation English (at other times his quoted speech is similar to Hannah's): "Toussaint dresses hair, he no news journal," or "Miss Regina, your mother very good."

The fact is, Toussaint could not have spoken this way. His entry into the English language came by way of courtly conversational French. He spoke the flawless French of Saint Domingue's aristocracy. French people learning English do, if anything, overemphasize the intransitive verb through their use of pronouns.

It would be almost linguistically impossible for Toussaint, as a French-speaker reaching into English, to omit the "is" in his declarations. He would more likely say, "Toussaint, he dresses hair, he is no news journal."

(Keep in mind, Lee was working from Mary Anna's notes and neither read nor spoke French.)

Lee probably had the year wrong when she wrote: "When the colored people in New York celebrated their release from bondage, on the 5th of July, 1800, they came to Toussaint to offer him a prominent part in the procession. He thanked them with his customary politeness, congratulated them on the great event of emancipation, but declined the honor they assigned him, saying, 'I do not owe my freedom to the State, but to my mistress.' "

More likely, Lee refers to July 1827, the date on which the New York State law freeing the children of slaves took effect. Toussaint had already been freed and was likely quite conscious of the fact he was not an American citizen.

Lee adjudges Toussaint a man "governed by a high and noble principle." He was a man, she said, "who reflected deeply" yet "had no theories of philosophy." She may never have moved in the circles where Toussaint's philosophical bent (if he had one) was aired. Lee may be correct, though given that neither spoke the other's language, there is a gap without a strong bridge. Toussaint's correspondents do note his wide range of interests, which isn't the same as having a philosophical bent. They relied on him, too, for current information on sociopolitical and cultural events. He attends concerts, the theater, and lectures as time allows; his friends acknowledge his widespread interests.

His white friend C. Phoenix, writing a jocular letter to Toussaint while on a six-week vacation in upstate New York, remarks, "I know that Mr. Toussaint is a personage of great taste . . . I have no news to tell you, Monsieur, but nevertheless we do expect to hear a great deal from you. Remember that you are to inform us of all that passes in the *World,* let it be either of a political, fashionable or literary nature."

From France, one friend keeps Toussaint well informed of the intimate and political details of the French court and ruling class, mentioning aristocrats Toussaint would have known in New York during their sojourn away from the Terror. His correspondents, whether in Le Havre, France, or on a Caribbean island, all presume his deep interest in current events. For example, Diego Moya provides detailed information on the French-Haitian negotiations regarding reparations.

None of this is indicative of anything but Toussaint's overall interest in what goes on around him. He may have been without a philosophy, and he may have been "unlettered" (not formally schooled) as Lee suggests. But she was working from the handicap of not being able to speak his language.

CITIZENSHIP

There is nothing in any of the material to suggest that Toussaint either had or was interested in seeking U.S. citizenship. There is documentary evidence that he regarded himself as a French citizen, and he probably understood, given the return of some of his friends to Haiti, that he qualified for Haitian citizenship as well. In modern terms, think of Toussaint as a "green card" holder—someone legally entitled to residence in the United States.

$\mathscr{S}$ELECTED $\mathscr{B}$IBLIOGRAPHY

Baxter, Catherine Schuyler. *A Godchild of Washington*. London: F. Tennyson Neely, 1897.

Breathett, George, ed. *The Catholic Church in Haiti, 1704–1785: Selected Letters, Memoirs and Documents*. Salisbury, N.C.: Documentary Publications, 1983.

Corson, Richard. *Fashions in Hair: The First Five Thousand Years*. London: Peter Owen, 1965.

Davis, Cyprian, OSB. *The History of Black Catholics in the United States*. New York: Crossroad, 1990.

James, C.L.R. *The Black Jacobins: Toussaint-Louverture and the San Domingo Revolution*. New York: Vintage, 1963.

McNeill, William H. *Plagues and People*. New York: Anchor Books, 1977.

Ott, Thomas. *The Haitian Revolution: 1789–1804*. Knoxville Tenn.: University of Tennessee, 1973.

Smith, Thomas E.V. *The City of New York in the Year of Washington's In-*

auguration, 1789. Reprinted by Joseph Veach, director, Museum of the City of New York. Riverside, Conn.: Chatham Press, Inc., 1973.

Stoddard, T. Lothrop. *The French Revolution in Santo Domingo*. Westport, Conn.: Negro Universities Press, 1914.

Watts, Sheldon. *Epidemics and History: Disease, Power and Imperialism*. New Haven, Conn.: Yale University Press, 1997.

I acknowledge the U.S. Catholic Historical Society's kindness in sharing Leo Raymond Ryan's monograph, *Old St. Peter's, the Mother Church of Catholic New York (1785–1935)*.

$\mathscr{A}$CKNOWLEDGMENTS

AND $\mathscr{P}$ERMISSIONS

This book originated during a four-way conversation at a lunch in Manhattan. The quartet was Eric Major, then director of Religious Publishing at Doubleday; Trace Murphy, Doubleday executive editor; my agent, Robert Ducas; and me. To all three my thanks for their enthusiasm for the project—and to Trace and his staff for their skilled editing.

My initial stop was to Marie Mullarkey and the Pierre Toussaint Guild in the New York Catholic archdiocesan center. My thanks to those who willingly shared information and files.

There are three existing books on Pierre Toussaint. The bedrock material is Hannah Farnham Sawyer Lee's *Memoir of Pierre Toussaint, Born a Slave in St. Domingo* (Boston: Crosby, Nichols and Company, 1854). The Lee memoir is augmented by more than four hundred letters in French to Toussaint from his friends, plus three three-ring binders' worth of letters from his adopted daughter, his niece Euphémie.

There are two fictionalized accounts of his life, *Pierre Toussaint: A*

Biography, by Arthur Sheehan and Elizabeth Odell (New York: P.J. Kennedy and Sons, 1955), and *Pierre Toussaint, Apostle of Old New York*, by Ellen Tarry (Boston: Pauline Books & Media, 1981). My thanks to Ms. Tarry, a Toussaint Guild member and Toussaint biographer, for an afternoon and evening of charming conversation.

The New York Public Library at 42nd Street provided easy access to its Pierre Toussaint Papers collection. The New-York Historical Society was equally helpful and provided most of the illustrations herein. I am grateful to both institutions.

The Rev. Joseph Tylenda, S.J., of the Woodstock Theological Center Library at Georgetown University could always be relied on for books and articles. To him I am particularly grateful for directing me to the George Breathett book on the Catholic Church in Haiti. My thanks to Sister Betty Ann McNeil, DC, archivist, St. Joseph's Provincial House, Daughters of Charity, Emmitsburg, Maryland; to Sr. Marguerita Smith, OP, archivist for the New York archdiocese; and to the archive staff at the Oblate Sisters of Providence, Baltimore, and the Sisters of Charity, New York.

I am grateful for permission to use excerpts from the correspondence of Saint Elizabeth Ann Seton in volume one: Regina Bechtle, S.C., and Judith Metz, S.C., eds. *Elizabeth Bayley Seton Collected Writings*, Ellin M. Kelly, mss. ed., 3 vols. (New York: New City Press, 2000).

The enthusiasm of Father Charles McTague was a tonic. Father McTague was the diligent and dogged seminarian who, in the late 1930s, located Toussaint's forgotten grave marker in Old St. Patrick's graveyard. His ingenious device for identifying the weather-worn lettering on the crumbling stone is worth a tale in itself.

Thanks go also to the vice postulator for the cause of Pierre Toussaint, Monsignor Robert O'Connell, a former pastor of St. Peter's Church, and to Archbishop M. N. L. Couve de Murville, retired archbishop of Birmingham, England (and author of the 1995 Catholic Truth Society pamphlet "Slave from Haiti: A Saint for New York?"), for an exchange of correspondence.

To take discovery one step further, and as a reminder of how Toussaint is viewed by many, an afternoon with five-year-old Joey Peacock, along with his brother and parents in Maryland, was fun—and provided information of a different type. As Joey laid out his toy cars on his bed, his parents, Lisa and John Peacock, talked about praying to Toussaint to cure Joey's scoliosis. The curvature of the boy's spine has been eradicated, and details of the case are before the Congregation for the Causes of Saints for consideration as a Toussaint miracle. There have been several other submissions to the Congregation.

When it was time to find out about Toussaint's fellow parishioner, Mother Adelaide of St. Teresa, OCD (Yonkers-born Joan Adelaide O'Sullivan), I could not have had a more pertinacious researcher than the Reverend Steve Payne, OCD, whom I now thank.

Gathering Toussaint materials was one major step. During the period when I was still dusting off my own forty-year-old French reading skills, I particularly relied on my daughter, Chris Jones. Fortunately she is a product of French, as well as English and American, universities. More, she is an archivist. Thank you, Chris.

In memoriam I am moved to thank a series of French masters at the 1526-founded Boteler School in Warrington, England (motto: *Deus Spes Nostra*, "God is our hope"). Specifically I mention "Spring Heel Jack" Seddon, who more than a half-century ago solidly drummed French into me.

Given that the Toussaint correspondence was written by people whose French was essentially eighteenth-century ornate, because most of them were educated in that century's closing years, I am grateful to Christine Casey and Frances Gray, who were on call when I ran into usage problems or was uncertain about the sense of a particular sentence or paragraph in one of the letters.

To two historians—the eminent Christopher Kauffman, invariably obliging with his time and talent and phenomenal memory, and Margaret Silsby, an authority on the women of Toussaint's circle—my grateful thanks.

PERMISSIONS AND SOURCES

The opening paragraphs of this biography are from C. L. R. James's book *The Black Jacobins*. I am most grateful to Ewan Thorneycroft of the Curtis Brown Agency in London for granting permission to use those, and incidental mentions.

For much Saint Domingue material I have relied on T. Lothrop Stoddard's *The French Revolution in Santo Domingo* (Westport, Conn.: Negro Universities Press, 1914) and Thomas Ott's *The Haitian Revolution: 1789–1804* (Knoxville, Tenn.: University of Tennessee, 1973). For insights into the Catholic Church in Saint Domingue at that time, I am indebted to *The Catholic Church in Haiti, 1704–1785: Selected Letters, Memoirs and Documents*, edited and introduced by George Breathett (Salisbury, N.C.: Documentary Publications, 1983).

For both detailed and general information regarding African-American Catholics in the United States, and for commentary on slavery, my thanks go to the Reverend Cyprian Davis, O.S.B., for permission to quote from his book *The History of Black Catholics in the United States* (New York: Crossroad, 1990).

Valuable information on French exiles and émigrés in the United States comes from Frances Sergeant Child's *French Refugee Life in the United States, 1790–1800* (Baltimore, Md.: Johns Hopkins Press, 1940).

I thank Thomas M. Paine, great-great-great-grandson of Hannah Farnham Sawyer Lee, Toussaint's 1854 biographer, for permission to use material on Hannah Lee from his privately printed *Growing Paines* (Wellesley Hills, Mass.), as well as for guiding me to, and granting me permission to use, his photograph of Hannah Lee as she probably looked at the time she and Toussaint last saw each other.

Shane White's *Somewhat More Independent: The End of Slavery in New York City, 1770–1810* (Athens: University of Georgia Press, 1991) provided excellent commentary and incidents regarding slaves and slavery in New York City. As did Christine Stansell's *City of Women: Sex and Class in New York, 1789–1860* (Urbana: University of Illinois Press, 1987).

I thank the Historic Hudson Valley organization for permission to quote from the manuscript "Reminiscences of Grandmother Schuyler" (S3028), arranged by Georgiana Brand Schuyler (after 1920), and from Historic Hudson Valley documents S1004, S1007.

❖   ❖   ❖

Early in the process, the Ladies of Avalon at Fair Lakes regularly placed their copying machines at my disposal. My thanks to them.

I say it every time, but that doesn't alter the fact that without my friend Jean Blake, no book of mine would ever be finished. Thank you, Jean, for all of your energies, inspirations, and encouragement. My colleagues Tom Fox, Tom Roberts, and Pat Marrin can always be relied on as sounding boards. Thanks, fellas.

First and finally, full credit to Margie, my dear wife, who has put up with having yet another book-in-progress scattered around the house. It's an invasion—papers that occupy, at various times, most of the flat surfaces.

Thank you, my love, for silently raising your eyebrows or closing your eyes to my customary messiness—now cleared away . . . almost.

ARTHUR JONES
ALEXANDRIA, VIRGINIA
VALENCIA, CALIFORNIA
1999–2003

$\mathcal{I}$ndex